Straight Girls and Queer Guys

In memory of Dora Carrington (1893–1932)

Straight Girls and Queer Guys

The Hetero Media Gaze in Film and Television

Christopher Pullen

EDINBURGH
University Press

© Christopher Pullen, 2016

Edinburgh University Press Ltd
The Tun – Holyrood Road
12(2f) Jackson's Entry
Edinburgh EH8 8PJ
www.euppublishing.com

Typeset in Garamond MT Pro by
Servis Filmsetting Ltd, Stockport, Cheshire

A CIP record for this book is available from the British Library

ISBN 978 0 7486 9484 6 (hardback)
ISBN 978 0 7486 9485 3 (webready PDF)
ISBN 978 1 4744 1102 8 (epub)

The right of Christopher Pullen to be identified as author of this work has been asserted in accordance with the Copyright, Designs and Patents Act 1988, and the Copyright and Related Rights Regulations 2003 (SI No. 2498).

Contents

List of Figures	vii
Preface	viii
Acknowledgements	x

Introduction — 1
   Unlikely Coupling and the Fag Hag — 2
   Politics, *The Heidi Chronicles* and Neoliberalism — 5
   Time Frames, Contexts and Case Studies — 10
   Conclusion — 13

Chapter 1: The Hetero Media Gaze — 15
   The Gaze — 16
   The Panopticon and the Political Economy of the Sign — 22
   Doris Day and Rock Hudson Trilogy — 25
   A Taste of Honey, *Darling* and *Zee and Co.* — 32
   Conclusion — 39

Chapter 2: Queer Gazes and Identifications — 41
   Queer Narcissism and the Gaze — 42
   Rope and *Suddenly Last Summer* — 44
   Swoon — 52
   Derek Jarman and Gregg Araki — 56
   Conclusion — 63

Chapter 3: Film and Commodity — 65
   Queer Spectatorship, Femininity and Camp — 66
   Kenneth Williams and the Carry On Films — 69
   Sunday Bloody Sunday and *Cabaret* — 75
   The Gay Best Friend in Contemporary Film — 81
   Conclusion — 87

Chapter 4: Television and Domesticity — 89
Domesticity and the Intimate Glance — 90
Love Sidney — 92
Tales of the City, *Will and Grace* and *Gimme Gimme Gimme* — 95
Sex and the City, *Girls*, *Queer as Folk* and *Looking* — 102
Bob and Rose and *Torchwood* — 110
Conclusion — 117

Chapter 5: Documentary and Performance — 120
Documentary, the Body and Liminal Performance — 121
Carrington — 125
Platonic Devotion and Marriage in Documentary — 129
Would Like to Meet — 136
Queer Eye for the Straight Guy — 138
Boy Meets Boy — 141
Conclusion — 144

Chapter 6: Youth, Realism and Form — 147
Social Realism, Queer Identity and Youth in 1960s film — 148
Beautiful Thing and *The Way He Looks* — 151
Glee — 155
Gayby and *G.B.F.* — 160
Conclusion — 166

Conclusion — 169

Select Filmography — 172
References — 176
Index — 184

Figures

I.1	*The Way He Looks*	1
I.2	Tom Hulce and Jamie Lee Curtis in *The Heidi Chronicles*	6
I.3	Anne Baxter and Farley Granger in *The North Star*	9
1.1	Doris Day and Rock Hudson in *Pillow Talk*	29
1.2	Rita Tushingham and Murray Melvin in *A Taste of Honey*	33
2.1	Montgomery Clift and Elizabeth Taylor in *Suddenly Last Summer*	51
2.2	Brady Corbet and Mary Lynn Rajskub in *Mysterious Skin*	63
3.1	Kenneth Williams and Hattie Jacques in *Carry On Doctor*	73
3.2	Glenda Jackson and Murray Head in *Sunday Bloody Sunday*	77
3.3	Jennifer Aniston and Paul Rudd in *The Object of My Affection*	84
4.1	Sean Hayes and Megan Mullally in *Will and Grace*	100
4.2	Andrew Rannells and Lena Dunham in *Girls*	106
5.1	Emma Thompson and Jonathan Pryce in *Carrington*	125
5.2	James Getzlaff and Andra Stasko in *Boy Meets Boy*	142
6.1	Fabio Audi, Tess Amorim and Ghilherme Lobo in *The Way He Looks*	152
6.2	*G.B.F.*	162

Preface

This book explores the representation of the heterosexual female with the homosexual, bisexual or queer male, within contemporary film and television forms, using the term straight girls and queer guys. While this coupling is often employed to characterise the female as a 'Fag Hag', framing a reductive terminology that clearly debases the straight girl and the queer guy, and there is a sense of mutual use, evident in the relationship appearing as a kind of masquerade or disguise for a 'regular' heterosexual coupling, I argue that the straight girl and queer guy archetype is an advancing and prolific form.

Through examining this archetype within films and television programmes mostly produced in the United Kingdom and North America, or at least addressing Anglocentric audiences evident in my case study on the Brazilian film *The Way He Looks*, this book foregrounds the notion of the hetero media gaze. Critiquing the foundational work of Laura Mulvey (1975) with regards to the cinematic gaze, and extending the work of later writers such as Jackie Stacey (1987) with regard to the homosocial female gaze, and Richard Dyer ([1989] 2000) in relation to the commodification of the queer male body, this book develops a conceptual framework that contextualises film theory with television studies and performance studies. Key aspects include: questioning the fixity of the dominant gaze as gendered, or socially exclusive; examining the significance of the queer gaze in relation to consumption; considering the importance of spectatorship, and the relationship to celebrity; exploring the significance of the televisual glance in relation to domesticity; considering documentary and issues of performativity; and examining the significance of youth and the context of social realism. These are explored by considering key case studies, which, while they are not examined in terms of chronological progression, offer a discussion, generally within the time frame of between 1948 and 2015, in terms of media production.

This includes examining prototypical representations of the queer gaze within the films *Rope* and *Suddenly Last Summer*, and the queering of male and female coupling in the performance of Kenneth Williams in the Carry On films. Also it includes the subliminal emergence of the hetero media gaze upon the straight girl and the queer guy within Hollywood films starring Doris Day and Rock Hudson, its more vivid representation within John Schlesinger's *Darling* and *Sunday Bloody Sunday*, and the impact of Christopher Isherwood's novel *Goodbye to Berlin* on the film *Cabaret*, as establishing an archetypal form. Furthermore, aspects of social realism are foregrounded in films representing youth, particularly evident in *A Taste of Honey*, *Beautiful Thing* and *The Way He Looks*. Also the explicit commodity of the gay best friend is vivified in *My Best Friend's Wedding*, *The Object of My Affection* and *G.B.F.* At the same time television form is examined, considering the enduring impact of the straight girl and the queer guy in popular situation comedies, such as *Will and Grace* and *Gimme Gimme Gimme*, and documentary and reality television representations focusing on aspects of devotion, and sometimes marriage, evident in *Boy Meets Boy*, *My Husband Is Not Gay* and the biographical drama *Carrington*.

However, a central premise of this book is that both the queer guy and the straight girl are abject others, as respectively female and queer, which while it implies a shared political vision, and the connectivity between feminism and queer identity politics, in fact offers an unstable and contentious cultural form. As part of this, the book considers the neoliberal, and post-feminist, context of the straight girl and queer guy union, which reveals the reliance on dominant identity forms, foregrounding a sense of absence as much as presence.

Acknowledgements

The concept for the book was developed from an earlier essay that I wrote entitled '"Love the coat": bisexuality, the female gaze and the romance of sexual politics' (Pullen 2010), for Andrew Ireland's edited book on the science fiction television series *Torchwood*. Also I was inspired by the work of Richard Dyer ([1989] 2000) and Jackie Stacey (1987), with regard to the commodification of the queer male body, and the development of the homosocial female gaze, respectively.

I would like to thank my partner Ian Davies, whom I consider to be a key contributor to and supporter of my academic work. Our many conversations over the ideas expressed in this book have often led to different approaches, and the development of new ideas. I would also like to thank Gillian Leslie at Edinburgh University Press, for being enthusiastic about, and ultimately commissioning, *Straight Girls and Queer Guys*. Besides this I would like to thank my copy-editor John Banks for invaluable work and excellent insight into the subject area. In addition I would like to thank Daniel Ribeiro, not only for producing the wonderful film *The Way He Looks* which I discuss in this book but also for giving me permission to use images from the film.

Finally, I would also like to thank various friends, colleagues and organisations who have inspired and supported my research: Craig Batty, Richard Berger, Bournemouth University Faculty of Media and Communications and the Fusion Investment Fund, Peri Bradley, Matthew Byrnie, Steven Capsuto, Hugh Chignell, the editors of *Continuum: Journal of Media and Cultural Studies*, John M. Clum, Fiona Cownie, Robyn Curtis, Pamela Demory, Bruce E. Drushel, Joshua Gamson, Dimple Godiwala, Robin Griffiths, Larry Gross, Graeme Harper, Kylo Patrick R. Hart, Trevor Hearing, Su Holmes, Alex Hunt, Andrew Ireland, Deborah Jermyn, Alexandra Juhasz, Stephen Jukes, James R. Keller, Shaun Kimber, the editors of *Media, Culture and Society*, Jill Lake, Iain MacRury, Catherine Mitchell, Felicity Pleister, Ken Plummer, Barry Richards, Christabel Scaife, Leslie Strayner, Sarah Street, Sean Street, Bronwen Thomas, Christa Van Raalte, Steve Wilson, Brian Winston and Jeffrey Weeks.

Introduction

In Daniel Ribeiro's groundbreaking film *The Way He Looks* [original title *Hoje eu quero voltar sozinho*] (2014, Brazil) which tells the story of the blind queer youth Leonardo (see Chapter 6), the subtitle 'not every love happens at first sight' offers an allusion to the notion of the gaze, a central premise of this book. We know that while Leonardo cannot possess the physical gaze, his sense of feeling, relating his close friendship with the straight girl Giovana, and the quest for his ultimate soulmate Gabriel, enables him to challenge normative perceptions of the gaze. This book consequently considers such opportunities, and tensions, in exploring the relationship between the straight girl and the queer guy within film and television, evident in drama and documentary forms. The straight girl and the queer guy relate to each other, while defining each character's identity potential, at the same time as they are constructed by the audience as subject to a dominant gaze.

For example, if we consider a publicity image taken from *The Way He Looks* (see Figure I.1), all three central characters are intimately framed as lying close together, viewed from above, along the edge of a swimming pool. Leonardo

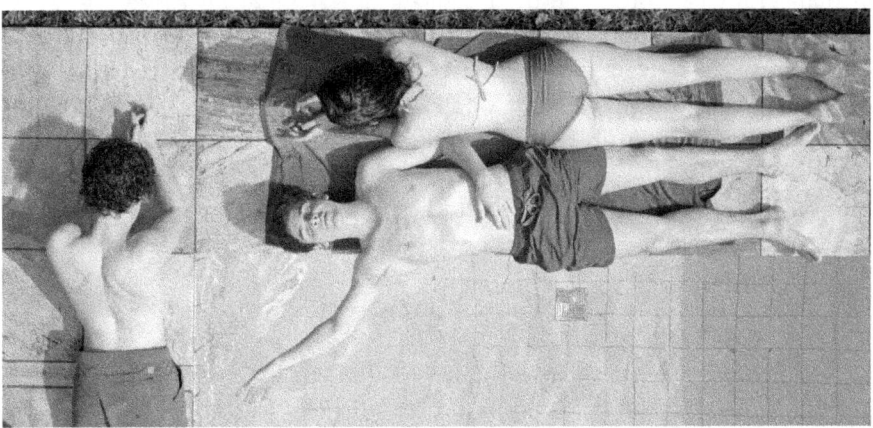

Figure I.1 *The queer youth characters of Gabriel (Fabio Audi, left) and Leonardo (Ghilherme Lobo, centre) are represented in juxtaposition to the straight girl Giovana (Tess Amorim, top), in Daniel Ribeiro's* The Way He Looks. *Image courtesy of Daniel Ribeiro.*

forms the central focus, as the only figure with his face visible, seeming to close his eyes as if resisting the direct sunlight whilst his body lies intimately close to Giovana, with her arm touching his, as he reaches out his other arm, seeming to rest in the swimming pool but in fact reaching towards Gabriel. At the same time, the medium of the swimming pool water, with a central focus on the drain, which might be symbolic of the cinematic or televisual camera as a medium able to frame these bodies, offers contextual resonance. These corporeal positions, framing one character in context to the other, at the same time alluding to limitations, subliminal narratives and diverse contexts of engagement, offer resonance not only to the meaning of *The Way He Looks* but also to the diverse representational contexts of the straight girl and queer guy within television and film.

Whilst the symbolic potential of Leonardo and Giovana within *The Way He Looks* as the queer guy and the straight girl is not a template for the discussions within this book but rather a theoretical model, I argue that it is the proximity of the characters, or representations, together, contained within, but also framed through, filmic and televisual industry technologies, forms and perspectives, that stimulates new ways of looking and reading. As part of this, the discussion in this book foregrounds the context of the hetero media gaze, at the same time relating historical and contemporary contexts.

Unlikely Coupling and the Fag Hag

Examining films and television programmes mostly produced in the United Kingdom and North America, or at least addressing Anglocentric audiences evident in my case study on the Brazilian film *The Way He Looks*, this book offers insight into the representation of the straight girl and the queer guy. I consider this as a developing archetypal form within contemporary western media, framing the significance of the hetero media gaze as contextual to the cinematic gaze (Mulvey 1975). As part of this, a conceptual framework is presented that makes connections to diverse theory contexts relative to film, television and performance studies, relating the subversive potential of the straight girl and the queer guy as an 'unlikely couple'. As Thomas E. Wartenberg (1999) tells us:

> The unlikely couple film traces the difficult course of romance between two individuals whose social status makes their involvement problematic. The source of this difficulty is the couple's transgressive make up, its violation of a hierarchic social norm regulating the composition of romantic couples. (7)

While in the case of the straight girl and the queer guy the notion of romance is either a historical context or an awkward subtext, in the manner that

Wartenberg explores heterosexual coupling that transgresses class, race and ethnic boundaries, this platonic coupling offers reference to wider notions of homosociality. This includes films that focus on the 'bromance' (DeAngelis 2014), heterosexual female identifications in a similar manner (Stacey 1987) and representations of the queer girl, in varying forms of coupling,[1] foregrounding notions of sexual equality or transgression.

However, the straight girl and queer guy coupling is often employed to characterise the female as a 'Fag Hag', framing a reductive terminology that clearly debases the straight girl and the queer guy (see Maitland 2007; Moon 1995). Hence my purpose is not to explore the semantics of the colloquial, rather it is to consider productive aspects of representation, and audience engagement. As part of this, I consider the straight girl and the queer guy relationship as a kind of union or alliance (see De La Cruz and Dolby 2007).

Within television and film, there could be a wide range of diverse case studies. This could include high-profile representations in television light entertainment, and popular culture. For example, the relationship between Larry Grayson and Isla St Clair, who appeared on British television between 1978 and 1982 as hosts on the popular game show *The Generation Game* (BBC 1971–2001, UK), may be considered as an iconic queer guy and straight girl coupling.[2] At the same time the contemporary success of Gok Wan, who offers fashion advice and body image support to heterosexual females in reality television shows such as *Gok's Fashion Fix* (Channel 4 2008–10, UK) and *How to Look Good Naked* (Channel 4 2008–10, UK), reveals the commodity use of the queer guy for the straight girl. Also the celebrated actress and comedian Margaret Cho, who has defined herself as a 'Fag Hag', including in her performances a routine where she philosophises about this identity (Cho 2002), forms a rich source of identification that has been referenced by a wide range of academic scholars (see Thompson 2004; Frackler and Salvato 2012; King 2014).

More significantly, the highest-profile coupling of the straight girl and the queer guy might be evident in the relationship of Princess Diana and the pop star Elton John. When Diana tragically died in 1997, at the funeral Elton John played a reworked version of his popular hit *Candle in the Wind* (Elton John and Bernie Taupin 1973), not only indicating his close relationship to her (see YouTube 2015) but also producing a record that would become the highest-selling single of all time in the United Kingdom. As part of this high profile, Princess Diana's commitment to gay men included aspects of AIDS activism, evident in her support of charities concerned for HIV and AIDS. Notably she was represented in the popular press as holding hands and in close conversation with gay male AIDS patients (see Princess Diana Remembered

2015; Thompson 2015), also forming a close friendship with Adrian Ward Jackson, who died of AIDS, publicly attending his funeral.

As Monica Davidson and Phoebe Hart tell us in their documentary *Handbag* (2015, Australia), the alliance between the straight girl and the queer guy might offer a generational and familial lineage (see Handbag 2015), in the manner of Princess Diana's close bond to queer men. This is evident where Davidson recalls that her grandmother, her mother and herself formed close bonds with gay men over many years. This included her mother's alliance with her gay best friend Bobby, where Davidson attests that 'they discoed together in the 90s, 70s and 80s, and when the AIDS crisis hit, she became a volunteer for the Names Quilt Project' (for the quilt see Morris 2011), referencing the strong bond between gay men and heterosexual allies at the outset of the AIDS epidemic (Shilts 1987; Jones 1994). As part of this, gay men are related as political activists, often in union with straight women and lesbians, with regard to pressing for the availability of AIDS drugs. This is vividly reported in Peter Adair's documentary *Absolutely Positive* (1991, US), and *How to Survive a Plague* (David France 2012, US), which features the ACT UP political movement. Also a sense of alliance is present in the organisation Straight Women in Support of Homos (SWISH), who take part in the New York City Pride event (see SWISH 2015), foregrounding a more carnivalesque approach. Hence the relationship between the straight girl and the queer guy provides a deep range of political and cultural interactions, intersections and alliances.

However, despite all this potential within activism, popular culture and light entertainment, I have selected my case studies not so much as defining the essential and historical narrative of the straight girl and queer guy relationship, or its sociocultural meaning, but rather as offering a theoretical model that can be applied across diverse media and representational forms.

Such a process not only explores the concept of union or alliance but also considers the objectification of the queer guy exerted by the straight girl that suggests a kind of sexual objectification, or emotional focus. At the same time it's important to note that the queer guy potentially relies on the straight girl, as offering a disguise to create the illusion that he is coupled with a desirable heterosexual female, engendering him as a normative citizen, apparent in the concept of the 'Beard' (a female who passes as a girlfriend for a queer male). Whilst the straight girl may also do this, these central ideas of union and use are key facets in working through the context of the hetero media gaze.

Politics, *The Heidi Chronicles* and Neoliberalism

As part of this, both the queer guy and the straight girl are abject others, respectively female and queer, implying a shared political vision and the connectivity between feminism and queer identity politics (Maddison 2000). However, as Mimi Marinucci tells us in her book *Feminism Is Queer: The Intimate Connection Between Queer and Feminist Theory* (2010), 'despite the [imagined] implicit connection they share, there is a history of tension between feminist studies and sexuality studies, both in general and in the more specific case of queer theory' (106). As Chris Weedon (1999) tells us:

> The queer movement challenges the very ideas of normality which underpin social institutions and practices. From a queer perspective nothing is natural, nothing is normal. Everything is a social and cultural construct and gender identities are acquired, at least in part, through performance... In theoretical terms, queer theory is in many ways postmodern, since it renounces any fixed notions of difference... Binary oppositions are replaced by a proliferation of differences which queer theory and politics refuses to hierarchize. (73)

The co-presence of a heterosexual female with a queer male problematises the normative gender binary dynamic that might be evident in feminist approaches, offering more of a connection to queer theory approaches. At the same time, as a representation of a male and female together, framing the sign and use value of dominant identity forms (Baudrillard 1981), there is a resonance in such a presence with notions of post-feminism (Coppock, Haydon and Ritchter 1995; Genz and Brabon 2012; Munford and Waters 2013). In this way, rather than connecting with the political dynamics of feminism, which might involve challenging the power structures held by masculine order, the union between the straight girl and the queer guy might be seen as a queer post-feminist identity construct. This might be apparent in offering these identities as subject to the process of the gaze, at the same time relating their usefulness or recognisability.

I argue that the imagined union between the straight girl and the queer guy suggests a form of alliance, which might stimulate some kind of revolution or drive to equality. At the same time, as both the queer guy and the straight girl are respectively and independently male, and heterosexual; they are indexical to the dominant powerbases. Hence their union is a complex identification resource, which relies not on stability and fixity but rather on shared difference, and also shared access to power.

This is evident in the many case studies discussed in this book, and is particularly apparent in considering the philosophical context of the television film *The Heidi Chronicles* (Paul Bogart 1995, US), which is based on Wendy

Figure I.2 Tom Hulce as Peter Patrone and Jamie Lee Curtis as Heidi Holland in The Heidi Chronicles. *Peter comes out to Heidi at an arts museum, while they are involved in political activism together.*

Wasserstein's 1988 feminist Broadway play of the same name. In *The Heidi Chronicles*, the lead female character of Heidi Holland (played by Jamie Lee Curtis) is an art historian who has a long-term relationship with a queer guy and paediatrician, Peter Patrone (played by Tom Hulce), as part of the context in exploring her life story, as an idealistic feminist figure. In a key sequence Peter comes out as gay to Heidi, after many years as a platonic friend (see Figure I.2). Outside a public art gallery both characters are protesting against the institution for not including women painters; they rush into the foyer, after Heidi responds awkwardly to hearing Peter's news:

> Peter: [shouting] Heidi, I'm gay! OK? I'm Gay! [sound reverbs echoing in the large building] . . . My liberation, my pursuit of happiness, and the pursuit of happiness for other men like me is just as politically and socially valid as [your feminist activism]. [Both rush back outside the building after being overheard inside]
>
> Heidi: I am going to hit you!
>
> Peter: Put up your dukes. Come on, put 'em up, put 'em up [then holding her arms, getting her hands to slap his body in the manner of a fight] That's

for my having distorted sexual politics. . . . That's because your liberation is better than mine. . . . And that's for being caustic, and paternal.

Mimicking a fight, but in fact aligning themselves politically, the characters in *The Heidi Chronicles* offer a performative insight into the diverse political challenges and life worlds of queer men, and straight girls, in relation to feminism. Despite this, the coupling of Heidi and Peter offers limited scope, as it is not until the end of the film that Heidi realises the depth of their abject communion, evident in Peter's work on the AIDS crisis. However, this focus on coupling, but also disparity, and not always comprehension and union, forms a central strand, in the straight girl and queer guy relationship. Central within this is the opportunity to personally connect and reflect, but also the limitations of the corporate, or institutional settings.

As part of this, the representation of the alliance between the straight girl and the queer guy is a product of self-reflexivity in contemporary society (Beck, Giddens and Lash 1995; Giddens 1992; 1995), and the context of neoliberalism (Saad-Filho and Johnson 2005). Where historically the representation of a male and female union within traditional media might be related to procreation, and the continuance of society, framing romance between the heterosexual couple as a key unit of cultural and social exchange, contemporary notions of identification that relate self-reflection and personal identification have become more central. As part of this the personal life worlds of individuals offer new scope in the development of self-reflexive narrative forms (Finnegan 1997; Plummer [1995] 1997; Pullen [2009] 2012). Hence the cultural capital of the straight girl and the queer guy foregrounds personal identifications, political goals and taste dispositions that evoke Pierre Bourdieu's notion of the habitus (1984). The straight girl and the queer guy are brought together not only through an alliance in their shared otherness, and potentially their shared access to power (as independently heterosexual and male) but also through shared senses of personal reflection, political articulations and taste dispositions that offer a cultural use value.

However, neoliberal media determine use value, as competition to gain access to power, in the manner that post-feminism frames dominant identity structures as relatable contexts of engagement. Hence the union between the straight girl and the queer guy might be seen as a queer post-feminist identity form, which, while offering a challenge to dominant forms of male and female coupling, in many ways is unit-based, suggesting exchangeability, in social commodity terms. As part of this, the straight girl and queer guy need to be represented as framing, and resonating with, the commodity potential of 'normative' male–female heterosexual coupling, as media corporations, producers and distributors are economies that rely on the dominance of heteronormative markets, as they are funded to address and to reflect their audiences. This 'heterocentric' unit potential is apparent in the manner that John Fiske (1994) considers as the notion of interpellation, relative to the process of hailing an audience, and the context of homophyly, where audiences may recognise themselves within the representational body. Consequently, the straight girl and the queer guy are part of this heterocentric value system. As part of this, the gaze inevitably must be defined as the 'hetero media gaze', following Larua Mulvey's (1975) examination of the dominance of male heterocentric commodity, even if neoliberal order (post-feminist order) suggests the potential to compete with, or be included within, the representational realm.

However, such inclusion, I would argue, is less about the selling of an identity, although clearly identity politics are important facets of political revolution; rather it is the process of identification, evident within the gaze. As Diana Fuss (1995) tells us:

> Identification is a process that keeps identity at a distance, that prevents identity from ever approximating the status of an ontological given, even as it makes possible the formation of an *illusion* of identity as immediate, secure, and totalizable. (2)

Hence a key facet of this book is arguing that the gaze offers a potential for identification, which reveals not a stable identity but rather the absence of identity. The straight girl and the queer guy are an unstable form, not coherently defined. They appear as a union that may be gazed upon, whose constituents equally may gaze upon each other, foregrounding a sense of process. While Henry Giroux (2011) argues that under a neoliberal order '[i]nstead of public spheres that promote dialogue, debate, and arguments with supporting evidence, we have entertainment spheres' (10) that focus on emotions and personal realisations, suggesting that these processes are insubstantial, I argue that the reflective potential of identification is central, in examining the constitution and utility of the gaze.

One example is an image from the wartime film *The North Star* (Lewis Milestone 1943, US) (see Figure I.3). The representation foregrounds the gaze of Anne Baxter upon Farley Granger (see Chapter 2), as lead actors set within a hayloft or barn. Whilst this film is not an explicit representation of the straight girl and the queer guy, in viewing this in contemporary times we are now aware that Farley Granger identified as bisexual, and later as gay, and he expressed comfort in sexual diversity (see Granger and Calhoun 2007). As in the discussion of Doris Day and Rock Hudson in Chapter 1, we are able to sense a certain sexual dynamic, which references the hetero media gaze but in fact subverts it, through self-reflection and refraction. Anne Baxter seems to

Figure I.3 *Anne Baxter and Farley Granger in* The North Star. *While later in life Farley Granger identified as a gay man, this early representation foregrounds his star identity as subject to the female gaze.*

gaze longingly at Farley Granger, suggesting sexual contemplation. However if we look more closely, her eyes offer a nuance of unattainability, as if reflecting on an imagined reality. While both characters lie down in the hayloft, the romantic place for impulsive sexual encounter, Farley looks directly away as if dreaming of another life, or a different intimate partner. Despite this there is comfort and ease in this representation, which suspends sexual desire, in preference for a sense of personal reflection, rather than a coherent identity form.

Hence the gaze is a subjective psychological process, rather than necessarily a fixing of an identity. As part of this, the gaze upon the straight girl and the queer guy references issues such as space and time differences. This is relative not only to the composition of the image, placed within a specific time frame, but also to the sense of time passing, and the possibility to review again, and reassess, the iconographic form. Hence, this book does not rely on an exact historical foundation, but rather focuses on time frames, in relation to theoretical and case study contexts.

TIME FRAMES, CONTEXTS AND CASE STUDIES

It is possible to argue that the 'unlikely coupling' of the straight girl and the queer guy emerged within modern literature, particularly evident in Christopher Isherwood's representation of Sally Bowles in his self-reflexive novel *Goodbye to Berlin* (1939), framing this as an archetypal representation of the straight girl who forms an alliance with the queer guy. Despite this it is inevitable that the union between the straight girl and the queer guy might be traced back to far earlier times. It is possible that such relationships were evident in opera houses in sixteenth-century Italy, with regard to the castrati (boys who were castrated, in order to retain a pure high singing voice) (see Barbie 1998); in the molly houses in eighteenth-centurycentury London, where cross-dressing male prostitutes worked and entertained (see James 2015; Weeks 1990); and in liaisons between gay men and prostitutes in the early twentieth-century London, who used the covert language of Polari to avert attention from the police (see Baker 2002). However as my focus concerns representations in mainstream film and television, the representation of Sally Bowles, who first appears in Isherwood's novel *Goodbye to Berlin* and later in the film adaptation *Cabaret* (see Chapter 3), seems to form the earliest representation. At the same time it is important to note that the exploration in this book focuses primarily on the notion of union or coupling, suggesting a kind of alliance; and consequently varying forms of straight female identification for queer men, such as online slash fiction, are not present in this book.[3] Hence the notion of the coupling is related within a theory-based context that references the development of new forms, based on relationship as much as identification.

Therefore, this book does not employ an exact chronological focus; rather it explores key case studies that are related to theoretical contexts, expressing this through the advance of time. As part of this, the first media case study is the Hollywood film *Rope* (Alfred Hitchcock) dated 1948 (discussed in Chapter 2), and the most recent case study is the television drama series *Looking* dated 2015 (discussed in Chapter 4). However in terms of historical origin, and adaptation, the earliest representation of the straight girl and queer guy in this book dates back to the early twentieth century, evident in the life story of Dora Carrington and Lytton Strachey, shown in the film *Carrington* (Christopher Hampton 1995, UK). Hence although a time frame might be evident in examining film and television texts between 1948 and 2015, in fact the analysis avoids an explicit linear chronology, and organises the material in relation to theoretical and conceptual ideas.

As part of this, the theory of the gaze is examined from the outset, tracing the significance of Laura Mulvey's early work in this area, and framing later critical work, in order to define the meaning of the hetero media gaze, foregrounding a textual analysis-based approach, in progressing through the case studies. However, the theory of the gaze is expanded, in developing a conceptual framework. This includes:

- questioning the fixity of the dominant gaze as gendered, or socially exclusive, and relating the context of the absence
- foregrounding the significance of the queer gaze, as a process of representation and consumption
- considering the importance of spectatorship, and the relationship to stars, as forming an identification resource
- exploring the significance of the televisual glance and its connectivity to female identity and domesticity
- considering opportunities within documentary for performativity, evident within the liminal frame, and the potential to transcend this
- examining the significance of youth and the context of social realism, relating both to the use of stylistic conventions and to its political attribution.

While these diverse theoretical contexts are expanded within the diverse chapters in this book, I argue that these are mobile conceptual frameworks, rather than fixed components in a machine.

As part of this mobile potential, which resists the formation of the machine but recognises the need for structure, while the book offers no specific time frame it does offer an examination of certain time periods, considering advances, and developing contexts. Hence in Chapter 1 a sense of emergence is presented in discussing the films of Doris Day, Rock Hudson and Tony Randall as a subliminal beginning of the straight girl and queer guy representation within Hollywood film. Later in this chapter I examine more explicit representations, evident in the films *Darling*, *A Taste of Honey* and *Zee and Co*. At the same time these filmic representations are further developed in Chapter 3, where the notion of spectatorship and star identity are more centrally examined, foregrounding the representation of Kenneth Williams within the Carry On films, archetypal representations in *Darling* and *Cabaret*, and explicitly commodity-oriented settings, as evident in *My Best Friend's Wedding*, *The Object of My Affection* and *The Next Best Thing*. This approach separates the filmic content within diverse chapters relative to theoretical contexts. As part of this, independent film is discussed in Chapter 6, relative to the notion of youth, as a central cultural force, in developing more contemporary approaches. Hence the social realist films *Beautiful Thing* and *The Way He Looks* are discussed in relation to popular culture and cult-oriented films, such as *G.B.F.* and *Gayby*. Through their connection to youth there is a sense of advance, and new beginning.

Such a new beginning is particularly evident in the case study on the television series *Glee*, which in Chapter 6 is framed within the notion of youth, contextualising advances in both film and television. As part of this, the context of social realism, and its foundation within 1960s British film and television, forms a central context of analysis. While realism is subjective, mostly relying on style and context, rather than any real essence, the case studies in Chapter 2, which relate to the queer gaze and its interconnection to heterosexual female identity, offer an intensity and connection to the 'real'. Notably, the prototypical representation of the queer gaze within Alfred Hitchcock's *Rope*, and its relationship to the later adaptation of *Swoon*, alongside the more recent work of Derek Jarman and Gregg Araki, stimulates a sense of co-presence, through acknowledging that the gaze may be complex, fluid and mobile, rather than fixed upon a hegemonic base.

At the same time in Chapter 4 the notion of the cinematic gaze is related to the televisual glance, which, that while it seems ephemeral, in fact, through its connection to female address and the locus of domesticity, offers a productive space for representation. Examining the prototypical representation of the straight girl and the queer guy in televisual form, evident in *Love Sidney* alongside more contemporary advances within *Will and Grace* and *Gimme Gimme Gimme*, foregrounds usefulness as much as parity. Despite this, transgressive potential exists, clearly evident in the later case studies of *Sex and the City*, *Girls*, *Looking* and *Queer as Folk*, where through differing dynamics the queer guy, or alternately the straight girl, as 'other', reveals a subjective dynamic that frames the mobility of desire.

As part of this, the final case studies in Chapter 4, which focus on bisexuality, alongside the case studies in Chapter 5, which foreground documentary approaches, relate as much to the tension between platonic relationships, as to the drive to sexual engagement. The fictional representations in *Bob and Rose* and *Torchwood*, alongside the real-life accounts within *My Husband Is Gay* and *My Husband Is Not Gay*, reveal a deep intimate connection, foregrounded not on desire for the male body but on the sharing of experience, and humanity, that transcends sexual attraction. This is also evident in the biographical film *Carrington*, and the reality series *Boy Meets Boy*, which are intense, political and subversive. While *Would Like to Meet* and *Queer Eye for the Straight Guy* seem to parody the notion of an authentic relationship, either heterosexual, homosexual or between the straight girl and the queer guy, the focus on performative elements in these reality series decodes the theoretical perspectives.

CONCLUSION

The representation of the 'unlikely coupling' between the straight girl and the queer guy focuses on their absence as much as on their presence. While in political terms it seems as if this union has offered increased scope for the representation of the queer male within mainstream media, evident in its coupling with, and address to, female representations, at the same time there is a lack of coherency in defining this representation. As a product of a neoliberal media environment, this limitation is not that surprising, as both the queer guy and the straight girl are at the same time abject, and enfranchised, evident in their complex relationship to queerness, femininity and heterosexuality. This blend of limitation and privilege, like the neoliberal order, offers a sense of being there and able, but also compartmentalisation and restriction.

In the manner that Farley Granger is gazed upon by Anne Baxter in *The North Star* (see above) the subtext may not be easily understood, as might occur with *The Way He Looks* (see above) where a sense of identity politics is explicit. Despite this, our processes of self-reflexive identification through theorising the gaze not only places us within the frame but also suspends the need for conclusion or ending. The straight girl and the queer guy therefore exist within a continuum, but it is not easily traced, or comprehensively understood.

As Peter evokes in *The Heidi Chronicles*, while the shared politics of feminism and queerness offers a sense of union for the straight girl and the queer guy, the lived experience and issues of self-knowledge takes precedence over political coalescence, or necessarily coherence. Despite this, I argue that the representation of the straight girl and the queer guy within film and television offers a source of identification possibility, with a particular regard to young people, as enabling new forms of social realism. Such a process might not fix an identity, but, through political articulation, offers scope in imagining new forms. These might independently support the life goals of the straight girl and the queer guy, in order to resist a disparate and individual sense of abjection; at the same time they might work together, as a political, cultural and social union.

NOTES

1. Representations of the queer girl, coupled with either the straight guy or the straight girl, offer similar insight to the focus of this book. Notably the television series *The L Word* (Showtime 2004–9, US) and *Lip Service* (BBC 2010–12, UK), plus the films *The Kids Are All Right* (Lisa Cholodenko 2010, US) and *Kissing Jessica Stein* (Charles Herman-Wurmfeld, 2002, US), offer insight into these potential alliances.

2. While Larry Grayson never came out, he publicly presented a queer male persona employing catchphrases such as 'What a gay day' and 'Shut that door', also referencing friends in his repartee called 'Slack Alice', and 'Everard' (implying an 'ever hard' phallic erection). Hence in the manner of Kenneth Williams (see Chapter 3) his public persona resisted a direct association with gay identity, but through camp allusion he coded himself as queer (see Independent 1995).
3. Slash fiction representations of Yaoi culture (see McHarry 2010), and homoerotic reformations of the *Harry Potter* and *Star Trek* narratives (see Berger 2010), foreground the online writing potential of mostly straight girls interested in queering male heterosexual narratives, for pleasure and fantasy.

CHAPTER 1

The Hetero Media Gaze

Clifford T. Manlove (2007), critiques the work of Laura Mulvey as regards the gaze:
> What is lacking in Mulvey's use of Freud and Lacan is a theory of the real, a register Lacan attributes to Freud. To begin with, according to Lacan, the gaze is not only an exchange between an active agent and a passive object. The gaze, rather, indicates a prior, more radical split within the apparently active subject. The gaze and its effects, are not gender or biologically specific. From a Lacanian point of view . . . women often have agency and desire in Hitchcock films, and are subject to castration no less than men. (90)

Manlove's analysis, foregrounding the work of Hitchcock, following a history of many academics who have critiqued, and developed, Mulvey's seminal work (see further below), emphasises a radical split in the apparently active subject. This reveals a sense of ambivalence and dualism, in framing male patriarchal order as controllers of the gaze. Women, or queer men, may be beholders of the gaze, revealing an imagined reversal of the subjectivity.

For example Richard Dyer ([1989] 2000: 124) cites a television advertising campaign for Levi's denim in the late 1980s, which featured a young male actor, Nick Kamen, in a launderette, as marking the beginning of a new period of the consumption of the male body, related as 'to-be-looked-at-ness'. This can be applied to images of masculinity with regard to both heterosexual female and gay male identifications (Neale 1983), revealing 'a shift in attitudes towards the male body' (Dyer [1989] 2000: 123). This is evident where Kamen in the television advert removes his clothes to reveal a well-toned body, dressed only in boxer shorts, having taken most of his clothes off so he may wash his jeans, placing them in the washing machine, accompanied by 'pebbles', making them 'stonewashed' (a semi-bleached appearance). This is accompanied by a range of onlookers at the launderette, including young teen boys, older males and females, and young teen girls who form the central conduit for viewing, represented as giggling and excited, peering over their magazines to gain a furtive glimpse.

Such a shift in the appropriation of the gaze related to the physical form, in many ways 'equalising' the imagined desirability of the male body to that of the female body, to mainstream audiences, offered new ways of seeing and consuming the male body. At the same time this advert has a homoerotic subtext, evident not only in the context that queer men might find pleasure in viewing Nick Kamen's body but in the choice of the popular song to accompany the advert, *I Heard It through the Grapevine*, a song that suggests a covert reading of secrecy and disclosure, implying homosexual desire. As Manlove attests, the gaze is a complex process, which is not purely male heterocentric, centred on gender, defining the modes and assets of patriarchal industry, and identity.

This chapter consequently considers the emergence of the female gaze, as executed upon the desirable young male body, foregrounding the concept of the hetero media gaze. This, I argue, is a mainstream gaze upon the queer male, not so dissimilar to the notion of the gaze on the female body, as related to histories within Hollywood film: however, the active viewer is the female spectator, rather than the male. In this chapter I develop this idea, looking at theories of the gaze, relating issues of genre and audience identification and consumption. Also I foreground a prototype for the hetero media gaze, examining the representation of Doris Day and Rock Hudson, within films where they were coupled with Tony Randall, in *Pillow Talk* (Michael Gordon 1959, US), *Lover Come Back* (Delbert Mann 1961, US) and *Send Me No Flowers* (Norman Jewison 1964, US). Also I examine more explicit representations of the straight girl and the queer guy, evident in three diverse films: *A Taste of Honey* (Tony Richardson 1961, UK), which features an effeminate queer youth who cares for a single pregnant young female, interested in the task of child raising; *Darling* (John Schlesinger 1965, UK), which features a young female seeking celebrity, finding camaraderie with a young queer male photographer; and *Zee and Co* (Brian G. Hutton 1972, UK), which features a temperamental housewife who challenges her unfaithful husband, with the support of a queer male friend. These films provide a prototypical foundation for ways of representing the straight girl and the queer guy, basing the notion of the gaze more directly on the opportunity of commodity for heterosexual audiences.

THE GAZE

Ben Brewster (1975) tells us that Laura Mulvey's original work on the gaze 'argues that the visual pleasures offered by traditional cinema reflect contradictions inherent in the patriarchal psychical order dominant in our societies, and that film theory should expose the mechanisms' (4–5). Hence the original purpose of her work was to reveal the patriarchal dominance of the film industry, and the inherent employment of a heterosexual male subjectivity, particularly with regard to how females are represented. However, her employment of theory focused on the use of psychoanalysis, in working through issues of spectatorship, and the dominant construction of identity. As Clifford T. Manlove explains in critiquing her work, her appropriation of Freud and Lacan is potentially problematic, through simplifying the notion of the gaze, as purely male, heterocentric and related to gender. Manlove explains: '[w]ithin ten years, many feminist film critics variously sought to question and/or redefine Mulvey's focus on three issues: gender positions in the gaze, heterosexuality of the gaze, and seeing the gaze as exclusively (male) pleasure in voyeurism' (2007: 85). Although there are many critiques and developments of Mulvey's work, one prime critique of Mulvey's notion of the gaze and her deployment of psychoanalysis concerned the focus on the phallus. As Manlove explains, citing the early work of Stephen Heath in 1978, 'psychoanalysis failed to account for the complexities of sexual difference, because it is defined in relation to the phallus (or its lack), which is ahistorical' (2007: 87).

However, historical contexts are significant, relative to the constitution of the iconic image. Furthermore, in defining the notion of the hetero media gaze, historical contexts of representation, performance and commodity are central in evaluating the emergence of new forms of the gaze, such as the gaze upon the queer male, within mainstream media. While Jacques Lacan's work on the 'mirror stage' (Lacan 1968) is relevant in philosophising the potential of the gaze, when 'the infant first experiences the joy of seeing itself as complete, and imagines itself to be more adult, more fully formed, perfect, than it really is, [reveals that] the self is constructed in a moment of recognition and misrecognition' (Creed 2000: 78), contexts of history relative to the life chances of the individual must also be relevant. For queer males, and heterosexual females, while equally they are prone to the misrecognition as fully formed, they are also situated as peripheral to male heterosexual dominance, and aspects of struggle, negotiation and alliance relative to historical progressions (or regressions). This should be relevant in considering the process of scopophilia, finding pleasure in viewing others, in opposition or contrast to themselves. At the same time, constructed as 'others' themselves (Hall 1997), in contrast to male heterocentric order, heterosexual females and queer males, and also a wide range of other identities that might be connected to sexual or gender diversity, are potentially unstable and fluid as social contexts, relative to histories of representation, and changing cultural forms.

This book makes attempts to situate these historical changes, relative to the usefulness of the gaze, as a mode of identity, performance and consumption. As part of this I argue that the notion of the dominant gaze, as defined by Mulvey, may be considered as a 'hetero media gaze', for its reliance on heterosexual-oriented gender dynamics, evident in the ownership of commodity, and the address to mainstream heterosexual audiences, framing the dominance of the male heterosexual. However, the notion of the hetero media gaze at the same time incorporates the significance of heterosexual female identity, which, although in Mulvey's work assigned a subordinate position, I argue is increasingly apparent in terms of address and genre (see below). Hence, heterosexual female identity is a significant mainstream asset, which forms a significant part of the contemporary media world. As part of this in considering the dynamic of the straight girl and the queer guy, central within the conception of the hetero media gaze may be the shifting 'usefulness' of cultural forms, relative to notions of 'use' and 'exchange', evident in postmodern media forms (see further below). However, before we examine the evidence of the case studies, which frame deeper cultural contexts relative to these notions, it is first important to consider the concept and process of the dominant hetero media gaze.

The concept of the gaze can be related in two contrasting, but contextual, ways. The gaze may be considered as:

- a subjective device, which might be related to issues of spectatorship, where one party looks upon another, and there are aspects of 'being used'
- a narrative representation of the gaze between two parties, in this case heterosexual females and homosexual males, as an enabling collaboration, which might offer 'usefulness' in storytelling.

Hence, the gaze, as defined in this book, is about use, and exchange, relative to the audience, framing mainstream production, and consumption, of the gaze. In many ways this suggests an alliance between parties that are used or objectified, involving complex relationships where both parties may objectify and use each other.

Laura Mulvey's analysis of Hollywood film concerned the objectification of women, framed as subject to the masculine gaze, which revealed the concept of 'to-be-looked-at-ness'. This suggests that male hierarchies within the film industry construct women, and they are represented as objects of desire, not only within Hollywood film but also within diverse western cultural forms, where women are subject to a voyeuristic focus. Many scholars have commented on, and critiqued, Mulvey's work. Among them is Mulvey herself, who has re-examined her own observations with regard to the subjectivity of the female body, suggesting that there are ways in which women can reject the male gaze (see below).

However. as Liesbet Van Zoonen (1994) tells us:

> Mulvey's dark and suffocating analysis of patriarchal cinema has lost ground to a more confident and empowering approach which foregrounds the pos-

sibility of 'subversive', that is, non patriarchal modes of female spectatorship. (97)

In this sense female audiences might be able to exert their own gaze, outside obvious connections to patriarchal power. Spectatorship might not necessarily be directly connected to the means of production which are androcentric, but may be employed by individual observations, and collective identifications. As John Fiske (1994) suggests, independent and subjective identification possibilities may be present, evident in the notion of active audiences. Also there may be a provision for a focus on the male body as an object of desire (see below). As David Gauntlett (2002) explains, this might progress Mulvey's theory which 'denies the heterosexual female gaze altogether [primarily discussing the] audience, both male and female [as] positioned so that they admire the male lead [character] for actions, and adopt his romantic/erotic view of the women' (39). Clearly, female identifications are present within media texts, even if dominant modes of media production may be patriarchal. Also the male body might be an object of examination, not only subject to the gaze of the heterosexual female audience (as evident in the concept of this book) but also subject to the gaze of the male homosexual viewer. However, as part of this process, the gaze might not just consist of subjective acts of visual pleasure: this foregrounds a disconnection between the viewer and the one who is viewed.

For example, Suzanne Moore (1988) tells us in relating Laura Mulvey's work on the female gaze that there are two types of visual pleasure, relative to Hollywood cinema.

> One revolves around an active objectifying look that requires distance between the viewer and the object on the screen. This is the voyeuristic or fetishistic look. The other involves identification with the screen image and so depends precisely on the dissolution of the distance between screen and spectator. (50–1)

These two contextual approaches reveal issues concerning the usefulness of the gaze. One approach reveals the disavowal of the person looked at, deconstructing their physical form, as a source of consumption from a distance. The other through framing identification, in the manner of social construct, offers a sense of closeness, and being together.

This opposition is highly relevant in the reading of Mulvey's work. For example Tania Modleski's 'A Master's Dollhouse: *Rear Window*' (in Modleski 2005) criticises Mulvey for her appropriation of women solely as objects of the heterosexual male gaze. Using the example of the Hitchcock film *Rear Window*, she considers that the female object in the film, Lisa, is not just a helpless glamorous socialite interested only in getting married, evident in a male heterocentric subjectivity, but is in fact a key agent in the film, who solves the crime mystery. In this sense she is not someone to be fetishised, contained and consumed, but is in essence someone whom we identify with as a heroine, established to some degree as an exemplar and role model of good citizenship.

The representation of the straight girl in relation to the queer guy in many ways relates to this. In a similar manner that Tania Modleski (2005) defines the character of Lisa in *Rear Window*, as connected to identification and citizenship, the straight girl is related as a democratic counterpart to the queer guy, offering equality in representations, and possibilities for identifications. This suggests a type of exchange of roles where the female is equal to the male.

However as Loraine Gamman (1998) tells us citing the work of Julia Kristeva (1977):

> [W]omen cannot simply exchange roles with men because thought and representation in the 'phallocentric order' are constructed in the context of a linguistic binarism that always equates masculine with hard/active and feminism with soft/passive. (17)

Hence, even if males are constructed as passive to 'stronger' females, such an evaluation is outside the linguistic binarism that is embedded within society. In this sense power is always 'male created', and there is a reliance on roles. Despite this Kristeva argues that the only way to move beyond this system is to 'refuse all roles'. As Gamman tells us, this would involve 'returning to the pre-Oedipal moment in the formation of the subject in language' (1998: 17), recognising the 'unspoken in speech, even revolutionary speech'. As Kristeva suggests, this might involve 'calling attention at all times to whatever remains unsatisfied, repressed, new, eccentric, incomprehensible, disturbing the status quo' (1977: 37).

Notably, Jackie Stacey (1987) tells us it is problematic to fully comprehend 'the relay of looks on screen [which potentially exist] between the audience and diegetic characters' (52), suggesting that an understanding of difference or otherness, is contentious. Significantly as Doane, Mellencamp and Williams (1984) state: 'it might be better as Barthes suggests, neither to destroy difference nor valorise it, but to multiply and disperse differences, to move toward a world where differences would not be synonymous with exclusion' (14). However, for the representation of the straight girl and the queer guy, there is a reliance on a kind of binarism, evident in emulating normative male–female relationships, which rely on difference. Such an approach assures some access to power, by presenting a 'regular' coupling. However 'regularity' relies on the binary norms of male–female relationships, framing masculinity as dominant.

Therefore the focus on the male spectator as possessor of the gaze makes it problematic for females to assume power. As Mulvey (1981) herself related in 'Afterthoughts on "Visual pleasure"', aspects of psychic transvestism are necessary if the female has any chance of becoming empowered. As Suzanne Moore suggests, 'a temporary masculinisation is the only way that Mulvey can offer active pleasure for the female viewer' (1998: 52).

Clearly, in films where women behave like men, such as *Alien* (Ridley Scott 1979, US) or *The Long Kiss Goodnight* (Renny Harlin 1996, US), there is scope for power. This is apparent where in *Alien* Sigourney Weaver playing the role of Ripley must become masculine to defeat an alien. Also it is evident in *The Long Kiss Goodnight* where Gina Davis, playing the role of Samantha Caine after a period of amnesia and transitioning back to her former identity as Charly Baltimore, gives up her maternal role to become an assassin. These films frame the need for the female to masquerade as the male, evident in assuming a masculine gender performance, framing authoritarian and instructive dialogue, which is not passive. As part of this the female is connected to masculine iconography in terms of physical prowess, such as an ability to handle weapons that reinforce the phallocentric, suggesting the possession of male genital organs, necessary for the roles. These films suppose that masculinisation is necessary, for the female character to gain access to power.

However, what about films where the main identifications are made between the same sexes? Jackie Stacey's (1987) groundbreaking work on female identification foregrounds the films *All about Eve* (Joseph L. Mankiewicz 1950, US) and *Desperately Seeking Susan* (Susan Seidelman 1985, US).[1] In these films, the male–female identification binary is subverted, and females identify with each other. Notably in *Desperately Seeking Susan*, the leading character of Roberta identifies not with the notion of finding the ideal male partner but with the life story of another female, Susan, whom she pursues with voyeuristic pleasure. While this is not a lesbian-identified film, although it clearly presents a subtext in this manner, it is the subversion of the male–female binary which is central here. Stacey (1987) suggests that film theory's reliance on psychoanalysis in construction of the gaze is the problem here. She argues for 'a more complex model of cinematic spectatorship . . . suggesting [a] need to separate gender identification from sexuality, [which is] too often in the name of sexual difference' (53). Despite this focus on sexuality and difference, established ways of viewing are dominant. Hence even if there is some kind of democracy between females (or males) who identify with each other in breaking down a reliance on gender expectations of performance, there is still a persistence of linguistic codes, which frame and form expectations of hierarchy and submission.

Despite this, Mary Ann Doane (1982) points out that gender performance may be 'complicated' with the potential of masquerade, offering the ability to deconstruct masculine hierarchies. She tells us that 'to masquerade is to manufacture a lack in the form of a certain distance between oneself and one's image' (82). If women perform a masquerade, as excessively male or female, they are presenting a synthesised relationship with regard to gender performance. Such agency can be transgressive. As Doane (1982) tells us:

> The idea seems to be this: it is understandable that women would want to be men, for everyone wants to be elsewhere than in the feminine position. What is not understandable within the given terms is why a woman might flaunt her femininity, in other words foreground the masquerade. Masquerade is not as recuperable as transvestism precisely because it constitutes an acknowledgement that it is femininity which is constructed as mask – as the decorative layer which conceals a non-identity. (81)

Hence, if we consider excessive female performance potentially as masquerade, although reasons for such excess are complicated, in doing this binary dynamics of gender performance are challenged. However the institutional gaze still determines a particular focus, potentially influencing behaviour.

THE PANOPTICON AND THE POLITICAL ECONOMY OF THE SIGN

Foucault's notion of the panopticon ([1975] 1995) offers insight into this, considering the manner in which prisoners were observed in the panopticon prison, and in which their behaviour was changed through the subjective gaze, as all-encompassing. Foucault considered the Victorian panopticon prison as a place that would offer no privacy for the prisoners, recalling how prisoners under the suppression of the regime often would lose grips on sanity, as there was no place where they could hide from observation. Rather than offering some improved social method of prison control, the panopticon prison was seen as an institutional failure, for its over-emphasis on observation, affording little scope for salvage or renewal. Similarly to Laura Mulvey's notion of the gaze within Hollywood cinema, the object of the gaze is contained within an institutional environment, determining appropriate behaviour. For example anyone subject to the panoptic gaze, such as the female body within Hollywood cinema or the incarcerated body within the panopticon prison, is unable to escape the power of the onlookers, and is contained. In order to survive this ordeal the female body must be compliant to the gaze, and willingly conform to stereotypical notions of female passivity and subjectivity, and the incarcerated prisoner must endure the gaze, maintaining compliant and passive behaviour.

Despite this, Majid Yar (2003) tells us that 'within [Foucault's] conception of Panoptic power, vision becomes synonymous with domination, [this] theorisation dispenses with notions of autonomy or freedom that would stand [for oppositional] power' (260), hence subjectivity in this form might be a little more complex. Potentially individuals possess the agency to make their own identifications responding to, and reforming, the dominant discourse, evident in the notion of active audiences (Fiske 1989).

In critiquing the panopticon and the subjective gaze, Yar considers that the relationship between visibility, subjectivity and discipline is relative to intersubjective relations, and opportunities for retelling stories. Yar considers that Foucault's evaluation of the panopticon 'overlooks the polyvalent and complex nature of our experience of vision' (2003: 258), and that this under-estimates 'the extent to which the subject has an active role within the reception of the gaze, and renders it impossible to give an adequate account of creativity and resistance' (2003: 261). Hence, although the institutional gaze might frame the object as passive, there are opportunities to respond through power resistance. This might allow for new articulations, and identity formations, within a postmodern media ethic that foregrounds 'incredulity towards metanarratives' (Lyotard 1979: xxiv), framing the emergence of 'micronarratives' (Jameson 1991), seemingly as signs of commodity.

As part of this, Jean Baudrillard's (1981) concept of the 'political economy of the sign' foregrounds the concept of use and exchange value, related to 'the logic of ambivalence, which corresponds to symbolic exchange [and] the logic of difference which corresponds to sign-value' (Lechte 2000: 61). This equates to the potential of the cultural symbol, evident in what it may offer through 'symbolic exchange', and the status that may be provided by the sign, as its 'sign value'. Whilst Baudrillard's work focuses mostly on the culture of consumption, and the consumer's imagined lack of potential within modern marketplaces, and also the issue of simulacra (discussed below), I argue that contemporary processes of audience identification concerning the potential of the gaze relates to the consumption of sign values. As Sean Nixon (1997) relates within Baudrillard's work:

> Drawing on his assertion about the centrality of the sign value of commodities and contemporary consumption, Baudrillard suggests that one principal effect of this 'play of signs' is to constitute a new dominant form of social communication. (184)

In this way audience identification, and engagements with the gaze, evoke a 'play of signs' foregrounding the sign and its useful exchange value. Female, and masculine, identity, and equally queerness, may be related as cultural signs, relative to the identification interests of the audiences. As part of this, the gaze may be a process that involves focusing on masculine, feminine or queer signs, relative to assumed social and cultural values.

In doing this, audiences may relate to the notion of homophyly. Kylo-Patrick R. Hart (2000) (drawing upon the work of Rogers and Shefner-Rogers) tells us that homophyly:

> [Defines] the degree to which [representational] characters [within fiction and documentary] are similar to the viewer. The greater the homophyly between the central characters in a narrative work and the individual viewing the work, the greater the chance that the work will be considered credible by that viewer, and the greater the chance that the viewer will be influenced personally by it. (59)

For example female audiences, who see representations that are similar to themselves within media texts, potentially expressing aspects of similar cultural interest, political stance or emotive context, may experience a deeper interest in the narrative evoked by the text.

For example, within soap opera the imagined sense of shared connectivity to the texts may be enabled, through female, male and/or queer audiences seeing positive or affirmative representations of characters that represent their daily lives. As Christine Geraghty (1991) informs us, 'Enjoyment will be affected by the way in which the woman viewer is herself positioned within the home as mother/wife/daughter' (40). Furthermore 'consistent recognition is given to the emotional situations which women are deemed to share' (47). Consequently female audience identifications within soap operas rely on a gender-oriented sense of group membership, evident in viewing self-like representations. However, these representations are simulations, or copies, of real-life narratives, which offer a sense of mimesis, focus and intensity, foregrounding the essence of a life world, or a character, through the means of media representation.

Such a representational intensity may be related to Jean Baudrillard's (1994) concept of 'simulacra', which reveals complex scenarios in the representation of identity. Hence, although the audience may recognise the similitude of the representation to their own identity, as a reconstruction and reformation, the representation may appear larger than, or beyond, real life. Baudrillard tells us: 'Simulation is no longer that of a territory, a referential being, or a substance. It is the generation by models of a real without origin or reality: a hyperreal' (1994: 1), revealing the distance between the original and the copy (or the hyper-real which is reproduced).

Such a distance is evident in the composition of the gaze within media texts, where the act of looking is produced in a manner that foregrounds distance. Hence imagined intimacies, evident in the representation of voyeuristic pleasure of one person looking at another, foreground a binary process of distance between the two, at the same time framing a sense of sameness or closeness, in the context of realism. As discussed above, the gaze is considered as on one hand an act of distance in looking upon and objectifying the body, and on the other a possible act of closeness through identifying with the social identity of the subject. Such a duality may be related to Baudrillard's idea of media representations as 'holograms', and the 'imaginary aura of the double' he attests:

> Similitude is a dream and must remain one, in order for a modicum of illusion and a stage of the imaginary to exist. One must never pass over to the side of the real, the side of the exact resemblance of the world to itself, of the subject to itself. Because then the image disappears. One must never pass over to the side of the double, because then the dual relation disappears, and with it all seduction. (105)

Hence, while audience identification through the composition of the gaze might generate closeness, empathy and shared experience, suggesting exchangeability, at the same time the issue of media reproduction is contentious. Baudrillard suggests that visual representation within contemporary media offers evocation through its disconnection from the real. Hence it is the over-constructed or hyper-real nature of the gaze that enables its usefulness, not necessarily its connection to a real representation, or realism.

As part of this, aspects of disconnection and fragmentation are central, rather than peripheral. Instead of the need for some meaningful, fully representative media representation that tells us exactly like it is, it is the process of the simulacra which enables an intense sense of seeing.

I argue that a postmodern gaze, which is deconstructed and fragmented, in terms of composition and look, offers new scope in working through the meanings of scopophilic visual pleasure. Hence, although we may consider that the hetero media gaze may describe the overlooking of those who own the means of production, in a similar manner to Mulvey's description of the male gaze as defined by Hollywood industry, I am arguing that the gaze is more complex in its relationship, relative to fragmented reading potentials, in terms of both aesthetic and narrative composition. As part of this, a trilogy of films starring Doris Day and Rock Hudson, offers insight into the covert reading of the straight girl and the queer guy.

DORIS DAY AND ROCK HUDSON TRILOGY

Doris Day, Rock Hudson and Tony Randall made three films together: *Pillow Talk* (Michael Gordon 1959, US), *Lover Come Back* (Delbert Mann 1961,

US) and *Send Me No Flowers* (Norman Jewinson 1964, US). I have selected this filmic trilogy to consider the representation of the straight girl and the queer guy, particularly foregrounding the friendship of Doris Day and Rock Hudson, alongside the appearance and participation in these films of Tony Randall, who may be considered as a 'third party', and in some sense offers a queering of Doris's and Rock's romantic potential. While in these films there is no overt representation of the alliance between the straight girl and the queer guy, Doris Day's friendship with Rock Hudson (who lived a covert life as a gay man in Hollywood) was well known (Hudson and Davidson 2007). I argue not only that their representation as a couple was informed by possible audience readings of their platonic friendship (and Hudson's queer identity), even though in the films they were represented as lovers, but also that those involved in production framed them in an ambiguous way, to offer some sense of queer pleasure (see Dyer 2001b), without express representation. In order to explore this potential, and relate the textual content to the notion of the hetero media gaze, I will first relate the context and the narratives of the three films.

There is no scriptwriting or directorial consistency within *Pillow Talk*, *Lover Come Back* and *Send Me No Flowers* which would have suggested the existence of some artistic master plan in the bringing together of Doris Day, Rock Hudson and Tony Randall. Despite this as the series unfolds, their appearance together offers a particular consistency in developing the narrative connotations.

Pillow Talk concerns the representation of Day as Jan Morrow, an interior designer, who shares a telephone 'party line'[2] with Hudson as Brad Allen, a composer. Morrow and Allen do not know each other, and the story unfolds, as Allen is using the party line too frequently, and as a consequence of this Morrow cannot use the telephone to operate her business successfully. She complains expressly to Allen on the shared party line, and an animosity develops between them, particularly fuelled by Morrow overhearing Allen seduce a wide range of women, developing contempt for him as a 'womaniser'. Tony Randall plays Jonathan Forbes, who is in love with Morrow, yet his affections are unrequited. He is also a mutual friend to both Morrow and Allen, without their knowledge. Morrow and Allen meet by chance in a restaurant, and a relationship develops between them through mutual physical attraction, with Allen concealing his real identity (as the troubling sharer of the party line). As part of this he assumes an imaginary identity as Rex Stetson, a simple character connected to the western and the southern states. A romance between Morrow and Allen (as Stetson) develops, with their mutual friend Forbes unaware of this. Ultimately Morrow discovers that Stetson is actually Allen, and, although she deftly punishes him for concealing his real identity, including taking on an interior design job for Allen who just wants any contact with her to win her over, with Morrow ruining the décor to make his apartment seem like a 'harem', eventually they accept their destiny as romantic partners.

Lover Come Back in many ways repeats the narrative formula of *Pillow Talk*, with Doris Day playing an advertising executive, Carol Templeton, and Rock Hudson playing a competing advertising executive, Jerry Webster. Once again at the outset, the characters are unaware of each other's real physical appearance, and later a scenario evolves where the Rock Hudson character pretends to be someone else in order to spend time with the Doris Day character. This occurs where Webster wins an advertising client whom Templeton was hoping to win, with Hudson as Webster exhibiting skills in social entertainment to gain the client, and Day as Templeton failing to get the chance to present her advertising campaign, which she had spent considerable time in developing. Templeton complains to the advertising board that Webster's practice in gaining business, based on parties, drinking and the procurement of glamorous women for male clients, should be penalised. Webster manages to fend off these claims by offering the main female witness against him, the lead in an advertising campaign, for an imaginary product called 'Vip'. As part of this deception, Webster actually makes Vip television advertisements for the actress to perform in, but these are stored with no intention to broadcast them. Templeton accidentally hears about Vip, and wants revenge on Webster, trying to win the account for herself, unaware of the incredulity of Vip. A scenario develops where Templeton mistakes Webster for the inventor of Vip in her pursuit of the account, and a romance unfolds between the two of them, with Webster pretending to be a socially naive scientist and inventor. Tony Randall plays the owner of the advertising company that Rock Hudson's character works for, and his role in effect enables the scenario where the Vip television adverts are actually broadcast, through a misunderstanding while Rock is absent. This reveals incompetence in Tony Randall as the unsuitable inheritor of his father's business, unaware of proper business conventions. Similarly to *Pillow Talk*, Rock Hudson's character is found out, and Doris Day's character initially rejects him for his duplicity, at one point leaving him naked on a beach. However, at the close of the film they are married.

Send Me No Flowers appears as an entirely different narrative, with Day and Hudson as a married couple, Judy and George Kimball, with Tony Randall as their neighbour and friend, Arnold Nash. The narrative revolves around Hudson as Kimball, a hypochondriac who mistakenly believes that he is dying after hearing a telephone conversation by his doctor concerning another patient, believing that it is about him. Kimball, thinking that he has little time left, tries to find a new male partner for his wife in his imagined remaining days, wanting to assure her future happiness. Randall as Nash is a confident to Kimball in this pursuit, commenting on the suitability of potential new male partners for Judy Kimball. As part of ensuring Judy's happiness, George buys cemetery plots not only for himself and Judy but also for any future husband. Later in the film Judy mistakenly believes that her husband is having an affair, after a scene where George warns a recent widow of the dishonourable intentions of a possible male suitor, with Judy mistakenly believing that George has romantic inclinations for the widow. George is thrown out of the marital house, but later is forgiven after the cemetery plot salesman visits the house, and the misunderstanding is resolved. The film closes with George rejecting his hypochondria, happy in his enduring and future relationship with Judy.

While there appears little formal coherence within this filmic trilogy, I argue that key themes persist and develop within these films. Primarily the notion of a covert identity, or the concealment of identity, is an enduring narrative. In *Pillow Talk* and *Lover Come Back* this concerns the concealment of the identities played by Rock Hudson, with the notion that, through the concealment of the 'real identity' of the characters, as in fact oppositional or in conflict with the Doris Day character, some sense of masquerade will take place, with the Rock Hudson character as the only character fully aware of the narrative contexts. This also occurs in *Send Me No Flowers*, where concealment of identity is less about romance or playfulness, but is about assuring a partner's future, in protecting them from 'the real story'. Hence, although *Pillow Talk* and *Lover Come Back* focus on Rock concealing his dubious amorous intents, and in *Send Me No Flowers* such concealment relates to withholding knowledge of impending mortality, the suggestion is that the Rock Hudson character is more aware of the 'full story' than Doris Day. While in effect in *Send Me No Flowers* this is a misunderstanding, I consider that it is the focus on withholding narrative expression, but persisting with a covert expression, that is central. Hence, in terms of audience's reading of the Rock Hudson character, his identify is codified as masquerade, in a manner that brings attention to form, but also deconstructs such form. Whether audiences or producers were fully aware of Rock's covert life as a gay man might be irrelevant. However, his covert life is coded in the narrative expressions within these films as masquerade, in holding back an identity that might be seen to be real, and the expression of an identity that might be seen to be a simulation, of a real life.

Such covert expression in narrative is also mirrored in the aesthetic forms within these films. For example within *Pillow Talk* a common formal feature is the employment of split screen representations. In many ways this appearance is a useful narrative tool in expressing two very different narrative worlds that might only be connected through conversation on the telephone line. In a scene mid-way in the film, Doris Day and Rock Hudson, as the characters

Figure 1.1 *Doris Day as Jan Morrow and Rock Hudson as Brad Allen in a split-screen representation in* Pillow Talk. *Rock Hudson is coded as queer and feminised, evident in his body deportment echoing that of Doris Day.*

of Jan Morrow and Brad Allen, are represented through the split screen as inhabiting two diverse but intimately connected worlds. Both are represented as taking bubble baths, at the same time as in conversation on the telephone: the characters are represented as facing each other, mirroring each other's poses. Notably, Rock Hudson lifts his masculine hairy leg covered in bubble bath foam, mirroring a similar action by Doris Day (see Figure 1.1). Hence the gaze is drawn upon the male leg, codifying the man as indulgent and leisurely. Rather than signifying the male leg as robust and on 'solid ground', possibly involved in exertive play, protection or defence, which might be associated with traditional masculinity, the leg is framed as an object of fetishism, mirrored with the female leg, connoting subjectivity. Furthermore with Hudson's leg raised, a pose of sensual passivity is connoted, inviting phallic penetration. Such a focus on passivity is dominant in all three films. In many sequences within *Pillow Talk*, *Lover Come Back* and *Send Me No Flowers* Rock appears partly clothed or face down upon a bed, suggesting leisure, passivity and subjectivity rather than agency or action. Key sequences like these, include in *Send Me No Flowers* Rock lying in bed as a feminised hypochondriac, connoting frailty and instability: and in *Lover Come Back* also lying face down on a bed, Rock is subject to an assault by Tony Randall, who uses a walking stick to poke at his body, signifying the male body subject to homosexual phallic order. Also his masculine identity is questioned in *Lover Come Back*, where Rock rubs off blue paint from Tony Randall's face, in the manner in which a mother might clean up the face of a child who has been out playing, signifying maternal domesticity, rather than masculine order.

Furthermore, a key narrative formula within the trilogy is the observation of Rock Hudson by internal characters within the narrative, framing the notion of the gaze or the panopticon. Hence, although I am indicating diverse ways in which the identity of Hudson may be textually read as queer, in counterpoint to Doris Day, constructing the duo as an unlikely heterosexual couple, in effect the masquerade and the simulacra are deliberately unveiled within the narrative itself, by 'onlookers'. These 'onlookers' could be perceived as representations of the audience themselves, yet they are represented as institutional or business-oriented characters, and as such may represent commercial knowledge of Rock Hudson, as a queer enigma within the Hollywood industry. In *Pillow Talk*, the narrative onlookers are connected to science, as medical experts. Rock is represented as a possible 'freak of nature' as a pregnant man, with a doctor and nurse observing him, and desiring to examine him in a scientific manner. This occurs in the film through a misunderstanding, where Rock takes refuge from being discovered by Doris Day, in a seemingly anonymous waiting room, unaware that he is presenting himself as waiting for a gynaecological examination. This is a recurring trope within the film, with the doctor who gazes at Hudson, trying to track him down, in the company of his receptionist, who forms the initial misinterpretation.

Similarly in *Lover Come Back*, Rock is again queered through observation. This time the observers appear to be two businessmen at a hotel, who recurrently see Rock with a range of different women. Initially they consider him as the ideal man, in his prowess in the art of seduction. However this changes abruptly, when they observe him returning home wearing only a female fur coat, after Doris Day had left him at the beach, on the pretence that they would swim together naked. Not aware that his appearance is due to the failure of an imagined heterosexual encounter, they codify him as a queer man. The characters attest, 'He's the last guy in the world, that I would have figured . . .', commenting that they figured him as a queer man, potentially returning from a night of homosexual promiscuity. While in *Send Me No Flowers* the onlooker character is less explicit, I would argue that this function is given to the man who sells the cemetery plot, in his observation that Rock is a sexually liberated man, in desiring to be buried with his wife and her new husband, suggesting the identity of a married man who is queer.

I would argue not only that these episodes frame Rock Hudson as a queer identity subject to the institutional and the scientific gaze but also that such observation offers a libidinal freedom which accommodates queer identity. Therefore, while Rock is represented as ultimately wanting to settle down and marry Doris Day, or in the case of *Send Me No Flowers* desiring to return to an assured future with his wife, there is a focus on sexual or social indulgence as much as assimilation. Such indulgence I would argue is framed within the trilogy of films as connected to freedom for sexual liberty, evident in *Pillow Talk* and *Lover Come Back* where Rock's characters desire sexual promiscuity. If we read Rock as an implicit, and potentially explicit, queer man, we can evaluate his sexual encounters as simulacra of queer desire, reformed as heterosexual sexual freedom within the films. Hence through the process or media representation the hyper-reality of the imagined real identity is transformed and revivified for a mainstream audience. Not only may this be evident in evaluating Rock as the subject of the gaze, as feminised and vulnerable, but it is apparent in reading him as a queer man liberated through direct access to his inner psychological and sexual desires.

Notably, all three films reference the psychological notion of the id as connected to sexuality. It is particularly evident in *Lover Come Back*, where at the entrance to a nightclub there is an advert for the 'Id Girl' in a reference to hidden sexual desire, and also it is apparent in *Send Me No Flowers*, where Rock is a hypochondriac, and this status is revealed as a problem in his psychological state. Also more directly the notion of the id as a representation or simulacrum of queer desire is apparent in incidents where Rock is deliberately coded as potentially homosexual. Notably the intimate relationship between Tony Randall and Rock Hudson offers evidence of this.

In *Send Me No Flowers* Rock and Tony share a marital bed, after Rock is expelled from his marital household, and both make comments about the coldness of their feet and the length of their toenails, foregrounding an intimate domestic narrative within a seemingly utilitarian context. Also in *Lover Come Back* such direct homosexual desire is framed within a key sequence where Rock is staying in Doris's spare bedroom, whilst still maintaining his deceptive identity as a potential client, rather than as a competitor. Doris in the character of Carol Templeton assures Rock in the character of Jerry Webster, concerning privacy, 'You have a lock on the door, and you have your own back entrance'. In this statement she potentially references covert sexual opportunity, and also signifies the sexual submission of such queer desire, evident in the 'back entrance' as a receptive sexual area for the active phallus. This is also apparent in *Pillow Talk*, when in a key sequence in a restaurant Rock as the imaginary character of Rex Stetson tells Doris as Jan Morrow of his home environment in Texas, illustrating the terrain of a mountain with the demonstration of a serviette raised as a model on the table. This is intercut with Allen (as Rex Stetson) suddenly seeing Tony Randall as Jonathan Forbes appear in the restaurant, and a return of Hudson's gaze towards Day indicating the potential of being found out as a deceiver, while the serviette remains still erect, seeming like a phallic object before Rock's body. Hence an acknowledgement of Hudson's queer desire is apparent, as the phallus remains foregrounded, framed after the arrival of another male, who may not only disclose his real identity but also provides a homoerotic proximity.

In addition, the representation of alcohol specifically within *Lover Come Back* and *Send Me No Flowers* offers connections to the id and the notion of liberated sexual behaviour. In *Lover Come Back* the representation of the party where Rock as the advertising executive provides the 'greatest party ever' to win his account offers resonance, presenting party revellers and the client himself as drunk and seduced by alcohol and the proximity of available women as sexual objects. This is counterpointed by the resistance of Doris Day as someone who does not drink, but later at the close of the film not only is she revealed to drink alcohol willingly but she also partakes in a binge party through consuming the alcohol-laced chocolates that are in fact the 'imaginary product' Vip made real. This realisation leads to the close of the film, framing alcohol as setting emotion and sexual liberty free. In *Send Me No Flowers*, alcohol is directly connected to Tony Randall as the character of Arnold Nash, who drinks excessively when he hears that his best friend, neighbour and later bed partner George Kendall, played by Hudson, might be dying, leaving him alone. Hence the notion of death is connected to the sexual drive, evident in the context of the id through the masquerade of alcohol inducement, where forbidden pleasure might be concealed. In this sense the representation of the coupling of Tony Randall and Rock Hudson offers more scope for libidinal pleasure based on instinct and senses than is apparent in the coupling of Hudson and Day, which is framed on an assurance of security and domesticity. The representation of alcohol offers a sense of 'revealing' through masquerade, evident in the character played by Tony Randall, where his emotions and feelings become deeply embedded.

Despite this, such representations of queer men in the company of straight females relies on a certain reading between the lines, and, although such analysis offers developed potential, more explicit representations of queer men in the company of straight females more directly frame the political mechanisms of representation. Hence, following the covert and subliminal potential of Doris Day, Rock Hudson and Tony Randall evident within their filmic trilogy, I now would like to explore three more films which may be considered as groundbreaking. These however are not within the genre of American romantic comedy, but are within the domain of British social realism, and responses to this.

A Taste of Honey, *Darling* and *Zee and Co.*

A Taste of Honey (Tony Richardson 1961, UK), *Darling* (John Schlesinger 1965, UK), and *Zee and Co.* (Brian G. Hutton 1972, UK) may be connected

Figure 1.2 *Rita Tushingham as Jo and Murray Melvyn as Geoffrey in* A Taste of Honey, *forming part of the British social realist film movement.*

not only in relation to the representation of the straight girl and the queer guy but also in their relationship to British social realism. Notably, *A Taste of Honey* and *Darling* may be considered as key texts produced by directors working within this domain (see Figure 1.2). Tony Richardson's *A Taste of Honey* and John Schlesinger's *Darling* are texts that follow the production of two of the most iconic British social realist films: Richardson's *Look Back in Anger* (1959) and Schlesinger's *A Kind of Loving* (1962). These earlier films focused on social inequalities within British society at the time, exploring issues of class relative to the opportunity, identity and discontent of young heterosexual males, as lead characters (see Hill 1986; Murphy 1992). *A Taste of Honey* and *Darling* develop or diverge from this androcentric formula, framing female characters as the central focus. While *Zee and Co.* has little connection to the directorial hierarchy of *A Taste of Honey* and *Darling*, I argue that this film offers a response to the tradition of British Social realism, in its focus on personal indulgence and intent, outside of a class-based world, in some senses framing opportunities of new materialism, foregrounding female agency, and the notion of post-feminism. The director Brian G. Hutton's directorial work previous to *Zee and Co.* included a focus on war films, notably evident in *Where Eagles Dare* (1968) and *Kelly's Heroes* (1970). Hutton's work may be considered as focusing on generic approaches to filmic form, framing production aspects, rather than auteur-based notions of film form framing the director's vision (see Grant 2008). This might offer insight into the relationship between the straight girl and the queer guy, for its reference to commodity, rather than artistry or intellectual perception, in a sense a rejection of realism. However, before we explore these textual possibilities, it is first important to relate the narrative and the context of the case studies.

A Taste of Honey, *Darling* and *Zee and Co.* all feature representations of the straight girl and the queer guy. However, it's important to note that only *A Taste of Honey* fully integrates this relationship within the closing narrative, suggesting the endurance and significance of this relationship. Hence in *Darling* and *Zee and Co.*, while the queer guy is framed as an important narrative context in relation to the straight girl, they are considered as narrative components, rather than coexistent within binary identification forms that might suggest equality. The diverse narratives are related below.

A Taste of Honey is an adaptation of the celebrated play of the same name by Shelagh Delaney. The central story concerns the life chances of a young girl called Jo (played by Rita Tushingham) who lives in relative poverty, with her mother Helen (played by Dora Bryan). Jo is about to leave school, and her mother offers little stability, evident in her promiscuous lifestyle, and her preference for finding a husband over caring for her daughter. Helen is depicted as rather cruel, telling Jo that her father was a simpleton, and that Jo had similar eyes to 'the village idiot'. Helen also fails to care for Jo, evident where Jo and her mother are forced to leave their accommodation, as Helen has not paid the rent. Later Helen abandons Jo, when she finds a potential husband who can support her, despite that man not caring for Jo, stipulating that Jo won't be able to live with them in their new house. Jo finds solace in the company of a black sailor, Jimmy (played by Paul Danquah), who is temporarily resident in the city, having sex with him after rejection from her mother and the new partner. Later, Jo, living alone, gets a job in a shoe shop, where she meets Geoffrey (played by Murray Melvin) who is a customer. Geoffrey and Jo become good friends, despite Jo humiliating him, after discovering that he is gay, saying that she will be friends with him only if he tells her about his homosexual encounters. Despite this the two become firm friends, sharing a low-rent apartment. Jo discovers that she is pregnant by Jimmy, who has now left the city, and Geoffrey offers her support, saying that he would marry her, and wants to raise the baby with her. Near the close of the film, Helen returns after her marriage fails, ejecting Geoffrey from Jo's apartment so she can live there. The film closes with laments from both Jo and Geoffrey that they cannot share each other's lives, and raise Jo's baby.

Darling is the third major film directed by John Schlesinger, who was openly gay (see Mann 2004), and who later produced the groundbreaking mainstream queer film *Sunday Bloody Sunday* (1971) (discussed in Chapter 3), which was a landmark for its representation of male same-sex intimacy, and the context of bisexuality. Hence, *Darling*'s focus on male queer desire offers a personal context of social realism, evident in the political connection to the director's identity. The central narrative of *Darling* concerns the relationship between Diana (played by Julie Christie), an aspiring actress and model, and Robert (played by Dirk Bogarde), a journalist, who both leave their long-term marriages to be together. However, Diana becomes dissatisfied with the relationship, making friends with Miles Brand (played by Laurence Harvey) who has connections within the celebrity world, and may be able to help her to advance her career. She becomes sexually involved with Miles, attending parties where group sexual activity takes place. Robert discovers Diana's deception, and breaks off their relationship. In response to this Diana throws herself into her career, at the same time making friends with the openly gay photographer Malcolm (played by Roland Curram), who is enthusiastic about her aesthetic potential as a photographic subject, and is playful in her company. Diana and Malcolm travel on holiday together to Italy, as part of her new success in an advertising campaign. On the isle of Capri, they spend considerable time together, with Malcolm finding a male sexual partner. Diana becomes annoyed that Malcolm is not paying attention to her, and seduces the man whom Malcolm had sex with. Diana spends a lot of leisure time in the company of queer men, including Malcolm in this grouping. Later she receives an offer of marriage from an older male who is part of the Italian aristocracy, whom she met whilst filming her advertising campaign. While she initially rejects this man, later, after seeing little advancement in her career, she marries him, moving to Italy, also caring for his family and household. However, she becomes discontented with this constriction, later returning to Robert in the UK. Robert ultimately rejects her, sending her back to Italy, and the film closes with her despondency, but her acceptance that she can no longer be with Robert.

Zee and Co. concerns the story of Zee Blakely (played by Elizabeth Taylor) and husband Robert (played by Michael Caine), who have an open sexual relationship. Zee is a housewife and her husband is an architect, and Zee is represented as possessing a non-restrictive household budget, able to take impromptu holidays, as she does in the film. At a party Robert meets Stella (played by Susannah York) whom he finds attractive, and they embark on a sexual relationship. Zee is jealous and volatile in response to this, and she embarks on a campaign to break up her husband's relationship with Stella. As part of this Zee visits Stella's dressmaking shop, and commissions work from her. Her plan is to find information concerning the life and interests of Stella, so she can use this against her. She consoles herself in the company of longstanding friend Gordon (played by John Standing), an effeminate gay man and hairdresser, who encourages Zee to defend her position. As part of this, Zee asks Gordon to 'chat up' Stella's shop assistant who is a young gay man, in order that Zee can get information from the 'little ponce' that she can use to break up Robert and Stella. Later, when Robert has moved out of the marital household and is living with Stella, Zee becomes mentally unstable, at one point attempting suicide. Despite this, she later seems to accept defeat in her loss of Robert to Stella, getting close to Stella as part of this. However, Zee uses this new intimacy to seduce Stella, aware that she has a homosexual past, found out through an intimate disclosure between the two. The film ends with Zee and Robert seemingly back together, as Stella is shamed for her homosexual tendencies.

I argue that the composition of the gaze within *A Taste of Honey*, *Darling* and *Zee and Co.* accommodates the notion of a queer subject, and a queer audience. In this sense, while these texts are generally addressed to the mainstream, there is a framing of aesthetic pleasure that incorporates queer sexuality. This involves a reformation in the aesthetics of the 'male gaze' that, instead of framing the female body as an object of pleasure or consumption, explores the queer subject, as a peripheral other. In the manner that Baudrillard considers the notion of the hologram, and the potential of the simulacrum, a duality is presented which counterpoints both inclusivity and exclusion. However, unlike the representation of the male (imagined to be) heterosexual body, such as the representation of Nick Kamen in the Levi's advertising campaign (see above), the focus is not on the consumption of the body, relating mechanisms and commodities of industry, but rather on the tentative and unfixed body, in the manner of the hologram. *A Taste of Honey*, *Darling* and *Zee and Co.* relate this potential, using the camera to gaze upon the ghostly presence of the queer male, as between places rather than situated as foundational, or clearly viewed.

Notably, this is evident where in *A Taste of Honey* the character of Geoffrey is constructed as 'peripheral' within the text, making him seem like a hologram, through refracting his direct gaze upon Jo. For example when Geoffrey first encounters Jo in the shoe shop where Jo works, he is represented as hesitating briefly three times as he looks through the shop window at the shoes on display, and his face is pressed closely to the door as he enters the shop. Hence the glass refracts his gaze, limiting his possession of a dominant gaze. Furthermore, Geoffrey is frequently constituted as lower in position than Jo in a number of instances where they exchange gazes, and a sense of lingering or hesitation is presented on behalf of Geoffrey. This is apparent when Jo first invites Geoffrey into her apartment, and Geoffrey takes time to gain the confidence to ascend the stairs, where Jo had looked down upon him inviting him to come in. Also in the apartment after Jo has discovered Geoffrey's homosexuality, and has offered him accommodation if he tells her about his sexual life, she is positioned above him, gazing down upon him. Furthermore such distancing is evident near the close of the film, when, after Geoffrey has been ejected from Jo's home by Jo's mother, he wanders around the public social space outside the apartment, as children tend to a bonfire. Geoffrey is represented as a ghostly figure, haunting this social space, offering a sense of lingering and longing, unable to move on but able to watch over, knowing that he must part, but having no place to go to.

Similarly in *Darling*, the sense of between places is evident when Diana and Malcolm spend time shopping in the upmarket store Fortnum and Mason in London. Prior to this sequence Diana has bought Malcolm some exotic flowers (streliza) as a gift, and the two exhibit themselves around the shop with Malcolm holding the tall flowers in hand, and Diana pressing the shop assistant to find exotic foods. However, rather than buying them, she embarks on a shoplifting spree, presenting the couple as outsiders to the normal behavioural decorum expected of customers in the store. This extraordinary behaviour is related to the gaze, where onlookers of the couple (notably an older female) become aware of her dysfunctional behaviour, and the couple are constructed as a queer couple, consisting of a female shoplifter, and a feminised man, evident in Malcolm holding the flowers, and unable to stop Diana in her shoplifting pursuits.

Later, when Diana and Malcolm consume the products that they have stolen, their gaze is inverted back, where in a drunken stupor they both terrorise two goldfish (which Diana had cared for for some time), pouring wine into their bowl, throwing food at them, and actually poking at them with a fork, killing them. Hence the goldfish, secure in a bowl on the domestic household table, represent an imagined security that could exist between the two, and this is disrupted and destroyed through their own actions, and their inability to fix themselves in a secure setting that is ordered. This malevolent sense of ghostliness, as existing outside and unable to find happiness in the home, however, prioritises Diana over Malcolm. Diana is represented as possessing not only the means of destruction but also the means of attention. This is further apparent where, when the two are on holiday in Capri, Diana seduces the waiter who had been a sexual partner to Malcolm, proving that she can ultimately gain attention, and Malcolm might not possess anything exclusively, coding him as subordinate to her. This counters the efficiency of Malcolm's gaze, which had been powerful in seducing the waiter in the first instance, represented as a libidinal exchange of looks between the waiter and Malcolm that resulted in their first sexual encounter. In contrast Diana simply rides off on a bike with the waiter to spend the night with him, connoting utilitarianism and bodily needs, rather than seduction and intensity.

In *Zee and Co.* the relationship between Zee and Gordon offers a similar inequality. In the only main sequence where Zee shares a scene with queer male friend Gordon, they are set within a restaurant. However, rather than sitting opposite at a table for a meal, they are represented at the bar, drinking together, with snacks in front of them. Whilst they may possibly be waiting for a table, we get the impression that this is a casual encounter, where Zee can offload her emotions concerning her discontent with her husband, for his attraction to Stella. While Gordon gazes at Zee with sincere support, in her venture to find evidence against Stella, with his eyes constantly looking at her, and offering support in his dialogue, Zee tends to look away whilst attesting her unhappiness. Zee parodies the idea of sustained attention and thoughtfulness, failing to sustain a gaze at Gordon in a manner that suggests equality. For example in conversation:

> Gordon: Now then, what's [Stella] like? [engaging look to Zee]

> Zee: A slob! Worse than that: a soulful slob! [looking down irritated] There is nothing more that I hate than soulful people. She is always a little out of breath. [looking up but away from Gordon mimicking, slightly tilting her head to mimic soulfulness], and always sees beauty in everything. Especially in shit! [looks mean directly at Gordon].

Zee's critique of Stella, framing the notion of soulfulness in relation to insincerity, parodies the value of a sustained or meaningful gaze. In this sense, she critiques her queer friend for his sustained gaze upon her, through indirectly looking at him, in a manner that denies a sense of mirroring. This is further evident where, on finishing this conversation, Gordon wants to tell Zee about his news of an attractive man whom he had encountered, and Zee retorts simply, 'I've got problems of my own', and does not want to hear his story. Such an imbalance engenders Gordon as supportive of Zee, but he is not valued as an equal. Notably, the scene following the restaurant conversation offers a vivid representation of this. That night Zee persuades Gordon to drive her to the house where her husband and Stella are staying, parking outside the house, where Zee shouts at the couple from the street. While this takes place we see Gordon firmly in the shadows, as the driver of the car, in support of her dysfunctional action, but not seen in full view. He is an enabler, but not an equal accomplice, in the events that they share or partake in.

Hence the queer men in *A Taste of Honey*, *Darling* and *Zee and Co.* are all constructed as enablers to the central female characters. Geoffrey in *A Taste of Honey* offers Jo confidence in getting herself together, so she can cope with the arrival of a baby, and can stand up to her mother as an oppressive figure. Malcolm in *Darling* helps Diana in her career and social life, not only producing the highest-quality photos that might advance her career but also accompanying her as a sincere close friend offering her moral support, even though she limits his potential to be an equal. Gordon's role for Zee is simply someone who can support her, with her taking every opportunity to use him, rejecting his own feelings as an equal. At the same time all these characters are framed by the public presences within the films, indicating to the audience possibilities of engagement. While in *Darling* and *Zee and Co.* these onlookers are generally middle-class or upper-class characters, such as the shoppers who witness Diana and Malcolm as shoplifters in *Darling* and non-specific restaurant-goers who may overhear Zee rant against the notion of soulfulness in *Zee and Co.*, in *A Taste of Honey* the onlookers, or imagined audiences, are children. Hence a key distinction between these films is the sense of realism offered by *A Taste of Honey*, which emulates discourses concerning social justice and the need for equality. Through framing Geoffrey as contextual to children, not only as characters within the film who accept both Jo and Geoffrey together, but also in suggesting that Geoffrey would make an ideal carer for a child, *A Taste of Honey* employs the media gaze with a political sense. Through avoiding discourses that might limit the connection between homosexuals and children, rejecting connotations of paedophilia, *A Taste of Honey* offers new concepts of the gaze that are progressive. This is not to say that *Darling* and *Zee and Co.* are regressive or counterproductive; rather, they exhibit a reliance on a female subjectivity that might be considered as post-feminist, in the shift of the female role to androcentric, but equally reliant on stereotypical subjectivities.

Conclusion

Carrie Tarr (1985) tells us that '*Darling*, though constructing a woman character whose very existence constitutes "trouble", has marshaled a formidable battery of devices to prevent possibilities of identification with the female point of view' (64). Hence, while the films discussed in this chapter seemingly present the straight girl and the queer guy to a mainstream audience, there are complications, with regard to female identification. As Tarr notes with regards to *Darling*, there is a 'comparative absence of any invitation to empathise with the woman and her predicament [at the same time lacking] any alternative controlling male discourse within the diegesis' (1985: 65). However, such an indirect address to female audiences, and a limitation of patriarchal order, I suggest do not limit the discursive potential of the texts discussed in this chapter. Rather, I would argue that the hetero media gaze is not formed exclusively through the means of production, or the production of identity, that might engage and positively speak to mainstream, or queer audiences; rather it is the philosophy of absence as presence which enables such connectivity.

Therefore the hetero media gaze, as related in this chapter to the concept of the 'male gaze', is less about looking and finding, and rather more about looking and sensing, finding presence where there seems to be absence. With the case studies that focused on Doris Day, Rock Hudson and Tony Randall, even though there was no explicit representation of queer desire, through adopting a covert reading, and potentially relating the life stories of the stars themselves, notions of the id, the libido and suppressed desire are potentially sensed by the audience. In real life Doris Day and Rock Hudson were the most celebrated straight girl and queer guy collaboration, even if many officially found out about this only after Rock Hudson succumbed to AIDS (see Hudson and Davidson 2007). It is this ghostly presence, as a sense of reality, that pervades these films, whether for contemporary viewers or retrospectively from a position of greater knowledge.

Similarly in *A Taste of Honey*, *Darling* and *Zee and Co.*, although these are more explicit representations of the straight girl and the queer guy, their discursive potential frames 'lack', as much as 'possibility', evident in the notion of the hologram (see above). The queer men in these films are largely constructed as enablers to straight girls, and through varying narrative approaches frame the abject position of the queer guy as an outsider who may be used, and is frequently denied. While in many ways the troubling representation of the straight girls in some ways problematises a positive reading of these characters, which might limit a female audience viewership, I argue that it is the shift towards a post-feminist approach to female identity which frames this commodity. This relates the female as equal to the heterosexual male, in their superiority to queer men. Although the representation of Jo in *A Taste of Honey* seems to suggest equality between the straight girl and the queer guy, later representations prioritised the life chances of the straight girl, framing a kind of inequality.

Hence, the contemporary relationship of the straight girl and the queer guy as produced within television and film in fact relies on this disparity, and I argue would not reach mainstream audiences, if it were not for this. At the same time the notion of the queer gaze itself is commoditised, and, as we discover in the next chapter, aspects of disparity might form a process not only of identification but also of consumption.

Notes

1. See also Jackie Stacey's book *Star Gazing: Hollywood Cinema and Female Spectatorship* (1993), which offers a development of these ideas.
2. A 'party line' is a telephone line shared by two users with separate telephones, to save the cost of having two exclusive lines. The users cannot make separate calls simultaneously but can hear each other's calls.

CHAPTER 2

Queer Gazes and Identifications

John Ellis (1982) tells us:

> [I]dentification involves both the recognition of self in the image on the screen, a narcissistic identification, and the identification of self with the various positions that are involved in the fictional narration: those of hero and heroine, villain, bit-part player, active and passive character. Identification is therefore multiple and fractured, a sense of seeing the constituent parts of the spectator's own psyche paraded before her or him. (43)

Hence, processes of identification are complex, allowing multifarious subjectivities and positions of viewing and reading. Part of this might involve the confrontation of personal desires and dreams, at the same time suspending personal subjectivities. For the relationship between the straight girl and the queer male, although I am suggesting an obvious representational interaction, as evident in Chapter 1, where covert readings may be possible in defining and working through this relationship, I want to consider the potential of narcissistic identification, where seemingly explicit representations clearly frame queer desire, offering a sense of fulfilment. This desire, however, may not be subliminal, suggesting some kind of repression: I want to consider expression and evocation that are more easily consumed.

Although we might consider that expressive and evocative texts that frame queer desire only followed the emergence of New Queer Cinema in the 1990s (see Aaron 2004; Benshoff and Griffin 2004; Ritch 2013), I would like to argue that earlier texts foregrounded this 'narcissistic' pleasure. Hence, following John Ellis's notion of the narcissistic gaze, in terms of spectatorship, and the likely engagement with heterosexual female identification, I would like not only to explore the emergence of explicit queer desire, as evident in New Queer Cinema, but also to consider prototypical cinematic texts demonstrating queer desire, which, while they may seem subliminal, involve complex formations of the queer gaze.

As part of this I explore the significance of *Rope* (Alfred Hitchcock 1948, US) and *Suddenly Last Summer* (Joseph L. Mankiewicz 1959, US), as prototypes of queer desire, relating the construction of the queer gaze. While both of these texts seemingly have no explicit homosexual characters, I argue that, through diverse forms of representation and character construction, these films are powerful queer texts, though they are seemingly inhibited through processes of adaptation for a mainstream audience.

I then relate the significance of one of the earliest films of New Queer Cinema, *Swoon* (Tom Kalin 1992, US), which appears as an adaptation of *Rope*, for its connection to the narrative of the murderers Leopold and Loeb in the 1920s (see Higdon 1999). While in many ways *Swoon* might be seen to make the supposed covert queer potential of *Rope* more explicit, I question this hypothesis.

Framing the explicit potential of New Queer Cinema, I then consider the work of two key auteurs in this area, Derek Jarman and Gregg Araki. As part of this I examine *Caravaggio* (Derek Jarman 1986, UK) and *Edward II* (Derek Jarman 1991, UK), which are historical adaptations of the life stories of queer men. I then examine *The Living End* (Gregg Araki 1992, US) and *Mysterious Skin* (Gregg Araki 2005, US), which respectively focus on AIDS and the sexual abuse of children. I argue that Jarman's and Araki's work, through a focus on the aesthetics of the painterly and historical image, represents the queer body as sensual, but also ephemeral. Such vulnerability encourages mainstream audiences to objectify and consume the queer body, adopting, in a sense, the notion of the queer gaze.

As part of this, while these case studies do not explicitly focus on the straight girl and queer guy relationship, they do consider the commodification of queer desire relating varying forms of subjectivity, related to the mainstream consumption of queer texts, foregrounding a focus on female viewership.

QUEER NARCISSISM AND THE GAZE

Robert Samuels (1998) has noted that while

> [T]he narcissistic subject needs to reinforce its ego by finding ideal images and forms that reinforce its own sense of ideal formation and body coherency, . . . the object [gazed upon] does not give one a sense of visual totality or control, and therefore a sense of bodily integration; rather the gaze object seems to fragment the illusion of a totalized body image. (112)

While Samuels considers in some sense that the gaze represents 'an inversion of narcissism', through its indirect connection with the totality of the body being gazed upon, I would like to argue for a sense of queer identification that might not rely on a need for wholeness. Hence queer audiences who might gaze upon seemingly fragmented objects, which may or may not literally represent themselves, might find narcissistic pleasure in recognising absence, framing the lack of a coherent self-like representation. Within a tradition of Hollywood film, which had denied the representation of queer men and women, the notion of absence is also relative to the potential for voyeurism. As Samuels (1998) attests, 'what the voyeur is looking to see is the absence of the ideal image or phallus and not its presence' (112). Consequently queer audiences to some degree are coerced into the position of the voyeur, as there is an expectation of absence, and yet there is a drive to continuously find representations of the self. Despite this, the process of the gaze itself enables some sense of material presence, involving reciprocity that connects narcissism and voyeurism.

Clifford T. Manlove (2007) tells us: 'because the gaze leaves evidence – a stain – it can also be *reversed*. [Potentially] becoming aware of the gaze – the viewer is introduced to the intersubjective presence of the gaze, resulting from its stain' (98). Using the case study of *Rear Window* and relating the agency of the character of Lisa, who travels from the security of her boyfriend's apartment to an opposite apartment, a scopophilic target, where we believe that a murder has taken place, Manlove demonstrates through this example the potential of the gaze to be returned from the point where it was originated. Where Lisa points at the wedding ring of the murder victim (that she has just found) now discreetly placed on her hand, concealed in view from those in the apartment she has broken into, but fully facing her boyfriend in the apartment opposite overlooking her, she returns the gaze, back at the audience. Lacan considers the notion of the stain, as evidence that the gaze has taken place: 'If the function of the stain is recognised in its autonomy and identified with that of the gaze . . . we can see its track, its thread, its trace, at every stage of the constitution of the world, in the scopic field' (cited in Manlove 2007: 98). Hence the scopic world invites a return of the gaze, through the agency of gazing, and leaving a trace of the gaze. Despite this, within cinema the gaze is often ephemeral, and fleeting, even if it is recurring. For example, although we do see Lisa point at the wedding ring in returning the gaze, this doesn't last long, and the normative conventions of film editing return with intercut shots between the overlooking apartment and the apartment overlooked. Hence the stain, as evidence of the gaze, soon fades away, and this is just a component of the narrative, even if it is rhythmically iterated. Despite this convention, *Rope* and *Suddenly Last Summer* offer a unique case study, in their relationship to the gaze, which I argue offers a sense of voyeurism and narcissism, in representing the imagined queer self.

Rope and Suddenly Last Summer

Rope (1948) and *Suddenly Last Summer* (1959) appear as contrasting filmic texts; the former is an innovative technical triumph from the celebrated director Alfred Hitchcock known for producing thrillers and suspense films, and the latter is the product of the iconic American playwright Tennessee Williams, known for an intense and literature-based approach. Also they come from different time frames, and from different political and social cultures. However, I have selected these texts not for their similarity, or even their difference: I am discussing them together for their potential to relate a prototypical queer gaze, which foregrounds absence as much as presence. However, before I examine the textual evidence I will first consider the diverse narratives, and historical contexts of these films.

Rope is an adaptation of a British play bearing the same name written by Patrick Hamilton, published in 1929. At the same time the narrative of *Rope* has been connected to the real-life story of Nathan Leopold and Richard Loeb, who abducted and murdered a fourteen-year-old boy, Robert Franks, in Chicago in 1924, for the foregrounding of two seemingly homosexual murderers, who involve themselves in the act of killing for the sensation and intellectual prospect of taking a life. Although *Rope* clearly references the killers Leopold and Loeb, evident in the class status of the murderers as students and intellectuals, Hitchcock's film closely follows the British play in terms of format. Hence the film is a cultural hybrid form blending a British fictional play with an American real-life narrative. At the same time, issues of casting are highly relevant in our reading of the film, with one of the central characters, Phillip, being played by Farley Granger (discussed in the Introduction), an actor who presented himself as bisexual, and later in his autobiography related his homosexual life (see Granger and Calhoun 2007).

Hitchcock's *Rope* is technologically unique in the mainstream Hollywood film industry, as in effect the film is a recorded play. Very closely following the format of the original play, Hitchcock uses no distinguishable editing, and we are given the impression that the entire film is one long shot, as if we were of watching a play in real time. This was an technical achievement, as the longest sequence that could be filmed at the time was ten minutes, and in effect the film consists of ten-minute shots which are edited together, to create the illusion of one long shot of eighty minutes. The sense of seamlessness and connection is achieved through joining the ten-minute segments by ending each segment as an obscuring of the camera lens, often achieved through placing the camera to focus on a character's back, achieving a sense of continuity. In terms of narrative the story concerns two young intellectual middle-class men, Phillip and Brandon, who murder a male friend of theirs, David. They strangle him in their apartment, immediately concealing his body in a large wooden chest. This is a planned event, with Phillip and Brandon considering the action of murder for some time, with the idea of holding a party after the murder has taken place, with David's body in close proximity to the guests, and the guests themselves wondering why David has not turned up for the party. Following the plan, after David has been murdered and concealed in the chest, a range of guests come to a party in the apartment, not aware that the food is served upon the chest where David's body is concealed. Guests at the party include David's girlfriend, Kenneth, a rival for David's girlfriend's affection, David's father, and also Brandon's and David's academic tutor Rupert. All of the guests are concerned regarding David's absence, and throughout the narrative Phillip and Brandon present themselves as equally unsure why David is not there. After the guests leave the party, Brandon and Phillip have planned to dispose of the body. However, Rupert, who returns to the apartment on the pretext that he has left his cigarette case there, interrupts them, leading to the discovery of the body.

Throughout the narrative we are given the impression that it is the intellectual teaching of Rupert that had inspired the killing. This is related to Rupert's interest in the philosophy of Nietzsche, and the notion of the superman (Nietzsche 1974), who feels intellectually superior to others, and considers those less superior as disposable. Rupert is represented as able to sense the emotions of Phillip and Brandon, and hence is able to solve the crime. As part of this closeness, we are also given the impression that he is jealous of Phillip and Brandon's relationship, with an intimation that he has previously been sexually involved with Phillip. However on Rupert discovering David's body, he is horrified that they have misappropriated his intellectual ideas, considering that Phillip and David possess no humanity.

Gore Vidal adapted *Suddenly Last Summer* from Tennessee Williams's play of the same name. Both Williams and Vidal identified as homosexual, or at least bisexual (see Pullen [2009] 2012; 2014), and their collaboration on this film offers a good opportunity to represent queer life, with Williams known for producing plays that reflected his life. As Raymond Hayman (1993) reports, 'more autobiographical than they seem [Williams's] plays are full of outcasts, misfits, and fugitives' (xv): the representation of himself and problematic issues that surrounded his family are key aspects of his work. This is particularly evident in *Suddenly Last Summer*, relating the representation of homosexuality potentially connected to Williams's own life, and mental health conditions pertaining to his sister. Hence the plotline of *Suddenly Last Summer* offers a direct connection to Williams's life through focusing on the troubling psychological state of a young girl called Catherine, after she has witnessed the death of her homosexual cousin Sebastian whilst on holiday abroad. In the story Catherine's aunt Violet is concerned for Catherine's psychological state, arranging for her to be examined by Dr Cukrowicz, who is a pioneer in specialist brain surgery, the lobotomy, designed to alleviate troubled psychological states. Dr Cukrowicz experiences a professional moral dilemma when Violet offers to fund the building of a new wing for the hospital that he works for, in return for the lobotomy operation on Catherine. The central narrative theme concerns the inappropriate intimate relationship between Violet and Sebastian, as mother and son, and Catherine's intrusion in this relationship, when she goes on holiday with Sebastian, when Violet is unable to travel. The character of Sebastian is coded as homosexual, in that he desires the company of young men whilst on holiday, and he uses his mother, and later his cousin, to attract them. Sebastian is murdered in the film by local impoverished youths, who, after taunting him at the beach, chase him through a medieval village and up a hill, eventually devouring his body as cannibals.

The casting of *Suddenly Last Summer* directly relates to the notion of the straight girl and the queer guy, with the character of Catherine played by Elizabeth Taylor, and the character of Dr Cukrowicz by Montgomery Clift. Taylor was a close friend to Clift, who was homosexual, and there were many instances where they supported each other within the social context of Hollywood (see Bosworth 1978).

Both *Rope* and *Suddenly Last Summer* present representations of queer sexuality that are subliminal or covert, not by design but as a result of the limitations of the Motion Picture Code, which as an industry monitor that commenced in the 1930s offered advice on the censorship of a range of explicit sexual and social representations (see Gross 2001; Russo 1987). In the case of *Suddenly Last Summer* Gore Vidal worked with Williams to adapt the play, with the hope that the representations might be more explicit, as later reported in the documentary *The Celluloid Closet* (Rob Epstein and Jeffrey Friedman 1995, US) there were problems in engaging with the censors in the department of the Motion Picture Code, who wanted to extinguish any direct references to homosexuality. Although the original play of *Rope* and the real-life story of Leopold and Loeb offer clear references to same-sex intimacy, and, although Arthur Laurents and Hume Cronyn, who worked on the screenplay, were expressly aware of this, there was no design to explicitly incorporate any form of sexual diversity. However, despite this imagined limitation in denying key elements of the actual narratives, I argue that these films produce powerful representations of the queer gaze, evident in foregrounding absence as much as presence.

I argue that a sense of absence as coding presence is evident in the notion of the voyeur, through the construction of the cinematic gaze. This is evident in both films; however, it is achieved through entirely different aesthetic production processes. In *Rope* it is achieved through a recurring sense of a relentless gaze, evident in the film's unique production process, as a continuous long shot without evidence of intercut shots or cutaways. In *Suddenly Last Summer* it is apparent where we are denied a visual representation of the face of Sebastian, yet we are presented with a composite image, blending an image of Catherine recalling the narrative and actions shots of Sebastian, where his body and movement are displayed but his face is obscured.

This sense of voyeurism offers an image of the queer male as to be looked at, or sought for, but, through concealing a vivid or explicit identity, this complicates an easy process of identification. Whilst this suggests negation, or limitation, I feel that, in terms of the psychological gaze, the construction of the queer male in this way is innovative. As Robert Samuels (1998) tells us:

> A central element of Lacan's theory of ethics is his belief that the foundation of all our guilt is our awareness of the way that we destroy the Real by Symbolizing it. Thus, our original sin is repeated every time that we speak or articulate something in Symbolic form. [Within film this potentially relates to how] linguistic transgression, punishment, and guilt are presented, [and] the 'projection' of different unconsciousness formations such as dreams, wordplays, slips, faulty actions, and jokes. (8)

Hence a tension between the real and the symbolic representation offers diverse scope in working through different discursive possibilities. Robert Samuels uses this process to consider the emergence of 'bi-textual' desire, evident within the films of Hitchcock, to allude to the notion of bisexuality. Hence a dualism is presented. Although Samuels does not apply this theory to *Rope*, I argue that this tension between the real and the symbolic is evident in the way that absence is demonstrated through the gaze. Hence the absence represents the Real representation, and potentially the Symbolic represents the visual gaze itself, as a sustained yearning that is not fulfilled.

For example in *Rope*, although the entire film may be considered as a sustained gaze, key sequences punctuate the idea of absence, and suspense, so that our desire to see something evidential will be fulfilled. Notably, in a key sequence in the film, there is tension that the body will be discovered while the guests are still at the party. Prior to this, Phillip (one of the murderers) is playing the piano, and Rupert (the teacher) is in conversation with him. What is notable about this prior sequence is that there is an allusion to an imagined sexual encounter between the two characters. Rupert (played by James Stewart) is standing looking down on Phillip who is seated playing the piano, framing a gaze between both characters which suggests encounter and intensity. The music that Phillip is playing is highly emotional, including dissonant notes that connote discord. Part of the discursive construction relates the imagined sexual history between the two characters, evident in the foregrounding of a metronome, placed on the piano. Rupert starts up the metronome and it represents syncopation with the rhythm of the music, reiterating a tension between the characters. At the same time Rupert at one point holds the metronome whilst it is working, seeming as if he is holding on to a phallic object, imagined to be the phallus of Phillip. This suggested relationship is further present in the conversation between the two, where Rupert challenges Phillip for denying his memory of a story recounted earlier in the evening regarding the inability of Brandon to remember his ability to strangle a chicken. In an allusion to the strangling of David, Rupert challenges Phillip's failing to remember this ability, recalling a time when they were both at a farm (presumed to be Phillip's family home), and Rupert tells Phillip, 'I remember you were rather good at strangling chickens'. Phillip admits this story, and an allusion is created, where 'the real' is made symbolic, making connections between queer homosexual activities, evident in the story of strangling a chicken as symbolic of masturbation between the two.

This foregrounding of queer sexuality as symbolic rather than explicit is then iterated again where a member of the party walks past the couple holding a pile of books that are tied together with rope, seemingly the rope that was used to strangle David. This then leads to a tension that a secret will be revealed, evident in the possible discovery of the body in the chest. However, rather than the film's focusing on the characters or imagined symbolic references, such as metronomes, chickens or rope, a visual space is opened up, purely foregrounding the chest, where the body is contained. The gaze of the camera is static, looking past the chest towards the kitchen through two open doors, and we simply hear a conversation between characters who are not visible concerning the imagined whereabouts of David, foregrounding notions of suspense inherent in the work of Hitchcock (Carroll 1996). At the same time the mundane domestic work of the maid is revealed, as she goesg back and forth between the kitchen and the chest, clearing away the food, drinks, tablecloth and candlesticks on top of the chest. For some time the camera stays in a static position, and this leads to the possibility of the body being discovered, where the maid aided by Rupert is about to put back in the chest the books that had been taken out by Phillip and Brandon to put the body in. However, this is resolved where Brandon simply walks into the scene to close the partially opened chest, keeping the body from view. Had the body been revealed, this would have made real the symbolic, framing queer desire, linked through the iconography of strangling, alluding to the queer phallus.

Such a focus on absence as presence is similarly evident in *Suddenly Last Summer*; however, rather than the technical process of the sustained gaze as occurs in *Rope*, there is a fragmentation that blends identities, effectively redirecting and refracting the gaze. Notably, although we never see the face of Sebastian, the queer male who is murdered in *Suddenly Last Summer*, in place of this we are presented with the visual representation of his female cousin Catherine. Hence, following the representation of the queer male with the straight girl, these identities are blended, offering some sense of oneness or union between the two characters. The film largely involves key sequences where Catherine recalls details of Sebastian's murder, and events leading up to this. As part of this, the aesthetics used by the film producers involves the production of composite images, foregrounding the face of Catherine in close up (usually to the right of the screen) recalling the events, and then, in the background of the screen, representing the actions she discusses. However, as discussed earlier, these background images as historical events never represent the face of Sebastian: rather the camera presents shots of his body involving images taken from the back or close-ups of parts of his body, which foreclose the possibility of seeing his face.

Such a direct focus on Catherine's face, and a rejection of seeing Sebastian's face, suggests that Catherine's face is symbolic of Sebastian. Hence through this union Catherine is coded as queer also, particularly evident not only in this aesthetic collage but also in her mental instability. Her troubled mental state directly relates to the notion of the 'other', as someone outside the normal social order, and someone who needs saving. Her aunt's interest in solving her troubled mental state, through encouraging her to submit to a lobotomy, in many ways codes her as queer. This offers an allusion to processes of electric shock treatment, and chemical castration, often used to treat homosexuals at that time, as reported in the documentary *Word Is Out: The Stories of Our Lives* (The Mariposa Film Group, 1977). Hence, while Catherine and Sebastian are separate characters, they are unified in their abject position as 'queer others'. The composite image used to represent the story of Sebastian's demise offers a dreamlike potential, in framing Catherine as Sebastian. Such a composition, however, is produced through juxtaposing the instinctive with the ordered, setting up a process of instability.

This is particularly evident where, earlier in the film, the textual content had focused on the idea of the primeval, and the deeply instinctive, rather than the ordered and civilised, alluding to the Dionysian and Apollonian drives within tragedy, as explored by Friedrich Nietzsche (1995) (see Pullen 2011). The former represents the shift to senses, indulgence and emotion and the latter concerns stability, the adherence to order and good citizenship. In many ways this might relate to the tension between instinctive queer sexuality extending from the personal body, in contrast to the restricting social order where sexuality may be institutionally controlled through observation, in the manner of the panopticon (see Chapter 1).

This is vivified in the film, in the representation of the garden at Violet's house, which was the design of Sebastian. Violet takes Dr Cukrowicz on a tour of the garden, not only stating that the primitive plants in the garden go back to the 'dawn of time' but also demonstrating the idea of the primitive when she feeds a Venus Fly Trap with insects that she has already prepared. In this sense she attempts to control the natural order, through observation and prepared nutrition, and a tension is created where the natural is powerful, but it is also contained. Hence the notion of the primitive and the instinctive is foregrounded in the film, framing both Catherine and Sebastian as part of this. In the manner that Violet engages with the Venus Fly Trap, and the Venus Fly Trap itself senses its prey without seeing it, the film represents Sebastian as observing and being observed, contained within an institutional order. However, the aesthetics of the film complicates the notion of any coherent visual representation. This is particularly evident where, in a closing sequence of the film, Catherine recalls the afternoon of Sebastian's death. A reconstitution of the gaze is offered, through presenting dreamlike composite images, framing both Catherine and Sebastian as one, yet in different time frames, foregrounding absence, and guilt, through voyeurism.

This sequence starts with Catherine recalling to Dr Cukrowicz what happened on the afternoon of Sebastian's death, in the manner of a therapy session. Also present and listening to this is Aunt Violet. Disturbing music accompanies this sequence, including the sounds of horns and percussion signalling malevolence. As the sequence starts there is a brief cutaway to Violet clearly listening, offering a closeup of her face with eyes downcast, and then an image of her hands placed upon a notebook imagined to be Sebastian's diary. Catherine recalls the afternoon when she and Sebastian ate at a 'shabby' beachside restaurant, and they were harassed by local impoverished youths. An image is presented of Dr Cukrowicz on screen left, with Catherine on screen right (see Figure 2.1). Catherine is looking away, and Cukrowicz in a lower position is intently looking at her. Between them in a central position is an image that she is recalling. This offers a representation of Sebastian and Catherine at the restaurant, with Sebastian's back to the camera, and Catherine facing him, her face in full view. This close juxtaposition, blending different images and different time frames focuses on parts of the body and utilitarian space, connected to notions of oppression and guilt. Violet's mouth, eyes and hands are related to memory and tactility, connoting her inappropriate relationship with her son. Catherine in conversation with Dr Cukrowicz in the imagined real time subverts the expectations of male and female engagement with her in a higher position looking away, while he subjectively gazes at her in an enquiring but submissive manner. At the same time the historical image of Sebastian and Catherine within a central position

Figure 2.1 *Montgomery Clift as Dr Cukrowicz and Elizabeth Taylor as Catherine Holly in a scene from* Suddenly Last Summer. *Between the two characters is a flashback picture, as part of a therapeutic sequence, where Catherine recalls time spent with the queer character Sebastian who was later murdered.*

foregrounds the back of Sebastian, as he looks at Catherine across the dining table. He is not framed by some rustic décor that might signify a beachside restaurant, but faces a utilitarian chain-link fence, designed to keep out local people. This frames the past as confinement, potentially offering some release through recounting the events in the present. Central within this is the limited view of the chain-link fence. Later we discover that behind this fence children and youths were staring and shouting at the couple, demanding food from them. This hidden context of impoverished youth, presented as part of a disordered world just outside the restaurant, and only three feet away from the couple behind the chain-link fence, offers allusions to senses of narcissism, guilt and voyeurism.

Sebastian, dressed in a white suit, with his back to the camera, directly faces Catherine in the restaurant. A sense of voyeurism is evident, as the camera codifies this engagement as private, through denying an image of Sebastian. At the same time notions of privilege and entitlement are apparent, in separating Sebastian and Catherine from the local people, relating some kind of social division. While disadvantaged others observe the couple, their gaze does not possess the power of the institutional panopticon, which might suppress and contain; rather they reflect a band of individuals who look on the couple for some sense of resolution. A sense of guilt is also present here, not only in the superior cultural and social position held by Sebastian and Catherine, who deny giving food to the onlookers, but also where, in conversation with Catherine, Sebastian mentions that he recognises some of the oppressive youths, potentially read as sexual encounters that he has now disposed of. This fragmented tension, which contains on one side of the fence a queer couple, potentially read as one privileged identity, and on the other a rebellious band of disenchanted local youths, breaks down when Sebastian is pursued by the youths. This is represented in the manner that a monster in a horror film is chased out of a local town, offering an allusion to the archetypal representation within *Frankenstein* (James Whale 1931, US). However the narrative ends with Sebastian murdered by this group. His body is deconstructed, through being cut up by the rabble, and his flesh seems to be eaten, as Catherine looks away and manages to escape.

The nightmare nature of the recollection seems to suggest that Catherine has escaped, while Sebastian has paid the price for his undeserved entitlement and privilege. Despite this, through the denying of any real representation of Sebastian's face, the sense of absence complicates our evaluation of the real and the symbolic. While Catherine represents the symbolic identity of Sebastian, and therefore signifies the death drive itself, for the inability to represent the real, the film, through denying a complete representation of actual queer lives, stimulates a process that challenges the symbolic order. Catherine may be coded as queer, but also she is coded as salvageable. This is evident where she finds resolution at the close of the film, in gaining the affections of a potential romantic partner, Dr Cukrowicz.

However, there is irony in this representation, as through the coupling of Elizabeth Taylor (as Catherine) and Montgomery Clift (as Dr Cukrowicz) at the close of the film a queer partnership is foregrounded. This is apparent as in real life; Taylor and Clift were the archetypal straight girl and queer guy (see Bosworth 1978). Hence the 'bitextuality' of the text is vivified both in fictional narrative and in social realist terms. Such a focus on social realism seems apparent in the film *Swoon*, which although it follows *Suddenly Last Summer* and *Rope* in a far later time frame, as a product of New Queer Cinema, potentially offers an explicit development of these narratives.

Swoon

Swoon is considered as a revolutionary cinematic film, in its constitution as part of the New Queer Cinema movement from the 1990s. As Michele Aaron (2004) tells us:

> New Queer Cinema is the name given to a wave of queer films that gained critical acclaim on the festival circuit in the early 1990s. Coined, and largely chronicled, by film theorist B. Ruby Ritch, New Queer Cinema ... repre-

sented an exciting prospect that gay and lesbian images and filmmakers had turned a corner. No longer burdened by the [need for, and inhibition of] positive imagery, or the relative obscurity of marginal production, films could be both radical and popular, stylish and economically viable. (3)

Many films may be considered under the aegis of New Queer Cinema. They include documentary texts such as *Paris Is Burning* (Jennie Livingstone 1990, US) and *Tongues Untied* (Marlon Riggs 1990, US), which explored issues of gender performance and race connected to queer identity (see Pullen 2007a). At the same time, New Queer Cinema includes varying cinematic dramas such as the work of Derek Jarman and Gregg Araki (both discussed below), which more directly reference connections to mainstream cinema. As part of the movement, I am initially focusing on *Swoon* for its connection to *Rope*, as an adaptation. Despite this, I am not attempting to establish a teleological journey; rather I want to consider the significance of New Queer Cinema as offering some kind of new constitution of the gaze, in relationship to queer desire. While later I will consider the work of Derek Jarman and Gregg Araki in relation to this, *Swoon*, as a key text of New Queer Cinema, may be considered as a historical reconstruction, contextualising the narrative of *Rope*.

Notably, within *Swoon* we are presented with an explicit representation of the narrative of Nathan Leopold and Richard Loeb. Hence, while *Rope* is clearly based on, or at least inspired by, the Leopold and Loeb murder case of the 1920s, the representation in *Swoon* clearly maps the historical narratives of the murder. This relates to recording key aspects of the crime, which led to their eventual incarceration and their ultimate demise. Hence in some sense the film is a biographical drama, which offers a historical record for posterity. While many might consider the coupling of Leopold and Loeb, who were passionate homosexual lovers and also murderers, as a macabre story to represent queer lives, in many ways this follows the ethics of New Queer Cinema, which saw less of a need to produce positive or affirmative images, but was more involved in conveying new freedoms of representation. Although I am not exploring the suitability of this text, as offering some kind of representational precedent, or suitability, as a paradigm for queer representation, I am interested in how the gaze is produced in *Swoon*, and its relationship to aspects of voyeurism, narcissism and guilt.

The film's central narrative records the intimate relationship between Nathan Leopold and Richard Loeb, aged nineteen and eighteen respectively when they committed the murder in 1924 (see Higdon 1999). The film explores their physical and psychological relationship, and their pursuit of crimes for personal pleasure, and to shock a community. The couple are represented as embarking on a range of petty crimes, such as throwing a brick into a window and setting a building on fire, and then later planning the murder of a young man. According to the reported life story of Leopold and Loeb, they murdered fourteen-year-old Robert Franks, after offering him a lift whilst out driving in their car, immediately bludgeoning him to death, then concealing his body within the undergrowth at the shore of a lake. This was a premeditated crime, which allegedly was planned over a seven-month period. A number of historical aspects are recorded in the film, including the murder weapon that was purchased (a chisel), the method of disposing the body and attempts to conceal the identity of the victim by pouring hydrochloric acid on the face and body. The film also maps a wide range of other historical details relative to the crime, such as the discovery of Leopold's glasses at the site where the body was discovered, which led to the police capturing them, and the ransom note that Leopold and Loeb composed before the murder took place, but which they released afterwards, as an attempt to confuse individuals as to what had actually happened. Furthermore as in *Rope*, the story foregrounds the philosophy of Nietzsche, and Leopold's fascination, as a student of the University of Chicago, with the notion of the Superman, who is able to rise above others, as superior, and is able to dispose of those considered as less worthy (see Nietzsche 1974). The film also records the murder of Loeb in prison in 1936, and the life story of Leopold, who was released from prison in 1958 and died in 1971.

Despite this vast inclusion of historical details presenting intercuts with actual historical footage from the time, the composition of the gaze within *Swoon* is quite different from that of *Rope*. While *Rope* sustains a gaze that offers absence as presence, through the technological process of the seemingly unending long shots (see discussion above), a sense of claustrophobia is apparent in Swoon. For example in an early sequence in the film, when Richard and Nathan are planning the crime, they are represented as in their student rooms. At one point Richard is on the bed wearing only his underwear with his chest exposed; he is looking comfortable and sexual, with the camera viewing him from above. Richard tells Nathan that he has bought typing paper and stamps, which will be used in the crime, suggesting that Nathan might want his 'payment' at that point. Richard is then viewed as face down on the bed, and we sense that Nathan is taking his 'payment' by climbing upon Richard for some sexual gratification. However, rather than seeing a shot from a distance, which might present both characters on the bed in some imagined domestic social setting, we are presented with tight closeups that focus on Nathan grabbing Richard's hands and arms, as if to hold him down, and a close image is presented, as Nathan writhes up and down upon Richard, suggesting sexual anal penetration. However when the camera draws back, we see that Nathan is still wearing his underwear, and this is some sexualised ritual, which might be perceived as formulaic and containing, rather than sensual and satisfying. Hence the sense of claustrophobia, employing the gaze in closeup on small details, forms a visual aesthetic process throughout the film.

This is further evident in a scene following this, with Nathan typing a letter, whilst Richard is on the bed using the telephone. A scene of apparent domesticity is presented, which might represent a content happy couple, with one working on a student essay and the other planning a social event with friends. However, we discover that the typewriter has been stolen for the purpose of being used in the forthcoming murder, and Nathan is typing the ransom note that forms part of their plan. At the same time Richard is using the telephone to invite friends to a party in their apartment, potentially as an allusion to the narrative of *Rope*. However the scene employs an extreme closeup gaze, at points with the camera focusing on the words that Nathan is typing, framing the aesthetic form of the typed word, and the structure of the typewriter in close up, establishing the typewriter as a menacing component.

Throughout the film there is an iteration of extreme closeups in this way, connoting claustrophobia and containment. This is directly related to the process of looking, gazing and consuming. Notably, over the opening credits of the film there is a visual representation of a romantic encounter between Nathan and Richard. They are both running through a disused and derelict building with the light bearing down on the couple from above, in the manner in which a cathedral window might spread light. A closeup reveals Richard taking two rings from his mouth, and placing one of these upon Nathan's finger, and then later receiving a ring on his own finger placed there by Nathan, in the manner that wedding rings might be used in an official ceremony. However, extreme closeups punctuate this scene, not only of the mouth containing the rings but also as the rings are placed on each other's fingers, as the hairs on their hands come into sharp focus. These images of the extremities and parts of the body offer a sense of fracturing, rather than coherency, which might have been achieved through representing the whole of the body. Later in the film, the focus on the mouth is again used to reflect the knowledge that Nathan's mother is now dead, and, through representing an image of a Star of David placed in a mouth, David states that since his mother's death he is no longer Jewish. The representation references a funeral tradition in Greek mythology, where coins are placed in the mouth of the deceased person to pay the ferryman Charon for a journey to the other side, the afterlife.

This sense of 'afterlife' is achieved through using closeups, of parts of the body, including the mouth and the hands, and generally framing non-human iconic symbols such as the wedding ring, the typewriter and the Star of David. A process is put in place where the gaze is sustained upon component mechanical parts, seeming to deconstruct the human and lived gaze, framing the mechanistic and the disconnected. Through constructing the gaze in this way, a reference is made to the disconnectedness of seeing, using the aesthetic closeup as a kind of voyeurism. Central within this is the focus on the eyes, as the process of seeing. As part of this the film focuses on the discovery of Leopold's glasses, often seen in closeup and examined as key forensic evidence. Not only do the glasses play an important part in the narrative, in setting up the discovery of the murders, evident in Leopold's carelessness in leaving them at the site of the murder, but also the film closes with a statement that he donated his body to science, and after his death a blind woman gained sight through the donation of his eyes. Whilst it's possible to read this as a final act of benevolence on the part of Leopold, to pay back to society for his heinous crime, I read this as a deconstruction of the gaze, which offers a sense of disconnected continuance, rather than a holistic conclusion.

Therefore in comparison to *Rope*, absence is made present within *Swoon*, potentially revealing more explicit evidence of queer lives. This is achieved not just by filling in historical and indexical evidence: there is a psychological undertow, through the use of fragmented closeups. I argue that these don't necessarily advance the story but they reveal a different layer of comprehension, or way of seeing.

While in many ways it's possible to consider that *Rope* is a superior text to *Swoon*, for its suspension of the real, evident in rejecting an obvious queer identity, apparent within the symbolic order, despite this *Swoon* nevertheless saturates the symbolic order, with forensic iconography in closeup, which is meaningful. Hence, the focus on the typewriter, the wedding ring, the Star of David, the glasses, the disconnected parts of the queer body and the eyes offer a rich source of identification and meaning. I argue that this relates not only to an examination of the queer skin as closeup but also to a sense of the queer body. This tension between skin and the body relating historical contexts, I argue is a key aspect of New Queer Cinema, and is particularly evident in the work of the queer directors Derek Jarman and Gregg Araki.

Derek Jarman and Gregg Araki

Derek Jarman (1942–94) was a political icon for gay identity, reaching wide audiences through his role as a progressive filmmaker, director and author (see Woolen 1996; Ellis 2009). Originally a fine arts painter, who became involved in the film industry as a set designer working on Ken Russell's film *The Devils* (in 1971), which established his industry credentials, he received heightened media attention (after 1986) through openly discussing his condition as a person with HIV/AIDS. From Jarman's first feature-length film, *Sebastiane*

(1976, UK), through to his last, *Blue* (1993, UK), he foregrounded his sexual identity, and (latterly) his condition with AIDS. Through his autobiographical[1] and political work Jarman and the gay community were creatively cast within artistic, intimate and often abstract frames. At the same time his work in aesthetic terms involves an innovative approach, not only influenced by his knowledge of light and the definition of social space and perspective, coming from his fine arts experience, but also applying these skills to the adaptation of historical narratives. This is highly evident in the case studies below on his films *Caravaggio* (1986, UK) and *Edward II* (1991, UK), the former exploring the life and work of an Italian Renaissance painter, Michelangelo Merisi da Caravaggio (1571–1610) and the latter relating the sexual life and demise of King Edward II of England (1284–1327).

Gregg Araki, born in 1963, is an innovative film director who is a celebrated key figure in the development of New Queer Cinema (see Hart 2010). Often focusing on dark humour, and little concerned for the production of overly affirmative or reassuring positive representations of the queer community, his work often engages with popular culture, examining the life chances of queer young people, trapped in inhibiting circumstances. Although his early work 'lacks slick production values' (Murray 1998: 11) and is clearly addressed to minority audiences in the overly determined focus on rebellion and angst, his later work is more developed, involving sophisticated aesthetic and editing processes, clearly appealing to more mainstream audiences. This contrast is particularly noticeable in the two case studies that I have selected, *The Living End* (1992, US), a road movie involving queer HIV-positive central characters, in comparison to *Mysterious Skin* (2004, US) an adaptation of a celebrated novel of the same name by Scott Heim (1995), which explores queer youth and age-inappropriate relationships (see Hart 2014).

I have chosen Jarman's *Caravaggio* and *Edward II*, and Araki's *The Living End* and *Mysterious Skin*, as an extension of my analysis of *Swoon* (see above). However, I am not relating these texts necessarily as paradigmatic of New Queer Cinema, I am considering their relationship to the queer gaze, and their address to heterosexual female and mainstream audiences. Hence I want to consider how the gaze upon the queer male is articulated in New Queer Cinema, as an important context in relation to mainstream appropriations of queer male identity.

Jarman's *Caravaggio* and *Edward II* both relate the distinctive lives of queer historical characters, who were known for their homosexual or bisexual activity. While the former has a unique contemporary script based on the life story of Caravaggio written by Nicholas Ward Jackson and Derek Jarman, the latter is an adaptation by Jarman of a Renaissance play written by Christopher Marlowe in 1594. Hence both of these films through varying processes of narrative production attempt to examine key historical figures who are connected to queer identity. In comparison Gregg Araki's *The Living End* and *Mysterious Skin* are modern fictional texts with screenplays written by Araki himself, with the former representing a contemporary original approach, and the latter as an adaptation of work by Scott Heim (see above). Although Araki's work by comparison to Jarman's seems less historically significant, a central focus on AIDS in *The Living End* (also present in *Mysterious Skin*) offers a distinctive documentary approach, in recording responses to the disease in that time frame.

In many ways, through Jarman's status as an HIV-positive film producer, and more directly within the narrative context of Araki's films, HIV and AIDS actually form a central context of identity, in both liminal and subliminal ways. This is achieved through relating HIV/AIDS directly, or through foregrounding blood, the body and skin as central contexts of engagement. Hence a significant narrative context of queer male identity within New Queer Cinema is the response to the AIDS crisis, represented in relation to the body, blood, skin and feeling.

This, I argue, relates to the notion of affect, framing the queer body, potentially referencing HIV/AIDS as subject to sensuality, vulnerability and agency. Gregory J. Seigworth and Melissa Gregg (2010) tell us that 'affect arises in the midst of in-betweenness: in the capacities to act and to be acted upon. [It] is found in those intensities that pass body to body (human, non-human, part body, and otherwise), in those resonances that circulate about, between, and sometimes stick to bodies and worlds, and in the very passages or variations between these intensities and resonances themselves' (1). This might be related to the notion of physical presence, foregrounding the context of memories, or histories. As Laura U. Marks (2000) has discussed in her seminal work *The Skin of the Film*, extending the work of Gilles Deleuze (1986) in relation to the movement image, the theory of 'haptic visuality' may be apparent, offering a connection to the sense of touch, which might trigger physical memories of smell, touch and taste, representing the body within social space, in creative personal ways. The queer body may be considered part of this, seeming like a site of feeling, contextual and articulated in relationship to other bodies, set within architectural social settings. Such potential foregrounds opportunities of performativity, related to history, memory and cultural register.

Notably within *Caravaggio* and *Edward II*, the body is represented as vulnerable and liable to bleed, prone to injury. In *Caravaggio*, a representation of a knife that is used in painting and also deployed as a murder weapon signifies connections between the artist's hand and the mortality of the queer body. In *Edward II*, a red-hot poker (heated in an iron forge) is represented as the murder weapon, used upon Edward II, thrust into his rectum, representing a punishment for queer desire. Added to this, a proliferation of the colour red in *Caravaggio*, blending references to red paint and blood expelled from the body, signifies the vulnerability and passion of the queer body, at the same time referencing blood as the carrier of the HIV virus. This is significant in *Edward II*, which was produced some time after Jarman had announced his HIV-positive status, framing blood as a central narrative strand. This is particularly evident when Edward II stabs a man strung up and tied to an animal carcass, withdrawing the knife close to his face and we see the blood glisten upon the metal blade. Also it is apparent when Edward's wife Isabella kills Edward's brother, who is tied to a chair; she bites into his neck like a vampire, and when she withdraws we see blood running down from his neck to his chest. References to blood within acts of vengeance within *Caravaggio* and *Edward II* frame the agency of the queer body, but also allude to its vulnerability.

With Araki's *The Living End*, blood plays a central narrative context, at the start of the film where Jon gets his HIV test result, and finds that he has tested positive for the syndrome, before he even meets his eventual soulmate, and fellow HIV-positive companion, Luke. Blood also plays a more subliminal and philosophical context in the film, where a married man is murdered by his wife, after she discovers that Luke has had sex with him, and a pet dog licks blood expelled from his body: and where later in the film Luke attests that AIDS 'is lying inside of me, but I can't see it'. In *Mysterious Skin*, not only does blood reference AIDS or HIV, where the lead character Neil who is working as a rent boy, bleeds from his rectum after being beaten and raped by a client, but also the film foregrounds the haptic presence of the disease. This is evident in a key sequence where Neil encounters a client who does not want to have sex, but simply wants to be held and touched. Undressing before Neil to reveal a body covered with Kaposi's Sarcomas (skin cancer lesions associated with AIDS), the client simply lies on the bed, while Neal touches his body, in the manner of caring and soothing. Hence the surface of the body as much as the internal workings (evident in the prevalence of blood) offers an affective surface for touching and sensitivity, referencing memories, and personal stories of feeling and resistance. While in *The Living End* AIDS is seemingly more apparent, evident in character actions and agency, within *Mysterious Skin* senses of the inside and the outside are blended.

Such a focus on the skin, and the surface of the queer body, is particularly evident in all of these films, including *Swoon*, my earlier case study. I argue that the sensitivity of the queer skin is highlighted by the aesthetic presence of light, and this relates both to contrast and to the definition of social space. As in *Swoon*, where there was a focus on the mouth and diverse parts of the body, through the emphasis on chiaroscuro (the contrast between dark and light), a focus was made in *Caravaggio* upon the sensitivity and feeling of the body. In emulating the use of light by the painter, *Caravaggio* offers a blending of painterly and filmic technology, using light to emphasise emotion and the definition of social space.

For example, early in *Caravaggio*, the young Caravaggio is represented as selling his works of art to the public, and an older man is represented as a possible client, interested in the paintings, but an allusion is created, connoting Caravaggio as a rent boy. The price of the painting is discussed, with a third male watching, seeming like a pimp setting up the transaction for the painting, but also for Caravaggio as a commodity. Following this sequence, we see Caravaggio partly clothed with his chest exposed. The client is bemused and enthralled, with trousers fallen down seeming as if he has just had sex, and Caravaggio laughs at the man, throwing a wine bottle from one hand to the other, at the same time running around the room in vertiginous motion, while the man attempts to follow him, losing his breath. The light glistens on Caravaggio's body as a social space is established, defining the two characters through the emphasis of reflective light upon the queer skin. The scene closes with Caravaggio holding a knife, taunting the client, saying 'I am an art object, and very, very expensive. You've had your money's worth', offering an allusion to the queer body, and the commoditised social space. In this sense, connections are made between the social space, and the representation of light as saturated on the skin, but a sense of motion defines a cultural space, which is coded as queer.

This sense of using space and light is also apparent in *Edward II*, where the notion of the onlooker and the audience is related, connoting childhood and imagined innocence. Edward's son, about ten years old, is represented as holding a battery-operated torch in the darkness. The child wanders in the dark, with only his face lit up by light from the torch, as if he is seeking some way out, or attempting to find treasure. The torch spreads across the room, and we see in the darkness a number of naked young men embracing each other, as if commencing a scrum in playing rugby. The light illuminates the bodies as they bend over, embrace and crowd together, pushing against each other mimicking the scrum 'warm-up', as if commencing rugby. A reverse shot of the child is presented as he gazes at the naked bodies, purely lit by the torch he is holding, with a sense of awe or trepidation apparent on his face.

Hence the construction of space is used within these films, using light to articulate distance and sensitivity, constructing the queer body as part, or framed within, social spaces relating to culture and feeling. For the representation of the queer body, this may offer transgressive potential. As Liam Kennedy tells us: 'To treat space as a social product . . . prompts fresh consideration of the instrumentality of space as a register of not only built forms but also of embedded ideologies. This entails a demystifying of space as natural and transparent so that it is a product with particular, localised meanings' (2000: 9). Central within this is the tension between heterosexual order involving capitalism, and the dominance of commodity and ideology evident in the mainstream film industry. This positions the queer as an outsider, who, while he may be peripheral, is mobile, and illuminated, as living within these social spaces.

In addition, this references tensions between sociality and materiality, in a manner that Adrian J. Ivakhiv (2013) considers as 'process relational' with regard to 'ecologies of the moving image' – 'a model that understands the world, and cinema, to be made up not primarily of objects, substances, structures, or representations, but rather relational processes, encounters or events' (12). Such encounters within cinema are less about fixing an identity, but rather contextualise the wider world, and the process of living through.

Central within these films is the notion of childhood as a process of living through, or attempting to live through, and its connection, or disconnection, from queer identity. Not only do *Caravaggio* and *Edward II* foreground the gaze, or the agency, of the youth or the child, evident in Caravaggio himself, and Edward's son, but also *Mysterious Skin* explores the notion of sexual desire in queer youth. Hence queer desire and the construction of the gaze are brought together. However, the gaze is often constructed as reflexive, directly addressing the audience, rather than exclusively exerted upon other characters.

Notably, the first time that Neil aged eight sees Coach, a man in his late twenties or early thirties, a youth sports leader and covert paedophile, who later preys upon Neil for sexual favours, Neil's desire for Coach is represented as reflective upon the audience, rather than upon the character. An image is produced of Neil's desire looking straight at the camera, in the manner that confessional discourse might be elicited, or that an aside might be spoken to an audience in breaking the rule of the 'fourth wall' in theatre drama that separates the audience from the stage. The image of Neil is accompanied with his voiceover:

> Desire sledgehammered me. He looked like lifeguards, cowboys and fireman I'd seen in the *Playgirl* [magazines] that my mum had kept stashed under her bed. And back then I didn't know what to do with my feelings. They were like a gift I had to open in front of a crowd.

However, through directing the desiring gaze at the audience, at the same time intercutting this with stills of men's faces that might have appeared in the *Playgirl* magazines, a dilution takes place that engenders the gaze as contemplative and reflective on cultural forms, rather than relating personal sexual agency. This is further elicited, in the reference to opening a gift in front of a crowd, as sharing the witness of his desire. This is a recurring aesthetic construction in the film, where characters often face the camera in executing the gaze, sharing this with the audience. I argue that such a process relates to the notion of absence as much as presence, in some sense denying any real form of gaze that might be subjective, or oppressive to queer youth.

This is particularly evident at the close of the film when Neil meets Brian, as a young adult. Earlier in the film, Brian experiences flashbacks, representing both characters at the age of eight, not aware that he had been sexually abused, considering instead that his trauma was related to alien abduction. Neil was complicit in the abduction of Brian, used by Coach to invite and assure Brian of his safety, before the sexual abuse took place. In a scene at the close of the film, there is a coming to terms, with Neil as a discontented queer youth who has been abused as a child, and who has embarked on a life of promiscuity, and Brian as a nerdy youth who has unresolved fragmented memories of his childhood. Through this Neil resolves Brian's quest to find out the truth about what had happened to him when he was eight years old. Neil breaks into the house where Coach had lived, taking Brian with him to explain what had happened when they were children. Referencing the presence of blood, evident when Brian as a child had returned home with a nosebleed, disoriented and scared unaware of his abuse, Neil explains:

> When it was over, we were getting dressed, your face looked like it had been erased, and you were just empty inside, and you just fell face first on the floor. When we pulled you up, your nose was bleeding.

This is accompanied by a visual representation in which we see Brian at the age of eight facing the camera with an empty, and distant, gaze before falling. Through the referencing of blood as symbolic of the queer body, damaged after abuse, a sense of loss, absence and erasure is foregrounded. Hence the gaze directed towards the mainstream audience foregrounds a sense of union and understanding, through sharing a sense of feeling, as reflexive. Notably, such senses of sharing are evident in the film, making connections to the union between the straight girl and the queer guy.

In *Mysterious Skin*, this is primarily evident in the close friendships that both Neil and Brian have with female characters. Neil is close to Wendy, who is considered as his best friend often accompanying him on his sexual escapades, and assuring him of his identity concerns. Brian develops a friendship with Avalyn, who helps him solve his quest to find Neil, sharing his interest in the narrative of alien abductions (see Figure 2.2). Besides this, both Neil and Brian are represented as possessing close bonds with their mothers, even if Neil is inappropriately influenced by his mother's promiscuous sexual behaviour, and Brian may be over-protected by his mother. Similarly in *The Living*

Figure 2.2 *Mary Lynn Rajskub as Avalyn and Brady Corbet as Brian in* Mysterious Skin. *Brian, as he reads extracts from his diary, is sharing stories of alien abduction; later we find out that these stories relate to child abuse.*

End, Jon recurrently consults his female heterosexual best friend Doris, who is protective of him. This is evident when he frequently telephones Doris on the road trip, and she is concerned that Luke is a bad influence on Jon. While in Derek Jarman's *Caravaggio* and *Edward II* there is little representation of compassion or understanding between queer male characters and straight female characters, I would argue that the representation of actress Tilda Swinton in these films contextualises her bond with Jarman, as his muse and close friend, who worked with him on many of his films. Hence, through varying character-based, and production cast contexts, the notion of the straight girl and the queer guy permeates the case studies of New Queer Cinema that I am presenting here.

Conclusion

The queer gaze is an essential component in thinking through the context of the relationship between the straight girl and the queer guy. Early representations of subliminal queer desire in Hollywood film, such as in *Rope* and *Suddenly Last Summer*, offered new ways of representing the queer male, as both a subject of the gaze and as one who could gaze upon others. The sense of absence and presence, related to notions of narcissism and voyeurism, is a key factor in the construction of the queer gaze, and its setting within mainstream cinema. Through a queer audience finding little representation of themselves, and through mainstream audiences finding only covert representations of queer lives, this sense of absence established a sensitised way of seeing and looking for queer identity.

While the later films of New Queer Cinema such as Jarman's *Caravaggio* and *Edward II* offered new scope and definition in establishing some historical and representational body of work, the rise of queer sensibility evident in these films offers new possibilities, but also reveals recurring limitations. While *Swoon* in many ways makes more explicit the context of queer lives that was seemingly missing in the contextual adaptation of *Rope*, similar processes relating absence and presence are evident. Hence while it's possible to fill in the representational and historical gaps, the psychology of the gaze is mostly enabled by the drive to seek out, or to consume, foregrounding aspects of voyeurism and narcissism.

However, the queer gaze within *Swoon*, similarly to representations within *Rope* and *Suddenly Last Summer*, relates absence and presence, in working out definitions of the Symbolic and the Real that might reveal some closeness to queer identity. While narcissistic pleasure might be found in the films of New Queer Cinema, evident in the potential for the queer gaze to reflect upon itself, similarly aspects of voyeurism through connecting to mainstream audiences are also present. Notably, the significance of straight females, either as central narrative characters or as supporting cast identities, stimulates the consumption of the queer male within New Queer Cinema, as subject to the heterosexual gaze as much as the queer gaze. Gregg Araki's *The Living End* and *Mysterious Skin* explore this potential, in framing a straight female-centric force, in supporting and developing the narrative. Hence, while the queer gaze might reflect upon itself, offering some sense of cultural introspection, at the same time mainstream audiences witness this reflection, and consume queer identity, as much as they identify with it.

At the same time such identification and consumption potentially relate to the notion of the star or celebrity, and, as we discover in the following chapter, their participation and representations stimulate new ways of examining and reproducing the straight girl and queer guy relationship, engendering it as a mainstream product for consumption.

Note

1. Jarman's autobiographical writings include *The Last of England* (1987), *Derek Jarman: Today and Tomorrow* (1991), *Modern Nature: Journals of Derek Jarman* (1992), *At Your Own Risk: A Saint's Testament* (1993), *Smiling in Slow Motion: Diaries, 1991–94* (2001).

CHAPTER 3

Film and Commodity

Richard Dyer ([1980] 2001a) tells us that

> Stars have a privileged position in the definition of social roles and types, and this must have real consequences in terms of how people believe they can and should behave. (8)

Focusing on the context of film stars, Dyer relates the possible influence that actors may have in taking on different roles, relating the perception of those roles by the audience. At the same time, he suggests that such perception might also relate to the personal identity of the star, in some way offering diverse identification potential to audiences. For example Dyer (1986) relates the significance of the Hollywood actor Judy Garland 'as having a special relationship to suffering, ordinariness, normality, and it is this relationship that structures much of the gay reading of Garland' (143). Hence, while Judy Garland as an icon of Hollywood cinema might not have explicitly taken on roles that exhibited a close relationship to gay men in terms of character representation, at the same time gay audiences related to her with a sense of close identification that might be considered as a union in the manner of the straight girl and the queer guy. This chapter consequently considers the significance of explicit roles such as representations of straight girls with queer guys. Also it relates the context of the star persona, or the life world of the star, developing the discussion in Chapter 1, which focused on Doris Day and Rock Hudson, to this process.

As part of this, the context of the spectator will be explored, framing the opportunity of gay subjectivity in reading the union between the straight girl and the queer guy. To explore this I will examine the representation of Kenneth Williams within a range of Carry On films, arguing that his imagined real-life friendship with female characters such as Hattie Jacques, Joan Sims and Barbara Windsor influences how we might read these films, contextualising aspects of camp representation and fantasy identification, which foreground irony and parody. I then explore the films *Sunday Bloody Sunday* (John Schlesinger 1971, UK) and *Cabaret* (Bob Fosse 1972, US), which offered the first explicit representations of the straight girl and the queer guy, contextualising the influence of the director John Schlesinger and the author Christopher Isherwood, respectively. After this, I examine three films together, *My Best Friend's Wedding* (P. J. Hogan 1997, US), *The Object of My Affection* (Nicholas Hytner 1998, US) and *The Next Best Thing* (John Schlesinger 2000, US), which I argue offer a commoditised representation of queer men with straight females. Central in these representations are the notions of spectatorship, femininity and camp.

QUEER SPECTATORSHIP, FEMININITY AND CAMP

In Brett Farmer's groundbreaking book *Spectacular Passions: Cinema, Fantasy, Gay Male Spectatorships* (2000), we are told:

> Cinema has long functioned as a vital form, for the production of gay male meanings and identifications to the point that a certain type of film spectatorship has become a veritable shorthand for male homosexuality in various cultural discourses. (23)

The notion of gay identity is inherently connected to aspects of film spectatorship, potentially related to the production of discourse for queer audiences (see also Bourne 1996; Clum 2000; Dyer 1984). Farmer considers gay male spectatorship and how fantasy is related to desire, examining how gay audiences have identified with certain narratives in Hollywood cinema, often finding queer pleasure in seemingly heterocentric story worlds.

For example, Farmer considers 'gay subcultural fascinations with the Hollywood musical [as a] facet of gay spectatorial formations' (2000: 69), considering how they 'articulate and shape [gay men's] innermost fantasies and desires' (77). Although the mainstream cinema musical may seem heterocentric in its adherence to 'normative' representational ideas, it also may be considered as a queer fantasy genre, evident in the performative aspects of excess and hyper-reality, where gay men are able to find pleasure, through reading traits of their identity, or imaginations of their life chances. As Al LaValley (1985) tells us, musical movies are often appealing to gay men as 'here they found hints of a utopian world and alternative world, one more congenial to their sexuality and repressed emotions' (cited in Farmer 2000: 75). So for example musicals such as *The Wizard of Oz* (Victor Fleming, 1939, US) offer a sense of escapism which, while it might not directly referencing homosexual identity, alludes to it in considering the context of the narrative, which focuses on outsiders and outcasts, and their search for acceptance, happiness and home. However, while these narrative worlds often seem to deny, or at least ignore, the express context of homosexual identity, the relevance of female identity, and the notion of feminine performativity, are central. Hence, in *The Wizard of Oz* there is a focus on feelings and emotions, relative to the contexts of bravery and isolation, framed within the life story of a young girl who is trying to get home. This places into focus the significance of female identity, and the potential to express emotions.

As Brett Farmer (2000) suggests, relating the significance of female identity and queer men:

> The gay camp celebration of female stars may also be seen to be motivated by, and expressive, of the many feminine identifications that circulate in and around male homosexual definitions and subjectivities. Because male homosexuality is widely represented in our culture as possessing strong, even constitutive ties with femininity, an active assumption of a male homosexual identity will potentially occasion marked identifications with the feminine at several different levels. (127)

Part of this, I would argue, is the alliance between the straight girl and the queer man within cinema, providing a meaningful social union that foregrounds feminine identity, evident within varying performative contexts. In some sense blending the subjectivity of the heterosexual female, who may be seen as prone to the male gaze (see Chapter 1), and the queer male, who is often constructed as an abject effeminate subject, these two identities together complicate any simple understanding of femininity and effeminacy. Such potential, I argue, is related to the possibility of camp performance, and camp identification within the audience.

David Bergman (1993) considers the notion of camp:

> First, everyone agrees that camp is a style (whether of objects or the way objects are perceived) that favors 'exaggeration', 'artifice', and 'extremity'. Second, camp exists in tension with popular culture, commercial culture, or consumerist culture. Third, the person who can recognise camp, who sees things as campsy, or who can camp is a person outside the mainstream. Fourth, camp is affiliated with homosexual culture, or at least a self-conscious eroticism that throws into question the naturalisation of desire. (4–5)

Hence in terms of femininity and effeminacy, camp performance concerns the notion of exaggeration and excess, relating this as a product of popular culture, revealing the representation of queer and female identity as performative, fluid, transient, and not necessarily static, natural and fixed. While inevitably camp is mostly associated with homosexual identity, it is the focus on denaturalisation which is pertinent in considering its political potential in gender performance. As Judith Butler (1999) considers in relation to this idea, 'gender is not a noun but a free-floating set of attributes' (33), and ultimately its formation emerges from within a 'matrix of power relations'. As part of this, Butler references the potential of the drag performer to adopt and parody varying forms of gender performance as artifice: such a powerbase offers the potential to deconstruct the hegemonic power-based dominance of masculine order.

However, as Fabio Cleto (2002) tells us with regards to the meaning of camp:

> Representational excess, heterogeneity, and gratuitousness of reference, in constituting a major raison d'être of camp's fun and exclusiveness, both signal and contribute to an overall resistance to definition, drawing the contours of an aesthetic of (critical) failure: the longing, in fact, for a common, constant trait (or for an intrinsic, essential, stabilising 'core') in all that has been historically ascribed to camp, or the identification of its precise origins and developments, sooner or later ends up being frustrating, challenging the critic as such, as it challenges the cultural imperatives that rely on the manageability of discrete (distinct and docile) historical and aesthetic categories. (3)

However, Cleto points out that histories and definitions of camp are hard to establish, indicating that while camp has associations with queer male identity, and notions of effeminacy, political intentions and distinctive outcomes associated with camp are hard to prove. Hence, although this chapter explores the straight girl and the queer guy in relation to camp performative traits, it's hard to assess distinct structures or political significances.

Therefore, for the purpose of this chapter, I am specifically focusing on the notion of camp in relation to the potential of mimicry or copying, relating both to the identity of the actor, and to the role that they are playing, in challenging sexual identity or gender performance norms. As Cleto tells us: 'The definition of '"Camp" in short, coincides with the definition of the element distinguishing original from copy' (2002: 17). Such a focus on the copying of an identity, referencing the original in the copying process, provides 'an ontological challenge that displaces bourgeois notions of the Self as unique, abiding and continuous while substituting instead, a concept of the self as performative, provisional, discontinuous, and processually constituted by repetitive and styled acts' (Meyer 1994: 2–30). In this sense a queering of identity takes place, where notions of social construction are challenged through a focus on fluidity, rather than fixedness.

In the case study that follows on Kenneth Williams, his articulations within the Carry On films potentially referenced his public persona as a camp performer. Notably, Williams had appeared on the *Round the Horne* radio show (BBC 1965–8, UK), and was popularly known for using parody, irony and 'double entendre'. This was primarily evident in his use of Polari, a covert language that was used by gay men in public to conceal aspects of their identity from the larger public and the authorities (see Baker 2002). Hence our knowledge of Williams as a celebrity who publicly affirmed the countercultural use of Polari, and considered camp 'as the greatest jewel, 22 carats' (cited in Cleto 2002: 1) in stimulating transgressive subcultural discourse, relates to our knowledge as spectators of his identity as an effeminate gay man. While within the Carry On films he would play heterosexual roles, a subtext would be present, not only alluding to his real-life queer identity but also apparent in his camp performance.

KENNETH WILLIAMS AND THE CARRY ON FILMS

Mark Campbell (2002) tells us that the Carry On films were 'a classic British film series that began in the 1950s, reached its heights in the 1960s and tailed off in quality until it ceased production in the late 1970s. [It foregrounded] a small repertory cast of actors and actresses appearing countless times in similar roles, [involving] ludicrous scenarios and hilarious dialogue' (7). At the same time the series mostly focused on the representation of male heterosexual desire, framing the female body referencing lascivious sexuality, in a manner that might be considered as bawdy, and 'lower-class'. Hence, a central narrative trope within the series was the male heterosexual gaze upon the youthful and/or healthy voluptuous female body, often framing the humour with closeups or direct references to the buttocks or the breasts, as a source of sexual salivation. This relates to contemporary English culture, and Donald McGill's bawdy cartoon seaside postcards, which offered insight into this, connoting possible unruly release. These were mostly popular in the early to mid twentieth century, and represented semi-naked bodies of holidaymakers, in compromising or embarrassing situations, with a suggestion of uncontrollable sexual urges, focusing on inappropriate partners or contexts (see Westwood and Rhodes 2007), at the same time making allusions to queer sexuality.

In the later part of the Carry On series, sometimes the jokes made explicit references to queer men, as occurs in *Carry On Abroad* (Gerald Thomas 1972, UK), where a queer male couple are broken up, after the more masculine partner rejects his effeminate boyfriend for a young sexualised girl. Despite this, a recurring feature of the series was the appearance of Kenneth Williams, who prior to joining Carry On was celebrated for his effeminate performances as an eccentric man within radio and television, evident in *Hancock's Half Hour* (BBC 1956–60, UK) and *Round the Horne* (see above), and the series capitalised on his humorous persona. At the same time, the series also included Charles Hawtrey, who similarly to Williams presented an effeminate camp identity.

From the outset, in the first Carry On film, *Carry On Sergeant* (Gerald

Thomas 1958, UK), Kenneth Williams and Charles Hawtrey are represented as foundational effeminate characters who would form the essence of the series as it evolved. This is significant as both were gay men, who, while they did not present a politicised version of queer identity, were popular with mainstream audiences, as disarming and entertaining camp men. With Kenneth Williams appearing in twenty-six of the Carry On films between 1958 and 1978, and Charles Hawtrey in twenty-three between 1958 and 1972, the notion of camp male identity was a recurring profile within the comedy film series.

While Kenneth Williams was often considered as an isolated character, who had a number of friends but was not intimately linked in terms of friendship with female actors, he nevertheless did offer security to them. This is evident in his marriage proposals at different times to both Joan Sims and Barbara Windsor, who were fellow actors in the Carry On series (see Stevens 2010), offering not a sexual relationship but one of convenience, to ensure both parties would not end up isolated. Hence, whilst Williams was not intimately connected to straight female actors in the manner of a close relationship, an aspect of alliance was present in these engagements. Added to this, he appeared with many female characters as potential love interest partners within the Carry On films. This included representations with Hattie Jacques in *Carry On Doctor* (Gerald Thomas 1967, UK) and *Carry On Camping* (Gerald Thomas 1969, UK), Patsy Rowlands in *Carry On Loving* (Gerald Thomas 1970, UK) and *Carry On at Your Convenience* (Gerald Thomas 1971, UK), and Joan Sims in *Carry On up the Khyber* (Gerald Thomas 1968, UK) and *Carry On Dick* (Gerald Thomas 1974, UK). These sequences offered a representation of Williams in close juxtaposition with female characters; however, the sexual advances by the female partners seemed inappropriate. Hence Williams was represented as coupled with straight female actors and straight female characters, offering a sense of union and alliance in the manner of the straight girl and the queer guy. Whilst I discuss this in more detail a little later, I would first like to explore the representation of Kenneth Williams and Charles Hawtrey in *Carry On Constable* (Gerald Thomas 1960, UK).

While the very early Carry On films did not necessarily offer camp excess, the casting of Williams and Hawtrey as effeminate characters developed. In *Carry On Constable*, the third Carry On film, Kenneth Williams and Charles Hawtrey are represented as inexperienced policemen, are drafted in to support the police force when there is an outbreak of influenza, and police numbers are low. Hawtrey is represented as a 'special constable' who would usually work limited hours and would not be fully trained, and Williams is represented as a junior constable, who is not fully qualified. At the outset both men are characterised as effeminate. The appearance of Hawtrey as a 'special constable' offers connotations to difference and queerness; at the same time his arrival at the police station bringing a budgerigar in a cage with him, and later wearing pyjamas whilst lodging in the prison cells, codes him as eccentric and domestic. Williams, as a junior policemen, presents himself as educated, seeming to understand the psychology of criminals and the public, yet this is a comical representation. This is evident where he leads an old lady across the road believing that she wants help, but in fact she has spent considerable time getting from the other side, and she attacks him for hindering her.

Also both are represented as sensitive or vulnerable, evident where Williams is fooled by a pickpocket who steals his braces, which results in his trousers coming down, and where Hawtrey tries to capture a cat that has escaped, but in this process he himself becomes vulnerable. Such a focus on exposing themselves, evident in Williams's trousers falling down, and Hawtrey placed in a lofty height, is also evident when both are represented in drag. They put on women's clothing in order to go under cover in a department store, hoping through this illusion to capture shoplifters. Notably, the representation offers a direct reference to 'camp', where, on both reflecting on their new disguises as middle-aged women, Hawtrey affirms to Williams, 'Do you know, I haven't done this since I was in the army, at a camp concert'. Here 'camp' relates both to a military base and to a stylised performance. At the same time, prior to this sequence when initially dressing as women, both Williams and Hawtrey admire themselves, appearing as if looking in the mirror, with Williams adjusting his hat glancing sideways at the mirror, curling his lips as if checking recently applied lipstick, and both fighting for a view of themselves in the mirror, parodying the idea of putting on makeup and going out. This sense of artifice is also evident when both men walk through the department store, offering an awkward appearance, with Williams clutching his hand to his chest, and Hawtrey holding his handbag close to his body. Hence a highly exaggerated representation of older females is presented, with queer men playing these female roles, yet there is a sense of knowingness, which is held not by the mainstream characters but by the queer men themselves. Notably, this is apparent when the female shop assistant does not immediately recognise that they are in fact men, and also it is evident when they confront a shoplifter who they think has stolen female underwear. A male observer of this incident (the chauffeur of the shoplifter) simply attests, 'Now come on, ladies', referencing the queer men. Hence this sense of queer pleasure is not represented as obvious or evident within the mainstream cast, rather a sense of knowingness is represented, where the queer characters are more knowledgeable, or more easily able to fool people. This is particularly evident in the representation of Kenneth Williams, as subject to inappropriate female attention.

As discussed above, Kenneth Williams, in character, was often represented as uncomfortable when presented with the sexual advances of women. Notably, his engagement with Hattie Jacques offered particular insight, in both *Carry On Doctor* (1967) and *Carry On Camping* (1969). In *Carry On Doctor* Williams plays a doctor called Kenneth Tinkle, and in *Carry On Camping* he plays a teacher called Kenneth Soaper, presenting characters who bear the same first name as himself, creating an allusion to his real identity. Opposite Williams in these sequences, Hattie Jacques plays the Matron in *Carry On Doctor*, and a teacher called Miss Haggard in *Carry On Camping*. Hence, in opposition to Williams's seemingly real character, Jacques was constructed as an older or spinster character. The scenario in these films, and in many of the queer couplings that Williams would be represented in with female characters, would focus on Williams's awkwardness in the company of sexually aroused (or sexually interested) female parties.

Notably, in these sequences a type of mock seduction takes place, where stereotypical female and male performances are inverted, and Hattie Jacques appears as the dominant masculine seducer, rather than the submissive female. In *Carry On Doctor*, Jacques as Matron visits Williams as Dr Tinkle, late in the evening, bringing a bottle of champagne to his room (see Figure 3.1). An awkward scene follows where Williams avoids the advances from Jacques, and this is laced with quips in dialogue. For example, when Jacques turns off the bedroom lamp, reaching across his chest as he is sitting on the sofa, Williams says, 'Matron no! I am not that kind of doctor', and she retorts, 'Don't deny yourself, Kenneth'. Here an allusion is made to both female and queer identity, evident in 'I am not that kind of "girl"', and the denial of hidden desire, which may be queer. Jacques then clasps his head in the manner in which a stereotypical male seducer might make advances towards a 'passive' female subject in amorous courtship, parodying male heterosexual desire.

Also in *Carry On Camping*, after a misunderstanding occurs between the two characters, Jacques as Miss Haggard believes that Williams as Kenneth Soaper had entered her bedroom at night to seduce her, when in fact he was subjected to a ruse, in which school pupils had changed the numbers on the bedroom doors, and he had entered her room mistakenly. In the morning, Jacques advises Williams that, rather than protesting against his (imagined) advances, she is interested in him, and he must wait till she is ready for him. Part of the conversation includes:

> Miss Haggard: A man has these uncontrollable urges from time to time.
>
> Kenneth Soaper: Only at Christmas and Bank holidays.
>
> Miss Haggard: I really feel very flattered that you would want to release them on me.

Film and Commodity

Figure 3.1 *Kenneth Williams as Dr Kenneth Tinkle and Hattie Jacques as Matron in a scene from* Carry On Doctor, *queering the art of heterosexual seduction.*

In this exchange, with Jacques set in a higher position than Williams, represented as descending a staircase while he is at the foot of the stairs, Jacques is coded as mistakenly confident as to the likely opportunity for romance. Her status as more ordered and confident than him, however, is complicated by her reference to desire, and the notion of 'releasing his uncontrollable urges on her'. In this sense an allusion is again made to queer sexuality, with regard to uncontrollable urges, and explicitly vivified in connoting the idea of ejaculation, in Williams not wanting to be 'releasing this' on her. Hence, the representation of Jacques and Williams in these sequences frames the straight girl with the queer guy, as involved in some collaboration, where notions of irony, and queer knowingness, are required in reading the text and the subtext.

While Hattie Jacques and Kenneth Williams were often cast as inappropriate lovers, Williams was often represented in collusion with female characters, framed within more explicit queer contexts. For example in *Carry On Cleo* Williams is coupled with Joan Sims, with Williams playing the part of Julius Caesar, Sims as his wife Calpurnia and Charles Hawtrey as Seneca (a soothsayer). Caesar is represented as under attack. A male guard draws his sword as if to kill him, and Williams retorts 'What are you doing with your thing?', and then, turning away from the man on entering another room, looks at the camera and says, 'Infamy, infamy, they have all got it in for me!' Soon after this, Sims as Calpurnia comforts Williams while he is recovering, in the presence of Hawtrey as Seneca. Williams lies motionless on the bed, and Sims cries, looking at him, saying, 'He looks a little wan'. Hawtrey adds, 'He looks like a big one, if you ask me'. Then Williams says, 'I cannot go without saying something for posterity', Sims affirms this and Williams adds, 'Then let our posteriors know this'. Hence, in this sequence vivid references are made to the queer male phallus, symbolic as the sword, and its possibility for penetration, where Williams references 'infamy' ('in for me'). At the same time the site of penetration, the posterior, is framed, with references to being 'one' (a queer). While all these references take place, Sims as the heterosexual female character is represented as complicit, in stimulating the queer humour, without any resistance.

Hence, the representation of Kenneth Williams and Charles Hawtrey within these Carry On films offers a sense of camaraderie where queer humour is represented, with the complicity of female straight characters. At the same time a sense of camp mimicry is evident, where straight girl and queer guy representations parody issues of gender performance, often with the females making fun of heterosexual male stereotypical representations of romance and desire. Added to this, I argue that the notion of the star persona is evident here, in the audience's possible assessments of the real lives of Williams, Hawtrey, Jacques and Sims. In this sense, the audiences are willing to engage with queer humour, knowing that heterosexual masculine hierarchies are being made fun of, through representing the queer male as the main conduit to express non-normative desire.

However, the expression of queer desire evident in reading the star persona of actors, relating imagined real lives to the cultural fictional representations that they stimulate, I would argue, is also contextual to the participation of writers, directors and producers. For example, although we are not fully aware of the sexuality, or the personal sexual politics, of the key producers who were involved in the Carry On films, other texts that represented straight girls with queer males often involved the creativity of queer writers or directors. For example, John Schlesinger, the director of *Darling* (discussed in Chapter 2) was an openly gay man, and in this film we can read his possible political intents in producing the evocative engagements between the straight girl as a central character and her queer friend who is a photographer. At the same time, Schlesinger produced a wide range of films, which included further representations of the straight girl and the queer guy, including *Sunday Bloody Sunday* (1971) and *The Next Best Thing* (2000). While I discuss *The Next Best Thing* a little later in this chapter, the discussion continues by examining Schlesinger's impact with *Sunday Bloody Sunday*, and the work of Christopher Isherwood in *Cabaret* (1972), which similarly involves the contribution of a queer author/producer.

Sunday Bloody Sunday and Cabaret

John Schlesinger's *Sunday Bloody Sunday* was a revolutionary British film, offering one of the first explicit representations of bisexuality and homosexuality within mainstream cinema. At the same time Christopher Isherwood's autobiographical book *Goodbye to Berlin* was adapted to create the Hollywood musical film *Cabaret* (Bob Fosse 1972, US),[1] offering a highly popular representation of a straight girl and a queer guy. Even though the contexts of these films – *Sunday Bloody Sunday* as a British film drama set in London in the 1970s, and *Cabaret* as a Hollywood musical film set in Berlin in the 1930s – offer little connection in cultural form, my discussion relates the impact of Schlesinger as a director in the former, and Isherwood as an author in the latter, relative to the production of queer representations for the mainstream. Hence rather than the implicit, or subtextual queer potential of Kenneth Williams (see above), and earlier films (see Chapters 1 and 2) which framed the queer guy as an accomplice to the straight female, these texts offer more connection to the imagined real life chances of the characters. Part of this, I argue, is the context of the queer director, or author, evident in the impact of Schlesinger in *Sunday Bloody Sunday* and Isherwood in *Cabaret*.

I argue that this may be related to self-reflexive potential, evident in media production, where directors and producers often reflect on their own life chances in the production of media texts (see Pullen [2009] 2012). As Anthony Giddens ([1991] 1992) argues, through this process 'in [the] conditions of modernity . . . the media does not mirror realities [in a passive sense] but in some part forms them' (27), related to reflexive thoughts of self-identity. This is particularly evident in Christopher Isherwood's work. He tells us in *Goodbye to Berlin* (the original source for *Cabaret*):

> I am a camera with its shutter open, quite passive, recording, not thinking. Recording the man shaving at the window opposite and the woman in the kimono washing her hair. Some day, all this will have to be developed, carefully printed, fixed. (Isherwood 1978: 11)

Whilst Isherwood 'came to rue this metaphor of the camera as misleading' (Bucknell 2000: 14), I would argue that this represents evidence of his emerging status as an interpretative and reflective personal character. This is particularly apparent in his autobiographical books *Lions and Shadows* (1947) and *Christopher and His Kind* (1977), which more directly place Isherwood as a the central storyteller, and focus of the texts.[2]

At the same time, as reported in the biography *Edge of Midnight* (Mann 2004), John Schlesinger's work is similarly self-reflexive. Notably, the film *Sunday Bloody Sunday* closely records a real-life relationship that Schlesinger had with his bisexual lover John Steiner. This is evident in key aspects of the film reflecting real-life events, such as Schlesinger being aware of Steiner's female lover and not having met her, the relevance of Jewish identity, the significance of a telephone answering service that he used, and the occasion of driving past his lover's flat, all aspects that appear in the film. Also this is something that John Schlesinger frankly admitted, noted in his tape-recorded diary: 'It's my story, my own bloody Sunday – my affair with a young man' (Mann 2004: 224).

I argue that the work of both John Schlesinger and Christopher Isherwood represents evidence of the emerging 'self-reflexive' queer male in storytelling. This directly relates to Anthony Giddens's ([1991] 1992) concept of the 'reflexive project of the self', where the individual in contemporary society identifies with personal visions of fulfilment, not necessarily informed by dominant structures or motifs. Isherwood in *Goodbye to Berlin* (the inspiration for *Cabaret*) and Schlesinger in *Sunday Bloody Sunday* produce texts that are fundamentally about themselves, expressing and prioritising the queer male as an integral part of the narrative. This may be related to the process of 'autobiographical thinking', which Giddens ([1993] 1995) describes not only as a central element of self-therapy but also as something that should be considered as a process which may engender change. As Giddens ([1991] 1992) tells us:

> For developing a coherent sense of one's life history is a prime means of escaping the thrall of the past and opening oneself out to the future. The author of the autobiography is enjoined to go back as far as possible into early childhood and set up lines of potential development to encompass the future. (72)

Hence Schlesinger's and Isherwood's work frames the notion of the autobiographical, not only placing themselves within the frame but also contextualising straight female characters as significant and foundational in recording the events they describe. I argue that both *Cabaret* and *Sunday Bloody Sunday* offer new insight into the relationship between the straight girl and the queer guy, particularly framing the notion of sexual agency.

In terms of storyline both *Cabaret* and *Sunday Bloody Sunday* integrate the straight female within the context of queer male sexuality. In *Cabaret*, the central character of Brian has a sexual relationship with a bisexual male (Maximilian), who also has sexual relations with the central female character, Sally. In *Sunday Bloody Sunday*, a similar relationship is represented, with queer male Daniel having a sexual relationship with bisexual Bob, who at the same time has a sexual relationship with straight female Alex (see Figure 3.2). Despite this, in *Cabaret* Brian and Sally are represented as close friends, while in *Sunday Bloody*

Film and Commodity 77

Figure 3.2 *Glenda Jackson as Alex Greville and Murray Head as Bob Elkin as a bisexual male and heterosexual female non-monogamous coupling, reflecting on their identities, in* Sunday Bloody Sunday.

Sunday the queer male and the straight girl (Daniel and Alex) are represented as competitors for the affections of the bisexual character. Nevertheless the key aspect in both films is the dynamics of a straight female, who would be considered as contextual or contrapuntal to the queer male. Notably, in *Sunday Bloody Sunday*, although Daniel and Alex are effectively in competition for the affections of Bob, in many ways they are the central male and female characters, and their relationship with Bob signifies their interconnection rather than their conflict. This is evident as this context frames the similarity of their desires, and life worlds, apparent in the sexual and romantic focus on Bob.

Such a focus on the bisexual character as the source of connecting the straight girl and the queer guy is apparent in both films. In *Cabaret*, Brian and Sally become closer when they both discover that they have been sleeping with Maximilian, revealing their connection through the third party, while in *Sunday Bloody Sunday* the closeness (or similar context shared) between Daniel and Alex is more philosophical, rather than explicit, related to shared disappointment. The film creatively expresses this connection, through relating the bisexual male as unattainable. This is achieved in the film through subjecting Bob to the heterosexual female gaze and queer male gaze, making him appear as untenable and outside the gaze, and hence uncontainable.

John Schlesinger creates a wide range of aesthetic compositions which foreground the bisexual male, as outside the controlling gaze. In a key part of the film where Alex (played by Glenda Jackson) and Bob (played by Murray Head) spend time together looking after children, and the household, of friends while they are away for the weekend, Alex and Bob play the role of surrogate parents. Despite this, a range of uncontrollable incidents take place, including the older child taking better care of the baby than either of the surrogate parents, the children smoking marijuana and the family dog being run over by a lorry whilst they are all out for a relaxing time in the park. The aspect of gazing is foregrounded, in a pivotal sequence with the children and Bob gazing at Alex through a plastic cubed prism, accompanied by fast-paced children's nursery rhyme music, suggesting incongruity and disturbance. Alex is at the sink in the kitchen, and distorted images of Alex are produced as she appears as an incongruous visual form, subject to the gaze of Bob and the younger children. This sequence is followed by a further image of Bob gazing at Alex and the children playing in the garden, whilst he is still in the house. We see him observe her, in some sense assessing her possible identity as a loving mother. However, his look is one of uncertainty and distance, as if framing the domestic and cultural space between the two, made more vivid in the following scene where he unravels a roll of transparent sticking tape, and, on hearing of her choice to leave her job, places his lips on the adhesive tape, looking at the image of his lips, as if recording his transience, and his rejection of her desire for him.

At the same time Alex is represented as gazing at Bob in the manner that one might gaze at a transient event that will pass and remain ephemeral, such as observing the phenomenon of the Northern Lights in wintertime (the colourful electrical atmospheric storm in the northern hemisphere). In one sequence Alex returns to bed after caring for the baby, she looks at Bob asleep on the bed, with the dog at the foot of the bed (before the fatal accident) and she holds Bob's hand briefly, with a look of longing and hopefulness. In another sequence she observes him whilst he is showering. She stands in the bathroom looking at his naked body through the plastic curtain, as the water flows down his body, and in the background we hear opera music, which connotes the presence of Daniel (played by Peter Finch). This is significant, as Bob has just returned from an afternoon with Daniel, and we imagine that the need for the shower is to cleanse his body, after having sex with another man. Alex observes this ritual, seeming to contemplate this prior event, reflecting on the transient nature of her relationship with Bob, vivid in gazing at the flowing water on the shower curtain, reflecting issues of sensitivity and tactility, but also connotes the inability to be held, or to hold.

In *Sunday Bloody Sunday*, Daniel also gazes at Bob, hoping that their relationship might become more permanent. However, rather than focusing on the ephemeral or transient body, Daniel focuses on an art installation water feature that has been produced by Bob, which is fixed in his garden. This outside, but not inside, presence – a construction of glass tubes, which is erect, and contains water as if flowing or crying – signifies the fixed, and yet unfixed status of Bob in his life. Daniel gazes at this structure from the confines of his house, with the water feature seeming to flow freely outside, never able to be brought in the house. While both Alex and Daniel are unable to contain or permanently possess Bob, as he ultimately leaves them both for a new life in America, the focus on connection and disconnection is permanently embedded in the film, apparent in all three characters using a telephone answering service, where only the telephone operator seems to possess a coherent narrative.

A lack of coherency, related to fragmentation, is particularly evident in *Cabaret*. This is not only apparent when Sally (played by Liza Minelli) works out that her new flatmate Brian (played by Michael York) is queer, and they work through a new relationship together, effectively sharing the sexual affections of bisexual Maximilian, but it is relative to the distinct political setting of the film, set in Nazi Germany recording the rise of Hitler in the 1930s. Hence Isherwood frames his own documented life, apparent in his diaries (and in *Goodbye to Berlin*), and is evident in the film as the character of Brian, contextual to oppression exerted by the Nazis on minority groups such as Jews and homosexuals.

While the film is essentially a musical, suggesting narrative diversion in the inclusion of performance sequences, *Cabaret* capitalises on producing oppositions between fascism and free-spiritedness. In many ways reflecting the historical times, connoting the end of the Weimar Republic in Germany, where civil liberties and freedom of expression were central contexts, which were ended by the rise of the Nazi party (see Kolb 2004), *Cabaret* creates an uncomfortable juxtaposition between rising violence and oppression and the continuing drive for personal expression, exhibited in music and club entertainment. For example, early in the film we sense the presence of Nazi supporters visiting the cabaret club where Sally Bowles is an entertainer, and a man who seems like the manager ejects the Nazi supporter collecting donations for the party. Soon after, a group of Nazis savagely beat the manager, as retribution. However, rather than purely a focus on the manager getting beaten up, there is a juxtaposition of this scene with a contrasting scene from the cabaret club. These two sequences are intercut, exchanging images of a few seconds between the two settings, imagined to be taking place at the same time. Oom-pah music (featuring a bass-oriented rhythmic brass band) forms a continuous soundtrack in this sequence, reflecting the music used in a performance scene in the club, where a number of male performers are dressed in traditional German lederhosen (leather shorts with braces). As the men in the club dance up and down in a comical manner, moving in time to the music, at the same time we see the manager punched and beaten, covered in blood, then kicked, having fallen to the pavement, presumably outside the club. The implication is that all this is happening without the audience being fully aware, blending the diegetic worlds, through the use of music, and the reference of bodily movements: in one scene representing comical playfulness and in the other signifying violence executed on a vulnerable body.

The notion of the vulnerable body is related not only to those who might object to the Nazis; it is directly related to those who might be oppressed by fascism, such as Jews, homosexuals and the sexually liberated. Hence Brian's arrival from England, desiring to work on his PhD in liberal Berlin, where he becomes a flatmate and good friend to Sally, frames the context of a queer man in union with a promiscuous girl, in opposition to the rise of fascism. While Brian's homosexuality, and consequently status as an outsider, is not immediately apparent to Sally, they develop a union soon after he announces his queerness. In many ways offering an archetypal and emerging foundational representation of the straight girl and the queer guy, the relationship commences with a sense of physical attraction felt by the straight girl for the queer guy, but this is rejected. In a key sequence, Sally tries to seduce Brian, but it becomes apparent that he is not physically attracted to her, implying that he is homosexual. She tells him, 'Why didn't you tell me in the first place? Look Brian, you are absolutely my best friend. And friends are much harder to find than lovers. Besides sex always screws up a friendship anyway, if you let it. So we won't let it!'

Their close friendship, however, becomes complicated after Sally meets Maximilian, a wealthy married man, who seduces her, after a time when Brian and Sally had become sexually intimate, when earlier Brian had consoled her over her father neglecting her. Although Brian and Sally are represented as lovers, this is constructed more as a union between outsiders who find consolation in their rejection than an explicit devotion. When it emerges that Maximilian is also having sex with Brian, seemingly as revenge on Sally for her promiscuity, in many ways it equalises their relationship. Hence all three characters are represented as involved in a union of intimacy. This appears notably in a key sequence when they are at Maximilian's country home, when in a state of mild alcoholic influence all three slowly dance together in close embrace, glancing at each other, sharing mutual desiring looks. In the large room, music reverberates to accompany this scene, as they move as if in slow motion, and they glance not only at each other but also away from each other and upwards to the glittering chandelier. This framing establishes not only their possible intimacy but also their distance from realism, evident in the iconography of wealth and privilege that they are distanced from but contained within. This sequence also resonates with a later scene relating deception, as Sally is unaware at this point of Brian's sexual engagement with Maximilian.

Hence this sequence foregrounds the liberty of gazing, but also relates the gaze as a commodity that might be deceptive or ephemeral.

Hence the representation of the queer guy and the straight girl is framed within a world of commodity, which, while it might enable social connections, also restricts attempts to find true love, or connect with some lasting partner. In *Cabaret*, whilst Brian and Sally are the central male and female characters, in fact their relationship is distanced from romance, and formed relative to commodity. This is particularly evident in comparing the relationship between Brian and Sally to that of another couple, Fritz and Natalia. Brian wants a lasting relationship and, on finding that Sally is pregnant, offers to marry her, and take her back to England, even though he knows the baby may be fathered by Maximilian, who has rejected her. Although Sally seems to desire this, ultimately she sells the fur coat that was given to her by Maximilian to pay for an abortion. The fur coat represents the commodity of her sexual favours, but also some exchange value that she can trade. While Brian is initially upset by her actions, as he had wanted to raise a 'unique' child, ultimately he accepts her transactional rationale. In contrast Fritz and Natalia, English language students of Brian, risk everything for love. Because Natalia is Jewish, Fritz initially conceals his Jewish identity for self-protection from the Nazis, at a time when anti-Semitism was rife in Germany. However, later Fritz reaffirms his connection to Judaism, purely so he can find true love and marry Natalia. While these two are not the central characters, they represent the heroic order, which enables them to be inspirational figures.

Hence the representation of the straight girl and the queer guy offers a consolation for the failure to find a lasting soulmate. While both *Sunday Bloody Sunday* and *Cabaret* are outstanding films, they frame issues of isolation and rejection in working through the potential of the queer guy with the straight girl. Despite this, more recent films have attempted to frame the notion of endurance and longevity, affirming the relationship between the straight girl and the queer guy, not as a substitute but as a new social form.

THE GAY BEST FRIEND IN CONTEMPORARY FILM

In the last part of the twentieth century three Hollywood films focused on the representation of the straight girl and the queer guy: *My Best Friend's Wedding* (P. J. Hogan 1997, US), *The Object of My Affection* (Nicholas Hytner 1998, US) and *The Next Best Thing* (John Schlesinger 2000, US). More recently the notion of the 'gay best friend' (GBF) has further developed in two films: *Gayby* (Jonathan Lisecki 2012, US) and *G.B.F.* (Darren Stein 2013, US) (see Chapter 6). Although I argue that the appetite for these representations may be largely due to the success of the television series *Will and Grace* (NBC

1998–2006, US) and the recurring presence of gay male characters within television drama and reality television (see Chapters 4 and 5), at the same time the commodity of the gay best friend may be considered as intertextual, engaging with notions of star identity. Hence, in a similar manner that Judy Garland and Doris Day may be considered as straight females offering identification resources for gay men, either seeming to exhibit the emotional context of queer male lived experience or represented as a collaborator or accomplice to queer male characters, the Hytner, Hogan and Schlesinger films represent the gay best friend as a fully functioning character, contextual to the presence of the celebrity or the star.

This is related to both males and females, as celebrity icons supporting queer identity. The openly gay actor Rupert Everett appears in both *My Best Friend's Wedding* and *The Next Best Thing*, not only potentially contextualising his real-life identity but also referencing earlier queer male performances in *Another Country* (Marek Kanievska 1984, UK) and *An Ideal Husband* (Oliver Parker 1999, UK). In the former he is represented as an upper-class queer youth, exhibiting sexual confidence in finding partners, set within the privilege of the private education system, and in the latter he references the identity of Oscar Wilde, starring in a seminal work, satirising the notion of the ideal 'heterosexual' husband. At the same time, three major icons of female celebrity and stardom appear in these films, playing the roles of the straight girl. The celebrated film actor Julia Roberts takes this role in *My Best Friend's Wedding*; the enduring television actress Jennifer Aniston (mostly known for her appearance in the situation comedy *Friends* (Warner Bros Television 1994–2006, US)) appears in *The Object of My Affection*; and the pop star and occasional actress Madonna takes this role in *The Next Best Thing*. The celebrities Rupert Everett, Julia Roberts, Jennifer Aniston and Madonna are centrally represented as star persona and queer supporter commodity storytellers in these films.

Hence, issues of commodity are explicitly represented in these films, suggesting that both the straight girl and the queer guy are bonded through necessity. Such a focus, however, complicates the idea of friendship, and the notion of finding the ideal partner. For example Deborah Thompson (2004) tells us, 'rather than the love and friendship between women and gay men the fag hag stereotype often seems to presume a failed object choice on the part of women, the hag' (8). Although Thompson is framing the reductive nomenclature for the straight girl and queer guy relationship, focusing on the abject notion of the 'hag' (a female connected to old age and uncertain gender identity), the idea that the relationship represents some consolation for not finding true love is a central narrative device within the three films. Consequently as Claire Sisco King (2014) explains, referencing the film *A*

Single Man (Tom Ford 2009, US), the representation of the 'Fag Hag' 'risks pathologising both the gay man and the straight woman. Making each as incapable of loving or being loved correctly' (191), implying that their relationship relates failure in finding the ideal partner. Certainly this seems to be a major narrative context, as is the complication between male and female 'normative' gender roles. For example Helene Stugart (2003) tells us that these texts 'reframe gay male sexuality as an extension of heterosexual male privilege predicated on [the] control of female sexuality' (80), suggesting that the 'women are portrayed as childlike, silly and cute, and often given to hysteria' (83), while gay men are related as stable. Despite this I would argue that *My Best Friend's Wedding*, *The Object of My Affection* and *The Next Best Thing* offer more complex insight into the relationship between the straight girl and the queer guy, which blurs distinctions in gender performance.

This is noticeable in considering the essential narrative contexts of *My Best Friend's Wedding*, *The Object of My Affection* and *The Next Best Thing*, which frame the female character as the central narrative protagonist, subverting normative gender expectations of performance. *My Best Friend's Wedding* concerns the story of Julianne Potter (played by Julia Roberts) who, on discovering that an old boyfriend is now about to be married, decides to break up this potential union through befriending the possible new bride who had asked for her support in the marriage plans. She uses her gay best friend, George (played by Rupert Everett), to support her in this plan, at one point getting him to pretend to be her boyfriend. *The Object of My Affection* focuses on Nina Borowski (played by Jennifer Aniston), who becomes pregnant, yet resists the notion of raising the child with the father, and rather desires to raise the child with her gay best friend, George (played by Paul Rudd), to whom she has become attracted (see Figure 3.3). Despite this, George feels trapped, later finding a gay male partner, but not initially disclosing this to Nina. *The Next Best Thing* concerns the story of Abbie Reynolds (played by Madonna), who becomes pregnant, seeming to believe that the father is her gay best friend, Robert (played by Rupert Everett), with whom she once had a drunken sexual encounter at the time of conception. She sets up home with Robert raising the child, but, when she finds a new male lover, embarks on a court case against Robert, seeming to deny him any legal role in raising the child, which proves not to be his.

Hence, while the straight girl and queer guy representations within these films frame the notion of affection and camaraderie, there is an over-emphasis on female agency which seems problematic rather than harmonious. This might be translated as the female masquerading as the male character, stimulating a kind of overdeterminism to be the leading protagonist. Hence in *My Best Friend's Wedding*, although we may consider the genre of this film as a

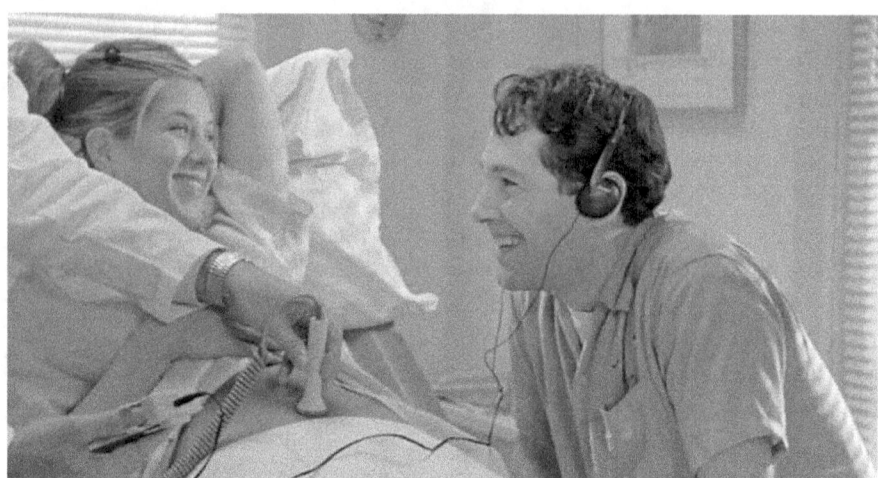

Figure 3.3 *Jennifer Aniston as Nina Borowski and Paul Rudd as George Hanson in* The Object of My Affection, *contextualising the queer guy as interested in raising a child who is not his own.*

'mad cap comedy' rather than a romantic comedy for its focus on a seemingly absurd plot, the straight girl is coded as masculine. This is evident in the text where Julianne is not only just considered as the best friend of the groom but also is related as 'practically the best man', given the task of holding the rings for the ceremony (a ritual associated with the role of 'the best man'), and taking part in masculine entertainments, such as attending a football game, excluding all other female characters. This complicates the gender dynamics, through foregrounding a female yet seemingly masculine subject as the possessor of the gaze, seemingly acting like a stereotypically masculine subject. Hence her desire is not a simple affective connection that would enable them to be together in a romantic sense, it is a desire founded on masquerade, involving an obsession to break up a marriage, rather than necessarily being able to form one. Within this the gay best friend is represented as an unwilling accomplice, highlighting the straight female's unrealistic obsession.

Such obsession and determination in forming the gaze, upon the subject to be desired and to be possessed, is similarly executed in *The Object of My Affection*. However, rather than the heterosexual male as the object to be possessed, it is the gay best friend. This is particularly evident in the seduction scene, where Nina attempts to have sex with George. Prior to this sequence Nina and George visit a shop for baby items, and whilst there George meets an old boyfriend who is a shop assistant there. A sexual tension is created as the assistant and George exchange seductive glances, with Nina looking on the couple, seeming embarrassed. Later in the apartment that Nina and George share, Nina expresses her insecurity, seeming not to want George to feel trapped. George assures her that he wants to be open with her, as she joins him on the bed that he is reclining on. They embrace, with Nina laying her head on George's chest, as George affirms that he does not think about men whilst he is with her. Although there is no indication that he is receptive to her sexual advances, they kiss, seeming like friends, and then she kisses him in a more sexual manner. She gazes up at him as if accepting that she must just accept friendship, but then proceeds to put her hand in his shirt, undoing it and kissing his chest. This leads to her kissing him again with a suggestion of reciprocity, then moving down to undo his trouser belt, as if about to commence oral sex. The telephone rings, and George looks up as if waking from a dream, swiftly answering the phone. Hence the straight female is represented as gazing, and desiring the unattainable queer male. Her act of seduction unfortunately establishes a discord in their relationship, where, although he wants to raise the baby with her, he feels trapped.

Hence while *My Best Friend's Wedding* misappropriates the seemingly normative gaze between the heterosexual female and the heterosexual male, through queering the female gaze as masculinised, the gaze of the straight girl upon the queer male in *The Object of My Affection* is constructed as oppressive and controlling. This offers resonance to the situation of the heterosexual female who is subject to the male heterosexual gaze in Mulvey's terms, similarly contained within an oppressive gaze. Hence although a union, and a bond, is created between the straight girl and the queer guy, in both films the female gaze is represented as problematised.

In *The Next Best Thing*, the coupling of the straight female and the queer guy similarly reflects these issues, more obviously framing issues of humiliation, in dealing with the rejection of the gaze. However, whilst in *My Best Friend's Wedding* and *The Object of My Affection* the straight females ultimately humiliate themselves, through overdetermining their desire for the straight male in the former, and the queer male in the latter, in *The Next Best Thing* the object of humiliation is the queer male. In many ways, of all three films discussed here, John Schlesinger's *The Next Best Thing* vivifies the abject position of the queer male as subject to oppression, evident in foregrounding the potential for humiliation. While the archetype of the straight girl as desiring the gay best friend frames a sense of camaraderie and shared experience between the two, similarly to the other films, I argue that Schlesinger deliberately employs the narrative formula of the courtroom drama, as a generic device, to offer discursive depth.

Through this formula, the notion of the female gaze upon the queer male is represented to some degree as a problematic corollary, for failing to contain or restrict the queer male. In the final courtroom sequence of the film, the queer male and the straight girl are represented as on opposing sides.

Rupert Everett in the character of Robert provides an emotional testimony, in arguing why he should be considered as the father of the child that he has raised:

> It seems like I spend my whole life thinking about blood. Worrying about blood. Blood, uh! It's like shit. We are all full of it. Its good it gets bad, but it's not who we are. Being a parent, a real parent, takes more than DNA. No one can hand it to you and no one can take it away. I have earned my right to be Sam's father. So no matter what you decide, Sam is my son, forever and always.

During this sequence, the members of the court respond in a way that reflects his hopeless position, with the judge herself acknowledging his important contribution in raising the child, despite not realising that he is not the father. At the same time Madonna, playing the role of Abbie, looks at him emotionally, despite rejecting his legal claims to her child. Central within this is the framing of a queer man who had formed a domestic alliance with a straight girl that had resulted in his caring for her child over many years. Despite this, owing to the forensic evidence of DNA, she was able to reject his status as the father of her child, even though he had raised the child thinking this.

Using the formal structure of the courtroom drama, framing the queer male as a vulnerable subject, yet not cared for by the dominant world, the director John Schlesinger foregrounds the problematic relationship between the queer male and the straight girl, as framing and commoditising desire, but ultimately coded within the heteronormative domain. At the same time he offers resonance of the notion of 'families we choose' (Weston 1991), where family ties are formed through kinship rather than necessarily blood ties. This is particularly resonant for the narrative, as the notion of the queer guy and the straight girl raising a child contextualises contemporary issues for queer family groups, suggesting that blood ties alone are not necessarily sufficient in forming close family networks.

While *My Best Friend's Wedding*, *The Object of My Affection* and *The Next Best Thing* do offer depth to the meaning of the relationship between the straight girl and the queer male, at the same time contextualising new concepts of family, all these texts reveal the problem of the desiring gaze, as framed within heteronormative worlds. While the straight girl cannot possess a desiring gaze unless she adopts the masquerade of the masculine dominant order, at the same time a corollary of this is either that her desire is devalued as incoherent or not meaningful, as occurs in *My Best Friend's Wedding*, or that her desire makes a commodity of the queer male in order to raise a child, as occurs in *The Object of My Affection* and *The Next Best Thing*. While such representations seemingly reflect 'mainstream depictions of fag hags [that] reproduce discourses of true love' (King 2014: 197) that are seemingly unattainable, such commodity, however, is less about finding a soulmate, whether romantic or platonic, but more concerns a drive to attain cultural capital, or at least to critique it.

Conclusion

The identity of the straight girl and the queer guy is complex and multifarious. Although the notion of star identity clearly plays a part in relating the role of the spectator, who might consume the notion of the star, or auteur, as a role model or as an identity to be consumed, the real lives of Kenneth Williams, John Schlesinger, Christopher Isherwood and Rupert Everett as queer males, and Hattie Jacques, Joan Sims, Julia Roberts, Jennifer Aniston and Madonna as straight females, offer insight, context and resource in exploring the 'possibility' of union. Such a union or alliance between the queer gay and the straight female may be framed in reading the performative potential of 'camp' as an aesthetic or discursive device; at the same time clearly there are aspects of 'knowingness' in reading between the lines.

Hence, the shared experience of the audience engaging with the potential of the star or the auteur offers a sideways glance at the potential of the straight girl and the queer guy, as a collaborative union. Despite this, the appearance of Kenneth Williams in the Carry On films, and the impact of John Schlesinger and Christopher Isherwood respectively in *Sunday Bloody Sunday* and *Cabaret*, foregrounds the significance of the queer male, relating senses of realism, connecting to real-life chances. I argue that this extends from the potential of self-reflexivity, and the willingness to speak about the intimate experience of the queer male.

At the same time, the context of the straight girl is central here, offering not only a counterpoint or context from which the queer male may express a connection or relationship, but also a resource to challenge notions of gender fixity. Specifically the opportunity of masquerade is central here, with the straight girl often taking on the mask of the dominant male. While it is tempting to consider that this is purely so she may gain access to power, engendering the queer male as an abject feminised object in comparison to her, in many ways issues of equality or equalisation are central here. Hence, when Hattie Jacques and Jennifer Aniston seem to seduce, or try to control, Kenneth Williams and Paul Rudd in their respective texts *Carry On Doctor* and *The Object of My Affection*, the queer male is not made abject through feminisation, but the straight girl frames the mask and the masquerade, challenging the notion of an essential or proper gaze.

While some might say that such a process is pure mimicry, and copying, which ironically reinforces the frame rather than the context, I argue that the liminal space created by the union of the straight girl and the queer male raises questions as much as it affirms answers. At the same time, the liminal space is related to the notion of personal feeling and the context of the home environment. This is particularly evident in the next chapter, where televisual form and its relationship to domesticity and female identity offer more scope for the straight girl and the queer guy relationship, at the same time as in many ways compartmentalising it.

Notes

1. *Goodbye to Berlin* (1978 [originally 1939]) was adapted into the play *I Am a Camera* (Van Druten, 1958 [originally 1951]) and then adapted into a film of the same name (Henry Cornelius 1955, UK). It was later used as an inspiration for *Cabaret*, which was originally a musical on Broadway, written by Joe Masteroff.
2. Despite this Christopher Isherwood tells us in *Christopher and His Kind* (1977) that his earlier autobiographical work *Lions and Shadows* (1938) was imbued with fictional licence, as he did not want to disclose the more intimate details of his sexuality.

CHAPTER 4

Television and Domesticity

As Maggie Andrews (2012) has pointed out, with regard to televisual form, the home environment and the context of femininity:

> Domesticity and the home is not merely bricks and mortar, it is a site of complex and changing social relationships, power struggles and identity formation which have been caught up in the wider shifts in social relationships in the twentieth and twenty first centuries. (xi)

Unlike film, which may be considered as presenting discrete texts to specific audiences often set within organised social settings (see Ellis 1982), television's broadcasting address to the home audience establishes its form as intimate, intertextual and focused on family life. As part of this, the address to females as heads of the domestic household, potentially paying concern not only to the utilitarian notion of organising or representing the household but also framed within the intuitive and emotive context of female identity, potentially offers scope in accommodating the 'other'. Part of this might include the emerging representation of sexual diversity, and its relationship to domestic, or feminised, environments. Hence, this chapter explores the development of the straight girl and the queer guy relationship within televisual form, enabled largely through the feminised domestic context of contemporary media.

Early television representations that explored the straight girl and the queer guy relationship included *Love Sidney* (Warner Bros 1981–3, US), a prototypical text that represents a middle-aged man (who is coded as queer) sharing his apartment with a young girl, who becomes pregnant and who later has a child. Later more explicit representations of the straight girl and the queer guy union were apparent in the serial drama *Tales of the City* (Channel 4 1993, UK) and the sitcom *Ellen* (ABC 1994–8, US), which established a cultural appetite that would be developed in *Will and Grace* (NBC 1998–2006, US) and *Gimme Gimme Gimme* – (Channel 4 1999–2001, UK), which focused on leisure and consumption. At the same time the notion of the queer guy in the company of females was equally apparent in *Sex in the City* (HBO 1998–2004, US) and *Girls* (HBO 2012 to present, US), where notions of female identification are counterpointed to the queer male experience. In contrast I examine the identity of the straight girl represented as contextual within queer male worlds, such as in *Queer as Folk* (Showtime 2000–5, US) and *Looking* (HBO 2014–15, US), framing issues of self-realisation and shared understanding. Finally I consider Russell T. Davies's *Bob and Rose* (ITV 2001, UK) and *Torchwood* (BBC 2006–11, UK), which might be considered as developments of his work in *Queer as Folk*, playing particular attention to the representation of bisexuality, and contexts of institution and authorship. However, before I examine my case studies, I want to consider the notion of televisual form, and its relation to domesticity and intimacy, relating the concept of television flow, and the significance of the glance, in contrast to the gaze.

Domesticity and the Intimate Glance

John Fiske (1994), extending the earlier foundational work of Raymond Williams (1992) concerning televisual flow, tells us that

> The television text, then, is composed of a rapid succession of compressed, vivid segments where the principle of logic and cause and effect is subordinated to that of association and consequence to sequence. Flow, with its connotations of a languid river, is perhaps an unfortunate metaphor: the movement of the television text is discontinuous, interrupted, and segmented. Its attempts at closure, at a unitary meaning, or a unified viewing subject, are constantly subjected to fracturing forces. (105)

Considering the potential of television form to offer the provision of fragmented moments that are connected through the continuity of scheduling, rather than through some generic homogeneity, Fiske focuses on the notion of discontinuity. According to this, unlike cinema, the television text appears within a collage of disparate meaning and understanding. Not only is this postmodern in its lack of an overarching metanarrative (see Lyotard 1979; Jameson 1991) but also any comprehension must be fleeting rather than focused.

Such potential may be related to the notion of the glance rather than the gaze. As John Ellis (1982) informs us in comparing film to television:

> TV's regime of vision is less intense than cinema's: it is a regime of the glance rather than the gaze. The gaze implies a concentration of the spectator's activity into that of looking, the glance implies that no extraordinary effort is being invested in the activity of looking . . . It is not that the experience is less intense than in cinema, rather it has a distinctive form of its own. In particular there is less separation between the viewer and the image than with cinema. Broadcast TV does not construct an image that is marked by present absence, its regime is one of co-presence of image and viewer. The image is therefore

not an impossible one, defined by the separation of the viewer from it, but rather one that is familiar and intimate. (137–8)

Hence through the televisual medium constructed as flow, unlike the cinematic gaze, there is little potential for intensity and rather a sense of transience is apparent. However, this does not necessarily reduce the potential of the gaze, glance or look: rather, as there is less of a separation between the image and the viewer, a sense of intimate co-presence is apparent. Such intimacy is evident in considering the reception of the broadcast image within the domestic environment, enabling a sense of inviting in and sharing.

As Lynn Spigel (1992) considers, relating the discursive construction of the television within family life in the United States:

> As [home] magazine continued to depict the [television] set in the center of family activity, television seemed to become a natural part of the domestic space . . . In its capacity as a unifying agent, television fit well with the more general hopes of a return to family values. It was seen as a kind of household cement that promised to reassemble the splintered lives of families who had been separated during the war. It was also meant to reinforce the new suburban family unit, which had left most of its extended family and friends behind in the city. (39)

Such a focus on framing the social and cultural potential of television firmly established a relationship to family and the notion of everyday life. This in part offered a sense of unification; the idea of bringing the family together in front of the television set. At the same time it related issues of community, foregrounding the life chances of displaced individuals within the domestic environment, looking for new opportunities of identification. Central within this was the significance of female identity.

As Judy Giles (2004) tells us:

> The feminine has frequently been represented as a refuge from the repressions and alienations of modernity, a symbolic space of redemption, nature and authenticity in which the injuries of modern living can be healed. In this version, the apparently timeless feminine values of intimacy and authenticity are set against the masculine experience of alienation and dehumanisation that constitute modern history. (9)

Hence the notion of the female as head of the domestic intimate household offers connections and understanding, framing problems of estrangement and alienation which might be evident in working through the trial of the modern world. Such potential, I argue, is connected to Anthony Giddens's ([1993] 1995) idea of 'the transformation of intimacy', related to strategies of reception and performance. As Giddens observes, 'Intimacy should not be understood as an interactional description, but as a cluster of prerogatives and responsibilities that define agendas of practical activity' ([1993] 1995: 90), framing 'intimacy as democracy' (184). I argue that female identity represented within the televisual cultural form, apparent in some sense as 'co-presence' making connections between the image and the viewer, offers the production of new feminised domestic space. As part of this, I argue, the relationship between the female and the queer guy offers an interesting intersection, which capitalises on the fleeting glance upon the queer guy, offering the notion of queer pleasure within television form (Doty 1993). However, this is not so much a transient queer apparition, but may be considered as an evolving substantial cultural form.

LOVE SIDNEY

Steven Capsuto (2000) describes an announcement by NBC network television to produce a new situation comedy in 1981:

> *Love Sidney* [will star] Tony Randall as a middle-aged, Jewish New York homosexual . . . Sidney finds new meaning in life after he invites a vivacious sexually active nineteen-year-old [girl], Laurie, into his home; together, they lovingly raise the bastard baby that she conceived during an affair with a married man. (160)

While Capsuto tells us that the Religious Right petitioned against the development of the show, for its focus on a queer guy who would be a co-parent of a child born out of wedlock, at the same time he reports that 'the program itself espoused extremely conservative moral values' (2000: 160). Hence, when the programme was eventually commissioned, with the homosexual identity of the main character intact but more subliminal than originally intended, there was a resonance of normative family values. Notably the central story concept that Sidney would confront Laurie, who was intending on having an abortion, offering to raise the child with her, offers a focus on family connected to procreation, as much as on family based on kinship groups. Hence, while in some senses the narrative foregrounded the union between a queer guy and a straight girl, as offering a new kind of kinship social relationship (see Weston 1991),, at the same time the notion of raising a child was central.

While this does not necessarily devalue the cultural meaning of the show, it frames the usefulness of queer identity in supporting normative family values, based on procreation. As part of this Steven Capsuto observes that

> What [Sidney] really wants out of life, he says, is family. Prudish, meddlesome Sidney is a stereotypical 'Jewish mother' type, much like his own oppressive mother, Yetta. His conservativism and possessiveness were apparently what

made his former lover, Martin walk out of his life. Burdened by that experience, Sidney became celibate and reclusive. (2000: 161)

The queer male character is represented as an isolated figure who possesses conservative values and rejects sexual relations. At the same time, he may be considered as a substitute for a matriarchal figure. Therefore, while in some senses the straight girl masquerades as the dominant male character (see Chapter 3) who may possess the agency of a liberated male, the queer male is constructed as an abject feminised other, who may be considered as a mother-type figure. Rather than possessing the oppositional identity of the heterosexual female in relation to the heterosexual male, this relationship is complicated through the processes of masquerade and sublimation. A complex mixture of identities and archetypes takes place, where the straight female masquerades as the dominant straight male, and in contrast the queer guy is subliminally read as the submissive female, also coded as a mother type.

Through this coding, references may be made to the notion of the gaze, and issues of sexual desire. As Sylvie Gambaudo (2012) tells us:

> Freud understood the experience of maternity as a form of momentary reparation for oedipal castration. While the oedipal experience ends the boy's fantasy of uniting with his mother, it also inaugurates his capacity for union with another woman. Hence the boy's oedipal moment castrates him at the same time as it 'phallicises' him. (785)

In this context, the queer guy represents an undeveloped, or problematic, psychological figure. Through his being represented as a mother type, but supposedly needing to transfer his desire from his mother to another female figure, there is no reparation for Oedipal castration, as he is unable to 'phallicise' in the imagined domain of the dominant symbolic order.

This is highly evident in the character of Sidney, who rejects a sexual life in favour of coding himself as maternal. In this sense he remains castrated. As part of this, he represents an uncomfortable blending of both the queer male, who may not fit within the imagined psychological order, and the abject female as the mother archetype. However, these two specific identities are not harmoniously blended, and a sense of ambivalence and uncertainty is present in reading the mask or the disguise.

The notion of ambivalence, and the suspension of ideals, are central in working through our understandings of the straight girl and queer guy relationship. Hence the televisual gaze is not a direct focus; it is a fleeting glance, reliant on the audience working through issues of identification and interpretation. For example, in a key sequence from the television pilot for *Love Sidney, Sidney Shorr: A Girl's Best Friend* (Russ Mayberry 1981, US), where Laurie is intent on having an abortion, Sidney frames himself in domestic and public spaces, adopting different familial disguises, in attempting to persuade her to keep the baby:

> [Laurie and Sidney in conversation in their kitchen]
>
> Laurie: Yes I want to have a baby, sometime. But not now, my career's beginning to break, . . . besides he [the father] wants me to have an abortion.
>
> Sidney: He wants. He wants. Who's he to want! We decide! . . . You're not poor. You're not ill. You're not alone . . .
>
> Laurie: OK. What if I do have the baby, who takes care of it? Who raises it?
>
> Sidney: Me! . . . [Arms stretched out, as if 'why not?'] . . . What did you give me for Christmas? . . . I want the baby.
>
> [Later at the Obstetric clinic, as both are sitting together in a crowded waiting room, while she is waiting for a consultation]
>
> Sidney: [hushed tone] Won't you change your mind?
>
> Laurie: Now I am here I want to go through with it.
>
> Sidney: [louder tone, as if to get the waiting room to overhear] Laurie, I have changed my mind . . . I will marry you! . . . I won't take it back this time, I really mean it. Don't feel trapped any more, I want the baby. Can you forgive me and learn to trust me again? I was wrong, terribly wrong, but I admit it. I'll make it up to you. I'll be the best father you have ever seen, and a hell of a husband too.
>
> [Applause from the waiting room audience]
>
> Laurie: Sidney [upset]
>
> [Laurie gets up, and walks out of the waiting room, and Sidney follows her]

The representation of Sidney and Laurie in the kitchen frames the domestic environment. The simplicity of Sidney's affirmation that he will care for the child not only references the mother figure, who might raise a daughter's child, but also it connotes the child, who might unrealistically argue why he wants to care for a baby, or another child, imagining it is like a Christmas present. In this sense Laurie the dominant figure who is intent on having an abortion, to ensure her career, is challenged by the notion of the family environment, not explicitly represented as a mother and a child but evident in symbolic performances of masquerade that reference these identities.

Furthermore, in the waiting room Sidney pretends to be the father of the child, offering a deliberate performance addressed to the audience, so that he may shame her into agreeing to keep the child. What is significant here is not only that this is an exaggerated hyper-real performance, presented as some realisation or catharsis, suggesting that this is unbelievable, but that a response is required from the audience in the waiting room itself. In this sense the notion of the domestic audience at home is reflected in the presence of the all-female audience in the waiting room. A sense of televisual glance, rather than a filmic gaze, is particularly apparent in this sequence, where both characters in intimate conversation are set within the waiting room, with their backs to the camera, and the audience are foregrounded as if watching over the couple. Hence, rather than the offering of a direct focus which might foreground their corporeal presence, as individuals in intimate conversation, a sense of co-presence is apparent, reflecting the audience as part of the text.

Through this sense of sharing with the audience, Sidney is related to different family roles. He is considered not only as the nurturing mother and the supportive child (evident at home) but also as the head of household as the father (apparent in public). Hence Sidney represents a queer male who mimics diverse family identities, in his attempts to form bonds with the straight girl, and thereby create a family for himself, where he is not necessarily the father, or the head of the household, but a composite representation, referencing notions of procreation and reproduction.

However, procreation and reproduction as signifiers of 'heterosexual' productive citizenship may be considered as oppositional to notions of leisure and introspection, which often signify 'queer' citizenship. While *Love Sidney* offers a focus on an imagined 'queer productive citizenship', through engaging with discourses of child raising, later representations of the straight girl and the queer guy are more explicitly focused on pleasure and self-examination.

TALES OF THE CITY, WILL AND GRACE AND GIMME GIMME GIMME

I argue that the notion of the queer guy with the straight girl was further developed, in texts such as *Tales of the City*, *Will and Grace* and *Gimme Gimme Gimme*. However, rather than the queer guy being represented as an ideal productive citizen, who might support a straight girl and an unusual family might be formed, the notion of 'queerness' became more embedded within the relationship, and the couple might be considered as independent subjects, relating some sense of shared queerness between the two.

Central within this is the connotation of personal indulgence relative to queer identity, which Alan Sinfield (1994) considers frames issues of 'effeminacy, leisure, idleness, immorality, luxury, insouciance, decadence and aestheticism' (3). While Sinfield's evaluation relates the impact of the celebrated literary figure Oscar Wilde, relative to the trials against him in the late 1800s, it is the focus on personal life chances outside issues of procreation and reproduction which offers insight into queer identity in this way. Such a process prioritises the notion of a superficial identity construct centred purely on self, rather than a resourceful identity that may contribute to society.

As Maria F. Fackler and Nick Salvato (2012) tell us in relation to the notion of the 'Fag Hag' (a reductive synonym for the straight girl):

> [T]he term is not only explainable by the way it defines the woman exclusively in relation to her best friend: there is a darker substrate beyond refusals both to use the term and to think critically about the friendships and queer intimacies that it continues to capture. (62)

Hence, the straight girl is signified as trapped within the orbit of the queer guy, not only coded herself as an improbable identity that is purely defined in relationship to her queer partner, but also bearing the burden of queer subjectivity. Hence I argue that, within the straight girl and queer guy relationship, the notion of queerness is shared between the characters, rather than solely attributed to the queer guy. This is particularly evident in *Tales of the City*.

Armistead Maupin's *Tales of the City* originated as a newspaper serial. It initially appeared (in a different form) as *The Serial* in 1974 in the Marin County (California) newspaper *The Pacific Sun*, and then later it was fully developed as *Tales of the City* in 1976, gaining high-profile attention in *The San Francisco Chronicle* (Gale 1999: 49). Achieving popularity, it was later transformed into a book (stimulating a number of sequels), and in 1993 it was adapted into a television mini-series (by Channel 4 (UK), and later Showtime (US)).[1] The original book and series are set in 1970s San Francisco and tell the tale of a diverse group of people centred on a rooming house headed by a transgendered woman and featuring gay, lesbian and bisexual characters, the central storyteller at the outset being the character of Mary Ann Singleton. While Mary Ann is the main straight girl, and her friendship with Michael Tolliver may be considered as the dominant straight girl and queer guy relationship, Mona Ramsey is also closely bonded to Michael. However, Mary Ann and Mona may be considered as bearing diverse traits of the straight girl in union with the queer guy. Hence, while Mary Ann is resolutely coded as heterosexual, Mona is coded as bisexual, yet both may be considered as 'queer' straight girls, who are bonded to the queer guy.

Notably, Mona is explicitly coded as the 'Fag Hag'. In an early sequence in the series where Mona and Michael go to the beach for the day, Mona expresses concerns to Michael (whom she affectionately calls 'Mouse'):

> Mona: Mouse, do you think that I am a Fag Hag? . . . Let's look at the symptoms. I hang out with you. We boogie at Busbys. I hardly know any straight men . . . You know, I really don't like most straight men. They are boorish, and boring.

While Mona affirms her identity as a 'Fag Hag', her queer identification is present not only in her willingness to focus on the companionship of a queer guy to the exclusion of finding a heterosexual male partner, but also in that her sexuality may be in part queer. This is literally evident when later we discover that Mona has had a lesbian relationship and soon re-embarks on this, and theoretically she cannot be considered as a 'straight girl'.

Also her queerness is apparent in her personal identity, relative to procreation. Although we are not aware of this at the outset of the series, we discover later that Mona is the child of their landlady Anna Madrigal, who is a male to female transsexual. Mona is not aware of this early on in the series, although it is alluded to in the narrative. This forms a sense of pervasive queerness, where we find out that Anna had sought out Mona to live in the boarding house with her, but Anna had not told her of their intimate relationship. In this sense the queer glance, which cannot be fulfilled until Anna announces her paternal/maternal relationship to Mona, offers a sense of suspension, where the straight girl is an object of queer subjectivity.

In comparison, Mary Ann Singleton is also coded as queer. This is not so much in reference to her sexuality or any question as to her 'queer' parents, but is apparent in her eccentricity and naivety, evident in coming to San Francisco and not being fully aware of the social life there. For example on meeting up with an old friend, Connie, whom she initially stays with, they are in a disco:

> [Mary Ann and Connie walk across a crowded dance floor holding drinks, as if looking for a good place to start dancing]
>
> Mary Ann: I thought that we would do something colourful, like go to China Town, for dim sum or something.
>
> Connie: Hon! You want to get laid. I wouldn't make China Town your first stop.
>
> Mary Ann: I didn't say anything about getting laid.
>
> Connie: You don't have to for Christ's sake. Look if you can't deal with your sexuality, you are going to get screwed up good in this town.

Mary Anne's innocence and naivety are presented as in opposition to the permissive society in San Francisco. Arriving there from Cleveland, she is coded as culturally and socially unaware. This is evident in many sequences, notably where she is represented as preferring to watch old television programmes rather than go out and socialise, and in her response to drug culture, such as when Mona offers her coke, and Mary Ann thinks it is the soft drink, not the hard-core drug. While it's possible to consider her as part of the mainstream, for her connection to 'normative' worlds, in the countercultural social world of San Francisco in the 1970s she is an outsider, and consequently coded as queer, through eccentricity and naivety.

Hence Mary Ann and Mona bear the burden of queer identity, as much as, if not more than, Michael, the actual queer guy. While Michael is clearly represented as a sexualised queer man, his main pursuit is to find an ideal partner, who can offer romance and emotional security. So the representation of the straight girl and the queer guy within *Tales of the City* does not so much focuson the everyday potential of the couple, it frames their difference from the mainstream as a countercultural couple. While Mona embarks on a lesbian relationship, and Mary Ann becomes more culturally aware, they are still represented as icons of difference, as straight girls who have a unique relationship with Michael, the queer guy. This offers a developed sense of queer alliance, where the couple are seen as equals. This tension is particularly evident in the situation comedies *Will and Grace* and *Gimme Gimme Gimme*, where the straight girl and the queer guy are represented as central characters.

Will and Grace (NBC 1998–2006, US) was the first television series to present the straight girl and the queer guy as leading storytellers, evident in the central characters of Will Truman and Grace Adler. The series follows the success in the United States of the situation comedy *Ellen* (ABC 1994–8, US), which featured a recurring representation of Ellen Morgan and Peter Barnes as a prototypical representation of a straight girl and a queer guy. While *Ellen* featured Ellen DeGeneres in the leading role of Ellen Morgan, who would come out within the television series as a lesbian (Tracy 1999), reflecting DeGeneres's own real-life identity (see Pullen [2009] 2012), it's important to note the precedence of Ellen Morgan and Peter Barnes as the straight girl and queer guy within the television format. This representation presented the queer guy as a close friend to the leading female character, at the same time offering an opportunity to present the imagined real-life context of the queer male, who in the case of Peter Barnes had a romantic same-sex partner, Barrett. While *Ellen* was a highly popular programme, and over 36 million people viewed the coming-out episode, the series declined in popularity after the character of Ellen Morgan became a lesbian. I argue that *Will and Grace* capitalised on the success of *Ellen*, developing the focus on the straight girl and the queer guy, inventively placing this as a central focus. However, the series considers the notion of potential romance between the straight girl and the queer guy. As part of this it highlights the failure of the queer guy to find the straight girl sexually attractive. Hence, although the series may be considered as progressive, at the same time it is embedded in a heterosexual female address.

In comparison *Gimme Gimme Gimme* presents a dysfunctional relationship between the straight girl and the queer guy, evident in the characters of

Linda La Hughes and Tom Farrell. Written by Jonathan Harvey, an openly gay screenwriter who produced the groundbreaking gay coming-of-age film drama *Beautiful Thing* (Hettie MacDonald 1996, UK) (further discussed in Chapter 6), *Gimme Gimme Gimme* offers an ironic representation. The series foregrounds the notion of the comedy farce, where unlikely events occur, and the focus is on eccentricity, extravagance and indulgence. Rather than representing the characters of Linda and Tom as potential soulmates who would be together if the queer guy were heterosexual (as occurs in *Will and Grace*), the couple are represented as competitors to each other for sexual encounters, and a selfish disrespect is present, in their humiliating each other and making fun of outsiders.

Despite *Will and Grace* and *Gimme Gimme Gimme* seeming like very different texts, connected only through their representation of the straight girl and the queer guy, and their format of the situation comedy, a sense of queerness proliferates within both texts, stimulating the notion of the domestic glance, offering the potential to stimulate co-presence with the audience.

Notably, both series present two sets of couples, who could be read as dysfunctional. In *Will and Grace* not only are the central characters of Will Truman and Grace Adler present as the queer guy and the straight girl, but so are the characters of Jack McFarland and Karen Walker. At the same time in *Gimme Gimme Gimme*, not only are Tom Farrell and Linda La Hughes the queer guy and the straight girl, but also Jez and Suze are a 'queer' heterosexual couple.

These contrasting couples offer a sense of mirroring in refracting the queer glance, in some senses intensifying the potential for a more direct gaze. In *Will and Grace*, the relationship between effeminate and stereotypical Jack and indulgent and gregarious Karen offers a deeper context to the main relationship between non-stereotypical gay lawyer Will and feminine interior decorator Grace. While the first episode of the series clearly identifies the queer couple as Will and Grace, and Jack and Karen have yet to meet, by the third episode Jack and Karen have become instant friends after initially meeting, with Jack announcing that he admires Karen's breasts, and Karen expressing intrigue at her new-found queer friend, agreeing to 'bounce' exposed bellies together as a celebration of their new coupling (see Figure 4.1).

Such a focus on playfulness, rather than earnestness, in defining the constitution of the straight girl and the queer guy relationship relates the notion of mirroring, rather than purely reflecting the meaning of the relationship. This is notably apparent in *Gimme Gimme Gimme* in the opening episode where Tom and Linda look at each other's reflections. In a supermarket Linda examines her distorted reflection in a sheet of metal appearing as a mirror. While she adjusts her glasses checking the way that she looks, a stereotypical

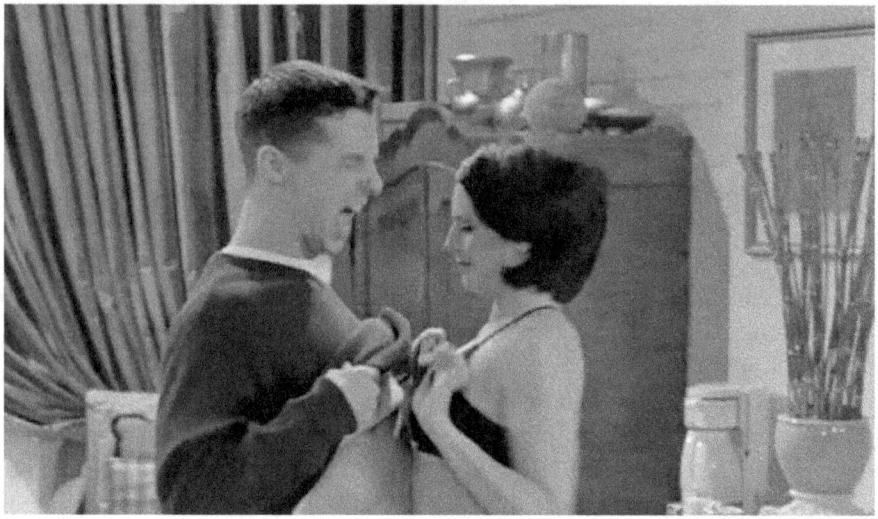

Figure 4.1 Sean Hayes as Jack and Megan Mullally as Karen share an intimate moment on first meeting *in* Will and Grace.

good-looking female reaches past her to pick up a container of milk, and Linda, looking at her with disdain, says 'Lesbian!', as if the girl has sexual desires for her. Then Tom arrives and looks in the distorted mirror as well, similarly looking at his face and hers at the same time. He says, 'You look as bad as I do', she retorts, 'Don't speak to me in public', and he then observes, 'Oh you have got a spot!'. She replies, 'No! I am just wondering what I would look like with a blonde streak like Ginger Spice'. This reflective moment not only foregrounds the aesthetic surface of the skin, referencing an ephemeral corporeal presence, but also it frames the carnivalesque humour, with Linda seeming as a dishevelled grotesque character, making connections to her imagined beauty, in deflecting imaginary sexual suitors. The distorted mirror, however, itself does not represent a distortion of her self-image, it represents knowingness that the televisual glance is ephemeral and unfixed. Whilst it seems to vivify her sense of self-delusion, at the same time it makes references to the distorted form itself, as unable to be set. Hence the couple in the supermarket, like the couple reflected back in the mirror, offer a reference to the co-presence of the audience in witnessing this event, framing the notion of the grotesque and the imaginary.

The mirror couple of Jez and Suze also reference this kind of abstraction. Notably, in the opening episode, Tom and Linda meet Jez, observing him in their apartment mostly viewed from behind, with him wearing just underwear: they believe that he must be a sexual conquest of theirs. However, they are unable to ascertain which one of them may have had sex with him, as they have no memory of this, because they were intoxicated with alcohol the night before. Later Jez turns up with Suze, we find that he is not a sexual conquest but a new neighbour and he is moving in with Suze into the flat below Linda and Tom. However, rather than seeming like a regular heterosexual couple, who might be shocked by Linda and Tom's antics, they are represented as equally eccentric, and similarly obsessed with sex.

This sense of equalisation, through mirroring identities, essentially coding heterosexual identity as queer, is also related to the characters of Will Truman and Grace Adler in *Will and Grace*. While the contrasting straight girl and queer guy relationship of Jack and Karen may seem the most 'queer', for the representation of overtly stylised and formulaic humour involving Sinfield's (1994) notions of 'effeminacy, leisure, idleness, immorality, luxury, insouciance, decadence and aestheticism' (see above) Will and Grace represent a more subtle critique of heterosexuality.

For example, if we consider the first episode of the series, comparing the opening and closing sequences, a sense of queerness is apparent. In the opening sequence where Will and Grace are represented as in conversation on the telephone, set within separate home locations, there is an implication that they may be lovers who are intimate and sexualised. However, as the conversation develops, we discover that Will's 'It's going to be a good one. I can feel it. I could talk you through it' actually refers to him watching the television drama *ER* (NBC 1994–2009, US). Furthermore, in conversation with Grace, Will makes references to his television 'clicker' (remote control) as an allusion to his phallus, commenting that, while George Clooney (the lead actor in *ER*) 'doesn't bat for his team', he hasn't seen Will 'pitch'. Hence, in a conversation that apparently seems like a heterosexual romantic encounter, references are made to the erect queer phallus, and the persuasion of queer ejaculation, that might challenge heteronormative worlds. Part of this involves framing the television audience's knowledge of the popular television series *ER*, and the subversion of heterosexual female desire, that might be apparent for the 'heartthrob' star of the series, George Clooney.

Such a subversion of television form also takes place in the closing sequence of the episode. Will and Grace are represented in a downtown popular bar, dressed as if they were bride and groom from a wedding. Prior to this sequence Grace had decided not to marry the man Will had not approved of, and, failing to turn up to the ceremony, they take refuge in the bar. With Grace dressed in a formal white wedding gown, including a veil, a comic representation is produced, where the audience in the bar are rowdy, celebrating the couple's presence there. Will and Grace enjoy the ruse, and, whilst drinking beer directly from the bottle, rather than seeming to celebrate a marriage, the couple act as if they are celebrating the victory of a favourite football team. This setting and narrative are highly significant, as the mise en scène references the television situation comedy *Cheers* (CBS 1982–93, US), which regularly depicted a drinking bar in Boston. This is likely to be an intentional allusion, as the director of this episode was James Burrows, a creator and producer of *Cheers*. Hence, *Will and Grace* references televisual form, in subverting and reimagining key mainstream series such as *ER* and *Cheers*. This enables a sense of queer glance to take place that reiterates and reforms heterosexual worlds, which are imagined to be stable. At the same time the audience are complicit in this understanding, suggesting a sense of co-presence with the characters in sharing this new domestic queer vision. However the notion of the televisual domestic queer glance is complex, particularly with regard to tensions between female- and male-oriented narrative environments.

SEX AND THE CITY, GIRLS, QUEER AS FOLK AND LOOKING

The queer guy forms a central context within the heterosexual female-oriented serial narratives of *Sex in the City* (HBO 1998–2004, US) and *Girls* (HBO 2012 to present, US). At the same time the straight girl plays a similar counterpoint of identification within the queer male-oriented serial narratives of *Queer as Folk* (Showtime 2000–5, US) and *Looking* (HBO 2014–15, US). While I am comparing a diverse range of texts, ranging from 1998 to 2015, I am bringing these together not so much to offer a linear and historical progression but more to consider the theoretical tension in locating either the queer guy or the straight girl as a minority reference within diverse gender-oriented texts.

Sex in the City and *Girls* are heterosexual female-oriented narrative serials, both set in New York City in the United States. These texts may seem to be closely connected, as both of these series are produced by HBO, they depict a central cast of four female characters who are best friends and each series has a central storyteller who is an author or writer. In *Sex and the City*, the series includes a voiceover by the central female character of Carrie Bradshaw (played by Sarah Jessica Parker), who is a columnist for a fictional New York newspaper *The New York Star*. While there is no voiceover in *Girls*, the central female character is Hannah Horvath (played by Lena Dunham), who is a creative writer with experience in academia.

Sex and the City was considered as a revolutionary television drama for its depiction of a central female cast, who would be represented as confident and self-assured in their professional and social worlds (see Akassand McCabe 2003; Jermyn 2009), particularly related to notions of post-feminism (Arthurs 2004). The series was created by Darren Star, an openly gay producer who was previously known for his work on *Melrose Place* (Fox 1992–9, US) and

Beverley Hills 90210 (CBS 1990–2000, US), which were foundational for their inclusion of gay male characters (see Capsuto 2000). *Girls* has been discussed as influenced by *Sex and the City* (Wilson 2012) for its references to sexual liberation, placing females as the leading protagonists in forming their own destiny. However, in terms of production, there is a more personal self-reflective nature, evident in *Girls* in the fact that the writer Lena Dunham plays the central character of Hannah. Although the series has no voiceover suggesting a personal narrative direction, in fact an intimate voice is present, evident in the direction of Dunham. Despite this both series may be considered as products of auteurs, which might reflect on their identity ideals. In *Sex and the City*, the discourse of Darren Star is evident in the voiceover of Carrie Bradshaw, while in *Girls* Lena Dunham places herself, directly within the narrative frame.

Such a focus on the auteur is equally present in the queer male-oriented series *Queer as Folk* and *Looking*, developed respectively by the openly gay screenwriters and producers Russell T. Davies and Michael Lannan. Notably, Russell T. Davies, prior to *Queer as Folk*, had worked for many years in the television industry, offering progressive narratives focusing on youth and sexuality (see Aldridge and Murray 2008). His work on *Queer as Folk* may be considered as groundbreaking television drama, featuring a central cast of gay male characters who are self-assured and relatively carefree. *Queer as Folk*, from the original television drama set in Manchester in the UK to its later adaptation as a longer-running serial drama set in Pittsburgh in the US, may be considered as a catalyst in changing the television landscape as regards foregrounding queer characters. While *Looking* may not have such an authorial provenance, it's important to note that not only might the series be influenced by *Queer as Folk*, for its central representation of gay men who are friends and living in a city (in this case San Francisco), but also that the openly gay director Andrew Haigh has been involved in the series, working with Michael Lannan. Andrew Haigh's groundbreaking work as a screenwriter, producer and director of the film *Weekend* (2011, UK), which offers a social realist representation of a queer male couple living in the city (in this case Nottingham, UK), offers a unique aesthetic and discursive style, in mediating notions of feeling and sensitivity (see Pullen 2014a). Hence a sense of collaboration between two queer male auteurs is present, constructing *Living* as an intimate text, connected to self-reflexivity.

The notion of self-reflexivity is central in considering the filmic gaze or the televisual glance. In the manner that the process of mirroring relationships (see above) offers a way to reflect on representational processes, placing the self with others in the frame, a sense of form is provided in looking at oneself, and considering others. Darren Star, Lena Dunham, Russell T. Davies,

Michael Lannan and Andrew Haigh may be considered as auteurs who reflect on their imaginations of identity, to some degree representing themselves and their political ideals within the texts.

However, the form of the straight girl and the queer guy seems like an ambivalent and unequal relationship, even if they share bonds and similar desires, and they may be presented with some equality. Ambivalence is evident in that the queer guy is male and consequently part of the dominant gender order, yet he may also be seen as an abject other for his failure to be heterosexual. Also ambivalence is apparent in considering the straight girl. As heterosexual she is connected with normalcy and the everyday; however, as a female, she is imagined to be subordinate to masculine order. Hence the televisual glance potentially reflects this ambivalence and inequality with regard to the straight girl and the queer guy. Media texts presented from a female perspective might prioritise certain issues of identification and political struggle, while texts presented from a queer male perspective would inevitably relate differing contexts of identification and political struggle. Hence, there are imbalances, and power contrasts, evident in considering the differing identification potentials of the straight girl and the queer guy relationships, even if there seems to be some harmony apparent in their union. At the same time as part of this, there may be an exchange in roles, where the queer guy might assume the guise of the straight girl, and vice versa, in order to express complex notions of identity extending from this relationship.

This possibility seems quite likely in considering *Sex and the City* in contrast to *Girls*, as the former was created by a gay man, mostly depicting females, and the latter more straightforwardly was written by a female, mostly depicting females. If we compare the representation of the female cast in *Sex and the City* in relation to the representation of the key queer male figure, and similarly do this for *Girls*, a certain dynamic is presented which conflates representational possibilities of gender and sexuality.

One episode of *Sex and the City* entitled 'All that Glitters', which forms the fourteenth episode of series four, mostly focuses on the main female characters' relationship to gay men, or at least gay social worlds (see also Buckley 2015). The central premise is that the lead storyteller Carrie makes a telephone call to her three best female friends (Samantha, Miranda and Charlotte), saying that she needs to go out for the night for entertainment, despite having an offer to stay at home with her fiancé, which she resists as it is Saturday night, and she needs to express herself. Samantha suggests that the girls go to a gay male disco called Trade. While they are there, all four females experience or develop more connections with their social and/or sexual lives. Carrie meets a gay guy called Oliver Spenser, who is a distributor of expensive shoes, who not only gives her a gay male porn film but also later socialises with her, gaining her access to an exclusive new club, called Bungalow 8. Miranda meets a male co-worker who she had not known was gay; she confides with him that she also has a secret that she wishes to keep from their fellow workers, that she is pregnant. Charlotte meets a gay friend who introduces her to a house fashion magazine photographer, which leads to her appearing in that magazine. Samantha, in the male toilets of the club, not only finds voyeuristic pleasure in looking at male genitalia but she is also given the drug Ecstasy for the first time. It is notable that Carrie's gay best friend Stanford Blatch is not present in the club, but later he meets up with her whilst she is with her new gay friend, Oliver Spenser.

In contrast is an episode of *Girls* called 'Triggering' which forms the second episode of series four. The lead storyteller, Hannah, has recently moved from New York to Iowa, to study literature there at a university. She is alone and none of the main characters visits her there. While she initially likes the new environment, she does not get on well with the other students, who are critical of her writing skills, which they consider are too personally reflective. Hannah becomes defensive and depressed. During this time her gay best friend, Elijah Krantz, visits her unannounced. Elijah's mood is eccentric and upbeat, and his arrival stimulates Hannah to relax and socialise with other people on campus. In a key sequence both Elijah and Hannah go to a party, which involves Elijah seducing a seemingly straight guy, and Hannah wrestling with other students in a paddling pool filled with blue slime.

In *Sex and the City* and *Girls*, the characters of Stanford Blatch and Elijah Krantz respectively represent the gay best friend, who is intimately connected to the leading female characters. Despite this, it's possible to argue that, in *Sex and the City*, the female character of Samantha is actually coded as the sexually active gay man. Notably in 'All that Glitters', it is Samantha's idea to visit the gay club, she joins in the sexual pleasure of the club, partaking in the voyeurism, and also takes recreational drugs. Added to this in contrast to the other leading female characters, she is considered as highly promiscuous, does not easily form romantic bonds with men and is coded as male in her attitude towards sex, engaging in this purely for pleasure. At the same time, in order to complicate this idea, in 'All that Glitters', through her taking Ecstasy and then having sex with her ongoing regular sexual partner, she experiences a psychological dilemma, when she becomes emotional and states that she is in love with him. Hence through her appearing in a gay club, which might in some way unveil her disguise (as a gay man), she has to be seen to be heterosexual, and consequently becomes romantic.

The notion of the queer guy is split between several characters in this episode. Not only are the gay guy that Carrie meets in the club (Oliver Spenser) and Stanford her ongoing gay best friend present, but also Samantha is coded as a composite of the straight girl and the queer guy. This is further evidenced in that Carrie, Miranda and Charlotte are represented as directly using gay men as a commodity, with regard to giving access to exclusive footwear, offering the ability to socialise in exclusive clubs, offering the role of confident in the workplace, and publicising social status in upmarket magazines. However, Samantha purely identifies with the gay sexual world, engendering this as part of her. While the central gay character of Stanford Blatch is clearly coded as gay, reductive stereotypes are employed in order to relate this, foregrounding effeminacy, psychological insecurity and attention seeking. Hence, I argue that the more socially developed gay character is Samantha, rather than Stanford, as she engages with issues of sexuality more directly.

In *Girls*, a similar process takes place. However, rather than a straight girl appearing as a masquerade of a queer guy, the gay character is a composite of the straight girl and the queer guy. Elijah's arrival in Iowa to support Hannah is no surprise, as they had historically been involved as boyfriend and girlfriend, and, through Elijah coming out to Hannah (in the first series), we understand there is a closeness (see Figure 4.2). However, Elijah's earlier coming out did not code him as purely bisexual: a suggestion is made that he was uncertain as to his sexuality, and he is willing to experiment with sexual intimacy. This is borne out in series two when Elijah sexually experiments with one of Hannah's best friends, Marnie Michaels, and he considers his possible identity as bisexual. He tells Marnie, 'People are prejudiced against bisexuals, though. It's the only group you can still make fun of', offering insight into hierarchical systems of abject oppression which assign bisexuality

Figure 4.2 *Andrew Rannells as Elijah and Lena Dunham as Hannah in the foreground in* Girls, *embracing in a moment of affection while playing in a swimming pool.*

as 'outside'. Hence, although Elijah is represented as the queer guy, he does not conform to regular stereotypes that surround gay men, which might disavow bisexuality.

Although his appearance in Iowa seems to be coincidental, I would argue that he represents the presence of Hannah's best friends, who are female. Notably, we are given this impression when Marnie tells Hannah over Skype that despite Hannah's enthusiasm 'No one is moving to Iowa', affirming that none of her female best friends will be visiting her. Hence Elijah is coded as the only intimate supporter of Hannah, at this time of psychological stress for her. Added to this, besides encouraging her to enjoy herself, and to set herself free at the party, which culminates in Hannah 'releasing herself' in the wrestling event, Elijah presents his body as in union with hers. Not only do Hannah and Elijah seem like eccentric girlfriends, but through madcap antics such as Elijah seducing a straight boy, and through him dancing frenetically with Hannah, with Hannah seeming to mimic the act of performing anal sex upon Elijah on the dance floor, an intimate sense of rapport is presented that codes Elijah as a soulmate. Although Elijah is coded as the queer guy, in many ways he is represented as an equal to the main female cast of best friends. Unlike Stanford in *Sex and the City*, who when in the company of the female cast presents himself as an 'other', Elijah takes on a composite role blending signifiers of the straight girl and the queer guy, seeming equally, if not more, enlightened.

While this is not surprising, as *Sex and the City* was an early representation of the straight girl and queer guy union in serial television, and *Girls* is a more recent production, it is the notion of blending identities, rather than revealing tensions between identities, which enables us to read *Girls* as a progressive text. At the same time, while *Girls* is produced as a female-oriented narrative, how might the representation of the straight girl and the queer guy seem in texts where there is a queer male-oriented focus? *Queer as Folk* appears as a historical precedent for the queer male community drama, and *Looking* is a contemporary contribution to this emerging genre. While *Queer as Folk* began as a UK television drama produced by Channel 4, I am considering the later adaptation of *Queer as Folk*, which appeared as a serial drama in the US, produced by Showtime.

Essentially the main character types are present in both series, with the US version developing the narratives (see Davis 2008). The central characters are Brian Kinney and Michael Novotny, who were best friends in school, and Justin Taylor, an underage lover of Brian in the first series. The episode I have selected as a case study is from series three, episode eleven. This episode is pivotal in the series, as it involves the friendship group of gay men, lesbians and heterosexual supporters challenging emerging political oppression, evident in the likely re-election of a politician who wants to limit the civil liberties of the gay and lesbian community. These limitations might include the closing of 'dark rooms' in gay clubs, where anonymous sexual encounters might take place. Brian, the leading male character, has been working as a publicist for the oppressive politician, believing that, despite the controversial politics, he is able to achieve personal gain. Brian's boyfriend Justin has infiltrated the publicity organisation of the politician, and sets up a demonstration at a public speaking event, with the support of gay and straight people. During the demonstration Michael's mother Debbie takes the leading role in this political challenge, presenting a placard with an image of a murdered young gay man, who was called 'dumpster boy', as the police had failed to investigate the case, and were unable to ascertain his identity, yet she had done this by her own efforts. In the series, there are three possible contenders as the straight girl in support of the queer guy: the leading character Michael's mother, Debbie, who runs a diner and an unofficial support network for queer youth; Justin's female best friend from school, Daphne: and Justin's mother, Jennifer. A sense of political collaboration is presented in the series, with the straight girl offering support to the queer guy.

In *Looking*, there is less emphasis on political struggles, and the straight girl is represented as a key narrative peer to the main cast members, rather than a supporter or a context. The episode that I have selected as a case study is from series two, episode seven. This focuses almost exclusively on the central gay male character, Dom, and his best friend, Doris, a straight girl. Doris hears news of her father's death, and she and Dom travel from San Francisco to Modesto by car for the funeral, accompanied by Patrick, another of the central gay male characters. Patrick comes along for the trip, as he is getting over a breakup with a gay guy who was committed to another man. Whilst in Modesto, Dom and Doris reminisce regarding their prior sexual relationship when they were much younger, and both support each other at the funeral. As part of this, Dom tries to find his own father's headstone in a cemetery, so he can come to terms with the fact that he never told his father that he was gay. After a car accident, where all three characters are slightly injured, at hospital Doris says that she considers Dom as family, and as part of this she wants to offer him financial support in his catering adventure, now she has been bequeathed funds from her father.

In *Sex and the City* and in *Girls*, the identity of the queer guy is mobile, a composite apparition in the former partly related to a female character, and in the latter the queer guy who seems to bear the traits of female identity not fixing a specific sexual form through allusions to bisexuality. In *Queer as Folk* and *Looking*, while the straight girl is the 'other' or the counterpoint in these dominant male-oriented narratives, I argue that mobility is equally apparent, yet this is related to agency rather than identification processes. Hence rather than introspection, or subjectivity in terms of identity, the straight girl as 'other' is a coherent, political and social form.

Notably in *Queer as Folk*, the straight girl is represented as an enabler and a supporter. She is someone who possesses a distinct political vision, concerning the abject suppression of the queer guy. Hence it is not so surprising that, in the case study episode, all three straight girls lead and direct the demonstration, leading to the final culmination, evident in the challenge by Debbie. As part of this the straight girls work in union with the lesbian characters, offering a female-focused union in defining political rights. At the same time, not only is the straight girl represented as a coherent form but also she is represented as an interpreter, or an insightful character. Hence when (in the second series) Justin forms a new relationship with Ethan, after finding discontent with Brian, Daphne argues why Brian has been more loyal to Justin than Ethan, who is secretive, offering a sophisticated argument that considers personal respect. Similarly, when Brian loses his job as a publicist for the politician, Debbie clarifies to him that he had integrity and a political vision, not accepting his own account of himself as complicit, and interested only in personal gain.

In *Looking*, however, aspects of integrity or personal vision are not directly related to political needs, rather they are framed within the personal, and the kinship group. Hence, not only is Doris as the straight girl an integral part of the dominant queer male social group but there is a sense of emotional equality evident in her engagements. For example, when Doris and Dom are driving to Modesto for her father's funeral, they reminisce regarding their failed heterosexual relationship, remembering her father at that time:

> Doris: My Dad loved you so much. Even after you told him that you were gay, he still wanted us to get married.
>
> Dom: And he even offered to buy the ring!

This sequence, filmed from the back seat of the car, as if from the viewpoint of Patrick, as both characters turn to each other in conversation and share this fond memory, frames the notion of both moving forward and looking back. Hence, the exchange of gazes between each other, the gaze forward as the road leads to Modesto, and the gaze backwards potentially in the rear view mirror that leads back to San Francisco evident in the reflection of Dom's face, offers a therapeutic potential that emboldens senses of kinship and sharing.

This sharing of feelings and memories, which stimulates reminiscences of the past and articulations of the future, plays a central role in this episode. Hence, rather than arriving early to meet relatives for the funeral, Doris suggests that all three of them check into a local motel, which she remembers had an inviting swimming pool, but she had never swum there. Doris, Dom and Patrick all jump in the pool, and playfully swim together, as if holding back the advance of the funeral, but also setting into place a sense of bonding and shared experience. Similarly later, when they are looking for Dom's father's headstone in the cemetery, not long after Doris's father's funeral has taken place, a sense of respect and shared reference is present. All three characters shout from the car as they drive away alongside the cemetery, that Dom is gay, offering a simplistic but thoughtful resolution in failing to find the headstone. Hence a sense of camaraderie and shared experience is present, in constructing the gaze as equal between all three characters, involving looking forward and looking back, suspending a subjective ending of the gaze, as continuously mobile and thoughtful.

While in many ways such a process is indicative of the televisual glance, rather than the filmic gaze, for its mobility and suspension, a sense of equality is presented, integrating the straight girl as a key component in the social group. While the queer guy within the female-focused texts such as *Sex and the City* and *Girls* seems less defined, appearing as a subliminal trait of a female character (as Samantha), or over-defined as a stereotypical but useful form (as Stanford) or as untenable yet philosophical through bearing traits of both identities (as Elijah), it seems apparent that, within the male-focused texts, the straight girl is offered more consistency, involving political and/or emotional strength.

Despite this, consistency and endurance might not necessarily equate to equality, within the larger social group. Potentially the fixing of an identity might be limiting, rather than enabling. Notably, in the following case studies that focus more directly on bisexuality, it seems apparent that a commercial appetite is present in relating the straight girl as able to convert the queer guy to become heterosexual, or at least find satisfaction in working through feelings of desire.

BOB AND ROSE AND TORCHWOOD[2]

Brett Beemyn and Erich Steinman (2002) tell us: '[s]ince the late twentieth century, bisexuality has seemed to be both everywhere and nowhere in popular culture' (3). The queer guy identifying as bisexual would offer a tantalising object of identification for female heterosexual audiences, presenting the queer body as a potential space of sexual encounter, framed within dominant heterosexual mainstream media frames. At the same time, through the potential threat of homosexual activity, the bisexual man could be considered as a source of unhappiness and contagion.

The notion of the androgynous bisexual man proliferated within the popular music culture industry, particularly achieving attention within the glam rock movement in the 1970s in the United Kingdom (see Auslander 2006). This is evident in the tabloid representations of popular musicians such as David Bowie, Marc Bolan and Elton John, who appeared as androgynous or effeminate. However, since the advent of AIDS in the early 1980s, bisexual men, in their likely contact with homosexual men, 'supposedly pos[ed] a hidden threat to heterosexual women' (Beenmyn and Steinman 2002: 3), in the possible transmission of HIV. This translated into an increased fear, and further demonisation of the bisexual man. This led to the commoditisation of the bisexual woman within Hollywood film. As Jonathan David White (2002) reports, the obsession with bisexual men was replaced with the 'equally stereotyped and ideologized bi woman' (42). Films such as *Basic Instinct* (Paul Verhoeven 1992, US) and *Showgirls* (Paul Verhoeven 1995, US) capitalised on these ideas, foregrounding the glamorous actresses Sharon Stone in the former and Elizabeth Berkley in the latter, as central sexual objects of desire, who would present a sexual commodity but be punished for their bisexuality.

Despite this, the commodity of the bisexual male would re-emerge within television drama, notably in Russell T. Davies's *Bob and Rose* (ITV 2001, UK), which foregrounded the representation of a female heterosexual character who would stimulate a (previously exclusively) homosexual man to fall in love with her, and reject a prior 'queer' life. Later, in Davies's science fiction drama *Torchwood* (BBC 2006–11, UK), the notion of the bisexual would be connected not only to heroism but also to active bisexual tendencies, falling in love with both men and women.

Bob and Rose is a television drama series, produced by Russell T. Davies, related to his personal life where he was aware of a gay man who fell in love with a woman and had fathered a child. Russell's interest in producing the narrative was that, the gay man had felt ostracism from his gay friends for becoming involved with a woman, and he wanted to consider this unusual relationship (see Aldridge and Murray 2008). Central within *Bob and Rose* is the premise that you fall in love with the person, regardless of their sexuality. The 'straight girl' dynamic is present in the series, in relation to not only the character of Rose, the ultimate object of Bob's sexual desire, but also the character of Holly as a more traditional 'Fag Hag', a longstanding heterosexual female friend of Bob. At the time it was broadcast, the series received considerable popular attention, leading to the invasion of Manchester's gay club scene by straight females 'looking for a Bob "convert" [to heterosexuality]' (Aitkenhead 2002: 7).

Torchwood is a series adaptation of *Doctor Who* (BBC 2005 to present, UK), a long-term mainstream children's television science fiction series which Russell T. Davies led to renewed popularity in the early part of the twenty-first century.[3] The invention in a supporting role within *Doctor Who* of the bisexual character[4] of Captain Jack Harkness, who would become lead protagonist within the more adult-oriented *Torchwood*, is evocative of Davies's support for sexual diversity. This series may be considered as an extension of Davies's influential work within this area as the writer of the groundbreaking television drama *Queer as Folk* (Channel 4 1999–2000, UK) (see above). Notably in *Torchwood*, the central heroic character of Jack Harkness is related as expressing sexual desire and feelings of romance for both a straight girl, Gwen Cooper, and Ianto Jones, a gay man, framing these possibilities within the science fiction genre.

Although Russell T. Davies produced both *Bob and Rose* and *Torchwood*, they seem like very different media texts in terms of their cultural and institutional relationship and settings. In many ways these texts form part of the larger work of Russell T. Davies, whereby he has consistently developed narratives that explore queer sexuality. However, as *Bob and Rose* ultimately closes with a queer man rejecting queer sexuality to essentially become heterosexual, it's possible to consider this text as retrogressive, or at least as old-fashioned. Notably, *Bob and Rose* engages with the common reductivetive stereotype, that, should a gay person find the 'right partner' of the opposite sex, they might reject their homosexual tendencies. While, in *Bob and Rose*, a key part of the texts involves Bob asserting that he is still gay, even though he has fallen in love with a woman, the notion that heterosexuality could be restored, or retrieved, is problematic for queer audiences, implying that they are happier if they fit in. At the same time, although Russell T. Davies was the leading scriptwriter, or at least executive producer, as *Bob and Rose* was produced for ITV, and *Torchwood* was produced for BBC Three (the first series), these associations offer very different cultural and institutional registers. ITV offers a mainstream lower- to middle-class adult address in its association with popular entertainment and drama, while BBC Three offers a youth cultural address in its focus on niche programming and popular culture.

Hence, while both texts are addressed to relative mainstream audiences, there are distinctions with regard to the target age group for the texts, and also there are ambivalences regarding issues of class and gender. In this way, *Bob and Rose* might be seen as directly addressed to lower- to middle-class females , while *Torchwood* may more directly connect to male youth audiences who might be more middle-class, in the focus on the science fiction genre, which is often associated with the concept of the 'nerd', and who might possess more sophisticated cultural knowledge. This suggests that *Bob and Rose* and *Torchwood* offer differing cultural and social perspectives within the bisexual continuum.

Despite this sense of diversity, it's notable that a female-oriented address is apparent within both texts, evident in the iconography and promotion. In *Bob and Rose*, the image used on the cover of the commercial DVD, forming part of the original promotional material, clearly foregrounds Bob as subordinate to Rose. This is evident in a picture of the couple embracing, both facing the camera directly. However, in subverting the traditional setting of the man positioned slightly higher in the framethan the female, as if indicating that he is able to take care of her, the reverse occurs, with Rose in the higher position. At the same time, not only are their faces close together, with her eye level above his forehead, but also she has her right hand upon his shoulder, as if signifying the notion of possession, or of taking care. While this could also signify the possibility that she is sitting on his lap, and might be in some ways submissive, this seems unlikely as her gaze appears more static as if in control, while his gaze seems more carefree as if resting rather than supporting. Similarly, if we consider the publicity surrounding *Torchwood*, a distinct female-oriented address is specifically apparent, in the contextual fan-oriented publications. For example the second issue of the *Torchwood Magazine*[5] prioritises on its cover images of the lead female character Gwen Cooper accompanied by the female assistant Martha Jones from *Doctor Who* (the original series of which *Torchwood* is an extension). This is then emblazoned with the headline 'GIRLS TALK'. These two images of lead female characters are not exclusively seductive or sexual images suggesting a male heterosexual stimulation, but they offer a sense of knowingness and agency, connoting leadership and direction. Hence the female characters are represented as in control, suggesting the prioritisation of their desires, feelings and potential discourses, connoting a reversal of the heterosexual male gaze that might objectify the female body.

Specifically within *Torchwood*, this translates to an objectification of the male body, framed through the identification of the lead female character Gwen Cooper. This is evident where Gwen discovers the covert operations of Torchwood through an encounter where she is called to a murder scene in her work as a policewoman. However, there is resistance, as Captain Jack Harkness, leading the Torchwood team, takes over this investigation from the police, and she is denied access. This creates a desire in her character to solve the murder and discover the mystery of the Torchwood organisation, which has been awarded special powers by the government and operates outside normative control. As the story unfolds, Gwen becomes more active, seeming to be a central protagonist in solving the investigation.[6] This translates to her elevated position within the narrative, at the same time framing her gender identity.

Notably, the first encounter when Gwen observes the Torchwood team, looking down on them from a high position in a multi-storey car park, is literally 'saturated' with female identity. Most apparent within this is the significance of the driving rain, falling down on the Torchwood team, as they stand over the body of a recently murdered young man. Captain Jack Harkness comments on the downfall, telling his team that he can taste the oestrogen in the polluted rain:

> There you go I can taste it, oestrogen, definitely oestrogen, you take the pill, flush it away and it enters the water cycle and feminises the fish. Goes all the way up into the sky then falls all the way back on me. Contraceptives in the rain! Love this planet. Still at least I won't get pregnant, never doing that again!

The opening words of Jack Harkness in the series directly comment on female identity, and issues of sexual influence. By indicating that he has been pregnant, he crosses the imagined gender divide, engendering himself as female, as well as male. As part of this he appears as exotic, in his distance from normative contexts of masculinity, which rejects notions of femininity and contexts of emotional exhibition. At the same time coded as bisexual, he appears as potentially subordinate to female characters, who may masquerade as male in opposition to his 'feminised' bisexuality. While *Torchwood* in many ways rejects this assignation, as ultimately Captain Jack Harkness is regarded as the leading heroic character, whom we discover to be in fact immortal, in *Bob and Rose* the gaze is more complicated.

Notably in *Bob and Rose*, the straight female gaze upon the queer male is split between two female characters, potentially representing diverse relationships to queer sexuality. In many ways, the character of Holly represents the straight girl who bonds with the queer guy, as she is represented as having a long-term non-sexual relationship with Bob. While Rose is a 'straight girl', she is represented as someone who does not necessarily bond with queer men, but just encounters a man she finds attractive, who happens to be queer. Through the series having two diverse representations of straight girls interested in queer men, a tension is established, as the gaze is not simply between the straight girl and the queer guy, and vice versa: the queer guy is subject to the diverse gazes of very different straight girls, and his gaze back to them is equally different.

This establishes a complex sense of the gaze, where desire and objectivity are embedded, relating differing emotions, histories and engagements. While the notion of unrequited love forms a central strand within many of the straight girl and queer guy relationships discussed in this book, usually this forms the context of a historical past, and often it's about a fleeting moment of early adulthood. For example in the television series *Will and Grace* (see above), we know that there had been an attraction between the two, and, whilst a lasting sexual relationship was not possible, a new platonic transparent friendship was formed. While the film *The Object of My Affection* foregrounds notions of hidden desire (see Chapter 3), ultimately this is explicitly presented to the queer guy, and there is direct pressure to respond. However in *Bob and Rose* the notion of suspense and complicity is present in the character of Holly, who we eventually find out has romantic feelings for Bob.

Hence two forms of the desiring gaze are apparent within *Bob and Rose*. Rose simply desires Bob as a potential sexual partner, risking her long-term relationship with her boyfriend Andy in order that she can be with Bob. In comparison, Holly over many years has concealed her sexual desire for Bob, and only reveals this when she discovers that Bob is interested in another female Rose. However it's important to note that Holly never reveals this to Bob but only confides it to Rose. This occurs near the end of the series, after the audience have become aware that Holly has deliberately intervened, making many attempts to stop Bob progressing with romantic relationships. Bob is unaware of this, consistently considering Holly as his best friend. In many ways Holly represents a stereotype of a 'Fag Hag', as she has suspended her own romantic life in order to progress a friendship with a queer man. While at the close of the series Holly is represented as restored to the straight world, as she accepts Bob's and Rose's relationship, and her new social life revolves around socialising with heterosexual women, not gay men, it is this tension between Holly and Rose that forms the central context of the gaze.

As part of this it's possible to argue that in fact Rose does not represent the straight girl, but is a cipher for a gay man. This is primarily evident in that Rose is represented as both masculine and queer. Notably, early in the television series she manages to discourage and fend off a potential rapist, coding her as psychologically and physically more able than the male taxi driver, who consistently harasses her, driving her off the normal route home, suggesting that he can have sex with her. Also living with her mother, rather than with her partner, subliminally she is coded as queer. More explicitly, when she embarks on the relationship with Bob, she codes herself as queer, telling Bob, after they have had sex in a toilet on a train, that she is 'practically a gay man'. Added to this, her social identity within the community may be considered as queer, particularly evident when Bob's mother, a gay rights activist, tells a crowd gathered after a demonstration (where she has tied herself to a bus with Bob), that her son is 'a gay man with a straight girl friend, and that's equality'. Hence by association, her sexuality must be queer, in that her partner in fact desires his own sex, and not necessarily hers.

Despite this, it is the notion of romance, and the idea of 'soulmates', that seems to form the central context of *Bob and Rose*. When Bob and Rose first meet, his lasting impression is of her humour. Bob and Rose had met after both had been looking for a taxi in the early hours of the morning, after Rose had escaped the potential rapist taxi driver, and Bob had rejected a male sexual partner for already having a devoted partner, coding him as disingenuous. When Bob and Rose share a taxi, and converse, there is an instant sense of trust and honesty. Later Rose turns up at Bob's house, tracing him through the phone directory. While she feels embarrassed that Bob discovers that she had called his home telephone, seeming like a stalker, they instantly have rapport. As part of this Rose makes a joke to Bob, saying that a pet dog or cat should have a name like 'Looks Like Rain', so that when calling for the pet at night a pretence might be produced which would disguise a personal concern for a beloved pet. The following day Bob recalls this to himself, and consistently muses over the joke or observation. This codes the couple as bonded by humour and sensibility, rather than purely sexual objectification.

Such a focus on romance, and the notion of the soulmate, is equally apparent in *Torchwood*. Notably, aspects of romance are present in Jack seeming to be eternally bonded to Gwen and Ianto, within differing contexts. This reveals not a stereotypical reimagining of male homosexual and bisexual promiscuity but the theatre of desire and the heroics of self-denial.

Despite this, everlasting romance is ultimately related to same-sex partnerships. In the episode titled 'Captain Jack Harkness' from the first series, we discover Jack's namesake within a nostalgic Second World War setting of servicemen in a dance hall. In this two men are situated within a generic narrative frame, which evokes the landmark film *Brief Encounter* (David Lean 1945, UK), relating issues of longing and deferred fulfilment, in the hope of eventually being together. Also in the third series of *Torchwood*, the love triangle of Ianto, Gwen and Jack comes to a close with the death of Ianto. Significantly, Jack is represented as more closely coupled with Ianto, particularly evident in Ianto's death scene:

> [Ianto is poisoned by gas in a heroic act to save the lives of others. He is dying cradled in the arms of Jack Harkness. Jack caresses his face as Ianto slips away]
>
> Ianto: It was good . . . Don't forget me.
>
> Jack: Never could.
>
> Ianto: In a thousand years' time you won't remember me.
>
> Jack: Yes I will. I promise I will.

Jack then passionately kisses Ianto at the moment of his death, framing his promise to remember him after a thousand years. As Jack remains immortal, and he must continue his life alone, 'for all eternity' he promises to remember the love he shared with Ianto. Despite this epic moment of same-sex love and affection, accompanied with emotive music, foregrounding intense character connectivity, following the heterocentric drive of *Torchwood*, the closing scene of this episode nevertheless foregrounds Gwen's emotive relationship to both Ianto and Jack, rather than Jack's desire for Ianto. As such this denies an exclusive homosexual representation, and provides continuing evidence of the narrative force within Torchwood, which prioritises the 'female (heterosexual) gaze', rather than a queer subjectivity or identity. Ianto's death represents a context for a heterosexual female interpretation, rather than a specific queer gaze that might focus and clarify.

While in many ways the queer gaze is translated to a queer glance, within both *Bob and Rose* and *Torchwood*, it is the reiteration of queer desire, framed within a female-oriented focus, which offers a sense of identity building. In these texts by Russell T. Davies, as a queer television auteur, we are aware that he has developed narrative forms that integrate queer characters, often making connections to domesticity and romance. *Bob and Rose* and *Torchwood* may seem like dominant hetero media texts, in their stimulation of bisexuality, seeming like a kind of queer heterosexuality, relating this to consumption more than identity. Despite this, they offer insight into the developing continuum of the straight girl and queer guy relationship, which, while it might foreground a heterosexual determination or experimentation, at the same time suggests a sense of ambivalence, and the need to read between the lines.

Conclusion

The televisual glance offers scope for shared experience and interconnectivity between the audience and the text. As part of this the straight girl and the queer guy relationship is framed within a domestic medium, where female address is a central part of this consumption. While early texts such as *Love Sidney* frame the queer guy as supporting the straight girl, in many ways assuming the roles of mother, father and child to the straight girl, this early focus foregrounded the usefulness of the queer guy, in terms of real social settings.

Later texts such as *Tales of the City*, *Ellen*, *Will and Grace*, plus *Gimme Gimme Gimme*, offer a deeper sense of equality, relating the life chances of both the straight girl and the queer guy. At the same time, issues of ambivalence are central in revealing the straight girl as the 'Fag Hag', seeming equally as queer, focusing on leisure, indulgence and aesthetics. Such a shift reveals the notion of shared experience, prioritising a sense of exchange. However, in texts such as *Sex and the City* and *Girls*, where the queer guy is the other, and in contrast in *Queer as Folk* and *Looking*, where the straight girl is the other, this exchange is complex. It seems that in gynocentric worlds, the female is usually the enabler, often taking on the role of the queer guy as occurs in the character of Samantha in *Sex and the City*, while at the same time suggesting distance from the 'real' stereotypical queer guy (Stanford). In androcentric worlds, the 'other' straight girl has an important role both in supporting the queer political world, as occurs in *Queer as Folk*, and in being an emotional social backbone, as occurs in *Looking*. This reveals a prioritisation of female sensibility, often at the cost of developing a meaningful queer guy identity. This is not so surprising, as not only is television a domestic media form, which relies on the iteration of female identity to frame and work through issues of intimacy but also such framing contextualises male identity rather than foregrounding it.

Despite this, in *Girls* the queer guy seems more robust, is insightful and does not rely on stereotypical forms, questioning issues of fixed sexual identity. As part of this, bisexuality is an important feature in *Girls*, and this context offers developed scope in *Bob and Rose* and *Torchwood*. While clearly these texts seem directly to address a heterosexual female viewership in suggesting the possibility of sexual reciprocation, at the same time there are opportunities for queer male identity that connect with the intimate, the eternal and the epic.

Televisual form may only seem to offer a glance, rather than a gaze, despite the fact that, through the union of the straight girl and the queer guy, the consistent glance implies not only a sense of rhythm, reiteration and reunion but also a sense of reformation, reconstruction and renaissance. Even if this is gynocentric, it offers a sense of wholeness and cohesion that makes connections as much as it reveals divisions.

At the same time, the notions of connection and division implies the significance of a political imperative, and, as we discover in the following chapter, through the participation of real-life social actors and the recording of actual historical lives, new opportunities are formed. For the representation of the straight girl and the queer guy, this establishes a new kind of veracity; at the same time it challenges the constitution of the liminal frame.

Notes

1. Regarding the books: *Tales of the City* (1978) was followed by *More Tales of the City* (1980) and *Further Tales of the City* (1982), all of which were adapted for television. Further sequels (not yet adapted) include: *Babycakes* (1984), *Significant Others* (1987), *Sure of You* (1989), *Michael Tolliver Lives* (2007), *Mary Ann in Autumn* (2010) and *The Days of Anna Madrigal* (2014).
2. The discussion of *Torchwood* is an edited and reformed version of the essay "'Love the coat": bisexuality, the female gaze and the romance of sexual politics" (Pullen 2010).

3. *Doctor Who* originally started as a television series in 1963 and ran until 1989. Russell T. Davies's reinvention started in 2005 (see Howe and Walker 2003).
4. Although theoretically the character of Captain Jack Harkness could be termed 'omnisexual', in the representation of his sexual interest in alien and non-human forms of life (in addition to men and women), I am purely considering his social constructionist human potential as a character. This situates Harkness as bisexual.
5. *Torchwood Magazine*, issue number 2 (April 2008), front cover. Published by Titan Magazines, London.
6. Also see Modleski (2005) for foundational discussion on the agency of females in Hollywood cinema.

CHAPTER 5

Documentary and Performance

Paula Rabinowitz (1994) tells us that

> Documentary performance and address is always about crossing boundaries – racial, sexual, class, gender, regional, temporal – as outsiders to a subculture enter into it, or as insiders from a subculture project it outward. (9)

Documentary form potentially allows the social space for minority identities to speak to the wider world, offering the potential to challenge representational norms, through social agency. As part of this, not only does the representation of the straight girl and the queer guy offer the potential to cross borders, framing the collaboration of individuals who may be seen as outsiders, but also such opportunity involves issues of performance and knowingness. Hence a sense of alliance is presented, offering a union between the straight girl and the queer guy, with the opportunity of performative political intent.

This chapter considers the representation of the straight girl and the queer guy within varying documentary media forms, considering the notions of social agency and performativity.[1] As part of this I examine the documentary biographical film drama *Carrington* (Christopher Hampton 1995, UK), which explores the relationship between the artist Dora Carrington and the writer Lytton Strachey in the early twentieth century. The relationship between Carrington and Lytton may be considered as a historical representation of the straight girl and queer guy relationship that not only offers cultural and social resonance but also foregrounds notions of devotion and intensity (see Holroyd 1994). I also examine the diverse documentaries *Fag Hags: Women Who Love Gay Men* (Justine Pimlott 2005, Canada), *My Husband Is Gay* (Benetta Adamson 2005, UK) and *My Husband Is Not Gay* (TLC 2015, US), which explore intense relationships between straight girls and queer guys – in many instances relating legal marriages and questioning issues of fidelity – and the problematic relationship to queer desire, and gay identity. I also examine the reality television shows *Would Like to Meet* (BBC 2001, UK), *Boy Meets Boy* (Bravo 2003, US) and *Queer Eye for the Straight Guy* (Bravo 2003–7, US), which foreground the straight girl and queer guy relationship within the confines and opportunity of television formats. Central within my analysis is the notion of performance, evident in biographical drama, documentary and reality television media forms, and how the union between the straight girl and the queer guy represents a subversion of the male gaze, reframing notions of liminal performance.

Documentary, the Body and Liminal Performance

Richard Schechner (2002) tells us that 'the underlying notion is that any action that is framed, presented, highlighted, or displayed, is a performance' (2), suggesting personal subjectivity and knowingness. However, those involved in documentary may be seen to engage with 'the encoding of history in documents' (Rabinowitz 1994: 18) and an evolution of media documentary form (Nichols 1991, 1994, 2001) predisposed to the idea of conveying actual social reality. Hence a tension is related between the notion of documenting some kind of reality and in contrast the potential of performative representations. As Marvin Carlson (1996) tells us, 'performance can work within society precisely to undermine tradition to provide a site for the exploration of fresh and alternative structures and patterns of behaviour' (15). As part of this, 'unable to move outside the operations of performance (or representation), and thus inevitably involved in its codes and reception assumptions, the contemporary performer seeking to resist, challenge, or even subvert these codes and assumptions must find some way of doing this "from within"' (172). Herein lies the quandary of those attempting to involve themselves in cultural resistance through participating in documentary performance: in order to influence or change the system you have (to some degree) to engage yourself with the mechanism you may be trying to critique or take apart. The representation of the straight girl and the queer guy within documentary form, I argue, foregrounds the notion of performance, relating the potential for 'embodied practice' which privileges the 'body as site of knowing' (Carlson 1996: 191) and 'resists conclusions, just as it resists sorts of definitions, boundaries and limits' (Carlson 1996: 189). The physical bodies of the straight girl and the queer guy may be considered as signifiers for sexual diversity, reframing representational opportunities regarding male and female unions.

However, within documentary form, such representations or performances do not necessarily foreground the notion of social reality, as Stella Bruzzi (2000) suggests:

> the closer one gets to the document itself, the more aware one becomes of the artifice and the impossibility of a satisfactory relationship between the image and the real. (21)

Hence, while the documentary representation of the straight girl and the queer guy suggests some access to actuality, the notions of artifice and performativity are equally central. In many ways the reappropriation of the heterosexual male gaze within documentary form relates an acceptance that reality can only be contextual, and that discursive opportunities may be mobile and fluid. As Bill Nichols (1994) has observed, although we consider documentary as a form which is complete and conclusive:

> more recently though documentary has come to suggest incompleteness and uncertainty, recollection and impression, images of personal worlds and their subjective construction. A shift in epistemological proportions has occurred. (1)

This shift in 'epistemological proportions' has engaged with the idea of individual agency. The individual may now be considered as the co-producer of the text, rather than the subject of an ethnographic project, which highlights the distance between the observer and the observed.

Consequently, contemporary documentary, or documentary drama, like reality television, does not not only raise what Nichols (1994) calls 'vicarious participation' (74); but also a corollary of this reconfiguration is the increasing profile of performance within documentary. At the same time, the 'anthropological unconsciousness' that Nichols maintains upholds documentary conventions involving 'whiteness, maleness, [the] body of the observer, the experimental [and the] canonical conventions of western narrative' (65) becomes diluted or distanced. Part of this might involve a sense of differentiation and destabilisation, as Marvin Carlson (1996) tells us:

> This removal of a center, a fixed locus of original meaning, brings all discourse, all action, and all performance into a continuing play of signification, where signs differ from one another but a final, authenticating meaning of any sign is deferred. (135)

Hence the notion of the gaze, stimulated through new forms of factual media performance, which foreground the straight girl and queer guy as a productive union, whilst displacing the hierarchy of male heterosexuality, at the same time suspends the need for authenticity. This suggests that the relationship between the straight girl and the queer guy may be considered as a deconstructed performance, rather than a coherent critique.

This may be evident in considering the case studies that follow, that through diverse forms – such as biographical documentary drama reliant on the reconstruction of history, contemporary documentary reliant on the context of non-diegetic music connoting humour, and reality television reliant on formats and intervention – foreground fragmented and incomplete narratives in revealing social reality.

I argue that, through these contemporary documentary forms, there is the potential to reform the liminal frame, offering a subversive imagination of the straight girl and the queer guy coupling. Central within this is the idea of 'liminal' performance, which Richard Schechner (2002) tells us derives from the word 'limen' – 'literally a threshold or sill, an architectural feature linking one space to another, [more] a passageway between places than a place itself' (58). The communicative property of the liminal performer has to recognise hierarchies and institutions which they perform within. For the straight girl and the queer guy, this may involve reflecting the normative liminal potentials of male and female coupling, such as referencing connotations to heterosexuality and romance.

At the same time, liminal performances are about ritual and transition, involving aspects of authorisation, authenticity and arrival. In terms of ritual, the liminal performer passes from one stage of life to another. We may consider this idea to be connected to the notion of documenting the performances of citizens, as occurs in documentary, reality television or documentary drama. There are certain ritual expectations involved with the documentary process, which involves authorising the 'citizenship' potential of the subject examined. When the performer appears before the camera, certain conventions are applied. The relationship between the producer or interviewer and the liminal subject is established, authorising them as worthy for exhibition, worthy for documentation, framing them as an enfranchised citizen. Therefore we may suggest that there is a liminal potential in the appearance of subaltern identities in documentary performance. This involves a ritual transition from unknown or unfamiliar identity to a 'suitable to be recognised' identity. For the straight girl and the queer guy, their 'unlikely coupling' may be 'normalised'.

However, as Marvin Carlson (1996) tells us, although liminal performance

> might seem to mark sites where conventional structure is challenged, this structure is ultimately re-affirmed ... Liminal performance may invert the established order, but never subverts it. (23)

Consequently, in order to provide meaningful performances within liminal frameworks, it is necessary to recognise established rules and contexts, such as the key contexts of heterosexuality and romance connected to procreation. In this way, while documentary provides the arena for performance, at the same time it comes with expectations, which relate to dominant ideology in society. Authorised ritual liminal transitions, for queer men within documentary form, necessarily have to connect to audience expectation, such as adhering to normative codes of identity or abjection. In this case gay men might be associated with isolation, promiscuity or effeminacy, as providing a coherent way of viewing them. This is evident within many of the case studies discussed in this book, and, in this chapter, notably the representation of Lytton Strachey within the documentary drama *Carrington* (discussed below) deliberately references the abject representation of queer man as effeminate and promiscuous. However, if a queer liminal performer transgresses this abject boundary, potentially appearing as cared for, interested in romance or masculine, the performance may be less likely to be seen as 'liminal', as passing through the threshold from one area to another – it may retain the cultural abjection, and may be considered as 'liminoid', as producing a new form outside the frame. This is apparent in the case of Lytton Strachey in *Carrington*, as not only is he coded as abjectly queer but also he demonstrates humanity, evident in his intelligent social awareness, personal sensitivity, romantic potential and caring for others, such as Dora Carrington.

Hence the liminoid performance, such as that demonstrated by Lytton Strachey, involving hybridity and challenge to order and renewal, challenges hierarchal norms, such as dominant representations and significations, and is more concerned with play, distraction and rebellion than with adherence to normality. Such a process extends beyond the liminal frame, challenging notions of the everyday and the regular. As Victor Turner (1982) tells us, considering contemporary society and culture:

> liminoid phenomena are often parts of social critiques or even evolutionary manifestos – books, plays, paintings, films etc., exposing the injustices, and immoralities of the mainstream economic and political structures. (54)

In this way, Turner makes the connection that liminoid performance often involves more free expression, foregrounding the personal political and ideological aims of the performers themselves, irrespective of dominant ideology. Lytton Strachey is indicative of this, not only in his relationship to Dora Carrington, as offering a transgressive reinvention of male to female coupling; also it is inherent in his artistic work, as innovating literary forms (see below). This type of self-reflexive expression, and potential bias toward play rather than convention, provides a carnivalesque potential, which Peter Stallybrass and Allon White ([1986] 1995) consider offers 'the possibility of shifting *the very terms of the system itself* by erasing and interrogating the relationships which constitute it' (58).

Consequently, the tension between liminal and liminoid potentials within performance are particularly relevant to the representation of the straight girl and the queer guy. The coupling of males and females evident within the liminal frame presents a coherent union directly addressed to mainstream audiences. The liminoid opportunity of reforming the liminal frame through the representation of a 'queer couple' not only extends and reforms dominant ideologies; at the same time it places the personal body, as a central discursive context. Lytton Strachey together with Dora Carrington involved themselves as key protagonists, in reframing liminal potentials, in situating their discursive and sensual bodies as both abject and affective sites of feeling and invention.

CARRINGTON

Dora Carrington and Lytton Strachey may be considered as iconic figures in examining the relationship between the straight girl and the queer guy. Offering a foundational liminal representation of the corporeal presence of the straight girl and the queer guy, the documentary biographical film drama *Carrington* tells the story of their relationship, based on the biography *Lytton Strachey* by Michael Holroyd (1994). While this suggests a reimagining of a cultural context, through shifting the focus from the queer guy (Lytton Strachey) to the straight girl (Dora Carrington) as the centre of the narrative world, Lytton (played by Jonathan Price) and Carrington (played by Emma Thompson) were intensely bonded (see Figure 5.1). Also, Carrington's final act of suicide in response to Strachey's demise two weeks earlier from

Figure 5.1 Emma Thompson as Dora Carrington and Jonathan Pryce as Lytton Stachey express their devotion to each other in the biographical film Carrington.

pneumonia not only frames her as a tragic and powerful figure but also reveals that their artistic and social worlds were deeply entwined.

Lytton Strachey was a celebrated writer who was a founding member of the Bloomsbury set, a group of influential literary writers in early twentieth-century Britain (see Holroyd 1994). Strachey was influential on biographical form, in writing *Eminent Victorians* (1918), which 'heralded a new age in this literary form, and turned biography into an art. Dismantling the notion that the biographer only assembles facts, Strachey interpreted, speculated, probed the psyche of the subject, and mingled the narrative voice with the subject's "inner life"' (Taddeo 2011: 112). Dora Carrington was a fine arts painter (see Hill 1994) who became a close friend of Lytton Strachey. In terms of practice, she was 'informed by Cézanne, but was inspired by the English pastoral tradition . . . Her work was inherently autobiographical; she painted places, people and possessions she loved . . . [However, her] artist's discipline was eroded as it became hopelessly undermined by her devotion to [Lytton] Strachey above her own' (Gaze 2001: 233–5). Lytton and Carrington were closely bonded in social, cultural and psychological terms, framing the biographical and autobiographical.[2]

The documentary drama *Carrington* offers insight into this union, establishing a liminal framework connecting both characters. This involves exploring the context of their engagement, while it involved intense mutual devotion, was essentially platonic. At the same time the film focuses on characters who were personally involved with the couple. These are mostly men who were connected to Carrington, including Mark Gertler, who was obsessed with Carrington and who encouraged Lytton to help him develop a relationship with her. Also they include Ralph Partridge, who married Carrington, and Gerald Brenan, Partridge's best friend, who embarked on a relationship with Carrington. In addition they included Beacus Penrose, with whom Carrington had a sexual relationship, focusing on her intense sexual desire for him, rather than his utilitarian desire for her. While Lytton is represented as consistently attracted to young men – as in the incident where he first meets Carrington, believing that she is a boy (because of her androgynous appearance), asking an old friend of his whilst looking at children playing in the garden 'Who on earth is that ravishing boy?' – only one male partner, Roger, is represented as sexually attracted to Lytton.

Despite a particular focus on desire for Carrington, evident in the sexual desires of a number of men for her, the desire for Lytton is central in *Carrington*. This is evident in Carrington's desire to live with Lytton, regardless of Lytton's failure to reciprocate his sexual attraction for her. At the same time, whilst Lytton expresses disgust for the female physical form, a social and physical intimacy exists between the two, more indicative of an enduring love and respect than an ephemeral physical attraction. This foregrounding of Carrington's desire for Lytton, and his deep love for her, is notable in the sequence where they first set up house with each other.

While earlier they had both conceptualised the notion of living together, and had visited a house in need of considerable renewal and decoration, later Carrington brings Lytton to the house, to see the fruits of her labour in domestic renovation. At the outset Carrington is coded as the male social agent, telling Lytton that if she were bigger (stronger) she would carry Lytton over the threshold of the newly decorated house, offering an allusion to the tradition where the groom does this to the bride on moving to their new home. At the same time Lytton is coded as submissive and female, seeming shocked when Carrington tells him not to go in a downstairs room that had been flooded from a burst water pipe, while she is resolute and confident, carrying his heavy travelling bags, and in contrast he wanders about carrying a lightweight box. Notably, when Carrington shows Lytton his newly decorated bedroom that she has been working on, a sense of union is presented that emotively bonds the couple. Lytton walks into the room that had been a squalid scene on his initial visit to the house. Carrington has now transformed the room, evident not only in clean and tidy furniture and decoration but also in a large mural covering the walls. Notably, the mural is a painting by Carrington, which depicts a scene like the Garden of Eden, including intertwined trees, owls perching on braches and cats climbing and reclining. Central within this is a depiction of a naked man standing, and a naked woman reclining, with one of the cats resting on her lap to cover her genitalia. This offers an illusion to Lytton and Carrington as the biblical characters of Adam and Eve, at the same time framing his desire for the naked male body and her situation as part of the picture but not necessarily a sexual partner. In this sense a pastoral scene is presented as an allegory of their relationship, deeply intimate as part of his bedroom. Her delight in producing this for Lytton is reflected in his awe and emotion on viewing the scene, commenting, 'It's remarkable!' As he says this, they exchange gazes, she puts down the suitcases that she has been carrying, and a sense of relaxed union and oneness is presented, in representing the couple as bonded.

However, despite the liminal frame foregrounding a focus on the desires of Lytton, as a pathway to union and fulfilment, Carrington is coded as an outsider and unfulfilled. A sense of isolation is presented, referencing the notion of the voyeuristic gaze, as one outside looking in, rather than as being within. This is particularly noticeable in the sequence where Lytton and Carrington have moved to a new house, and guests are invited there for the weekend. Prior to this, Carrington finds out that she is pregnant by Beacus, and decides to have an abortion, telling Lytton, 'I can never have a child, unless it was yours'. She has been convalescing after the abortion, and Lytton has been caring for her. Initially Carrington and Lytton are outside the house at night, looking on the building from the garden as the guests are observed within the illuminated rooms. On observing one room, where the guests seem to play table tennis, Lytton comments, 'Do you suppose that they are going to play that wretched game all night?' This scene offers a reference to an earlier scene in the film, when Lytton and Carrington observe an upper-class party in a house, viewing it from outside, observing dancing and buffoonery, and Lytton tells Carrington that young men in the war are dying to preserve this privileged and absurd way of life. This codes Lytton and Carrington as of one mind, as sharing ideologies; however, within this sequence Lytton then leaves Carrington, and goes inside. Carrington remains outside alone, continuing to observe those within the house.

In a sequence that evokes the mise en scène of Alfred Hitchcock's *Rear Window* (1954), where the actor James Stewart is represented as looking on a range of different apartments across a courtyard from his own anonymous apartment, with life going on: as he is wheelchair-bound and purely an observer, a sense of voyeurism is presented, framing notions of disconnection and lost agency. In *Carrington*, as the camera pans behind Dora Carrington looking on the house as she is in the garden, standing before an old tree stump covered in moss, she is represented as looking on the different couples or individuals in the illuminated rooms of the house. Her ex-husband Ralph Partridge is represented as content with his new wife Frances; they walk across a room, embrace and turn the light off. The camera then pans to another room where Lytton's sexual partner Roger stops playing table tennis, puts down the bat, then is observed as going from one room to another and arriving in Lytton's room, where Lytton is sitting at a table. Roger leans down and kisses Lytton on the head, and then both gradually climb the stairs as if going to bed. Then the camera pans upstairs as Carrington sits down on the tree stump, continuing to observe Ralph and Frances now in a bedroom, and in the next bedroom Beacus, the father of her now aborted foetus, looking out, presumably wondering where she is. Then the camera focuses on Roger and Lytton: now they are in the bedroom, as Lytton gently kisses Roger, as a preliminary to sex. However, unlike *Rear Window* where there is a sense of intrigue, relaxation and wonderment, evident in the accompanying jazz musical score, this sequence from *Carrington* offers a connotation of knowingness and irreversibility, counterpointed in the emotionally laconic contemporary orchestral music composed by Michael Nyman. Hence Carrington is represented not as possessing the dominant gaze, able to securely observe and watch over, as is often suggested with regard to *Rear Window* as a metaphor for the cinematic eye (see Mulvey, 1985), but as a fractured component of the gaze. With Carrington sitting in isolation in the garden, as eternally outside, not only is her desiring gaze for Lytton rejected but she observes such deflection of the gaze. Lytton's choice of Roger, an unsuitable partner, who ultimately rejects Lytton – foregrounded when earlier Lytton had offered him a key to a new apartment that they were to share, and Roger had simply replied, 'No you keep it, I would only lose it' – reveals the impossibility of equality within the reciprocal gaze for both Lytton, and Carrington.

While later, when Carrington commits suicide, using a shotgun on herself, unable to go on living after Lytton's death, suggesting some kind of eternity in fixing the gaze, it is the tension between the straight girl and the queer guy as exhibiting differing desires, but sharing life chances and life goals, of affection and camaraderie, that is central. The representation of the straight girl and the queer guy within contemporary documentary also contextualises this issue. However, rather than the framing of this within a historical world based on art and literature, as occurs within *Carrington*, notions of the everyday are central in working through, this social and domestic relationship. At the same time, the notion of the platonic relationship, and the context of marriage, offer insight into meaningful connections between he straight girl and the queer guy.

PLATONIC DEVOTION AND MARRIAGE IN DOCUMENTARY

The documentaries *Fag Hags: Women Who Love Gay Men*, *My Husband Is Gay* and *My Husband Is Not Gay* offer a liminal framework for the representation of the straight girl and the queer guy, mostly foregrounding deep emotional platonic relationships, and in many instances the context of marriage. However, these documentaries seem like very different texts. *Fag Hags: Women Who Love Gay Men* is a seemingly light-hearted documentary focusing on three couples of gay men and straight women, with one couple having been married to each other. It frames the discourse with footage of the comedian Margaret Cho, and includes an ironic YouTube video pop song *Gay Boyfriend*, making comical connections to the notion of the 'Fag Hag'. In contrast *My Husband Is Gay*[3] and *My Husband Is Not Gay* directly examine the issue of marriage, with the former generally focusing on married couples who have broken up their marriages (with one exception who remain together), after coming to terms with issues of sexuality, and the latter examining couples who are determined to be together, connected by the Mormon religion.

Notably, *My Husband Is Not Gay* may be considered as a problematic text for its focus on the denial of gay identity, and its potential support of gay conversion, a process where individuals are encouraged to reject their same-sex attraction and become heterosexual. Undoubtedly, such a process restricts human liberty, and there are many accounts were individuals have experienced extreme oppression through engaging in 'conversion therapy', including incidents of suicide (see Human Rights Campaign 2015). Despite this, I am discussing *My Husband Is Not Gay* for its focus on gay desire, which might not be initially apparent in considering the context of the programme. While my case studies seem diverse, offering a mixture of best friends and married couples, some of whom want to stay together, and others who want to separate, all three texts are bonded through exploring the personal discourse of queer guys and straight girls, bonded by social and sexual attraction of varying forms.

In terms of identity, it's important to note that, while few of the texts mention the notion of queer identity, all present a direct relationship to gay identity, relating this as a liminal framework. Even while *My Husband Is Not Gay* resists the notion of gay male identity, preferring to consider the male partners as heterosexuals who are subject to 'same-sex attraction', or SSA, the relationship to gay identity is central. While this suggests that *My Husband Is Not Gay* is an unusual text, for its focus on rejecting queer desire and the liminal potential of gay identity, it works through the straight girl and queer guy relationship, attempting to resolve problematic aspects of sexual desire that are seen to be in conflict in their marriage unions. As part of this the couples seem to be bonded by discussing their desires as much as their identities. Hence, although *My Husband Is Not Gay* seems to reject gay identity, in fact it emboldens it, framing gay identity as an irresistible subtext that cannot be denied.

This leads us to consider how the relationship between the straight girl and the queer guy is framed within documentary form. Unlike the first case study, *Carrington*, which may be considered as a biographical documentary drama, and the later case studies in this chapter, *Would Like to Meet*, *Queer Eye for the Straight Guy* and *Boy Meets Boy*, which might be considered as reality television and format-based, these texts present themselves as documentary, in conveying some kind of actuality. Despite this, *Fag Hags: Women Who Love Gay Men*, *My Husband Is Gay* and *My Husband Is Not Gay* have an unusual relationship with verisimilitude. Notably, all three documentaries rely on contexts of humour, irony or parody, particularly evident in the use of non-diegetic music that might accompany the discourse. While in *Fag Hags: Women Who Love Gay Men* this context seems more suitable, and it is acknowledged in the text by the inclusion of Margaret Cho, a stand-up comedian, and the comedic video *Gay Boyfriend*, this relationship is not so obvious in *My Husband Is Gay* and *My Husband Is Not Gay*. I argue that the notion of irony is central here, in conveying the meaning of the texts. As Claire Colebrook (2004) tells us, 'recognising irony foregrounds the social, conventional and political aspects of language:

that language is not just a logical system, but relies on assumed norms and values' (15). These ideas might be challenged through relating the potential of ambivalence in questioning a specific meaning, and also offer the opportunity of 'reading against the grain'. Hence, in representing a married couple who might be experiencing problems in their relationship, considering notions of fidelity or untruthfulness, it seems incongruous to use humorous music as an accompaniment. While this could suggest a light-heartedness, in encouraging mainstream empathy, conversely I argue that the use of music in this way is ironic. Through these texts using comedic music, there is a counterpoint representation, suggesting a duality juxtaposing seriousness with humour, connoting an alternative, or at least ambivalent, reading.

As Annahid Kassabian (2001: 3) relates the idea of 'identification' in connection to music used in film – using the term 'assimilating identifications' that may be applied to music 'scored' for films, while 'affiliating identifications' may be used to discuss music 'selected' for films – the composition or selection of music implies a duality, and a certain hybridity in forming the meaning. Using notions of assimilation and affiliation, the music becomes part of the identification world; although not explicit, it is connotative and contextual. For example, if we consider a key sequence in *My Husband Is Gay*, when couple Sam and Dave are initially introduced in the documentary, the accompanying music and visuals seems a little incongruous to the dialogue:

> Dave: We are the real *Will and Grace*. [Switches from image of the couple on the sofa with Sam's head looking down, after hearing Dave's comment, to both on the streets in a crowded shopping centre, with cutaways to images of young men whom we imagine to be desirable to Dave]
>
> Voiceover: Dave came out to Sam a year ago, but to everyone's surprise they have decided to stay married and living together. [The image morphs to a wedding shot of Dave and Sam's wedding day with Dave looking directly at the camera, and Sam looking away]
>
> Sam: [now in home, with a close up of her face] But everyone else could tell [that he was gay] apart from me. [Followed by shot of Sam's eye's reflected in a car rear-view internal mirror, looking sideways, whilst driving the car, with a road sign just ahead]

While in the prior sequence, which discussed Sarah and Matt, the accompanying music had been in a minor key, offering an emotional reflection of the sadness that Sarah had experienced in considering the needs of her daughter, on finding out that Matt was gay, in the discussion of Sam and Dave the tone swiftly changes. Rhythmic jazz-style music with saxophones and horns is heard, implying leisure and easiness. Horns are played in a recurring motif or riff, with syncopated staccato chords played by the horns. At the same time the images selected – such as Dave looking ahead, or at others, signify his desire to leave or to be uncontainable, while the images of Sam seem to offer connotations of personal reflection, or lack of direction – present a complex mixture of deceits and uncertainties between the couple. Despite this, the music seems upbeat, as if presenting some irony, while at the same time the image of the couple on their wedding day, presented with the text font in the style of a wedding invitation, seems like a direct parody of the meaning of weddings.

Although I would not argue that these documentary texts would be considered as 'mockumentary' (see Hight 2010), providing a coherent ideological parody, of a particular documentary context such as the meaning of weddings, a certain irony is present in the selection and juxtaposition of images and music. I argue that this directly foregrounds the hyper-real and simulacra, rather than the explicit representation of social reality. This is particularly noticeable in *My Husband Is Not Gay*, where a sense of distance and stylisation is presented, problematising the notion of the dominant gaze.

In *My Husband Is Not Gay*, while all queer male contributors coupled in matrimony or identifying with the Mormon religion state that they do not identify as gay, there is an uneasy tension in relating desire and identity. These contributors freely state that they identify as subject to SSA (same-sex attraction), admitting desire for sexual relationships with their own sex, and imply that they may be considered as MSM, men who have sex with men (see Avert 2015; Joseph 2005). Those identified as MSM are considered to engage in sexual relationships with their own sex, but do not consider themselves as gay, in terms of social identity. Hence, the only difference between someone who is MSM and gay would be that the latter presents his identity in the wider social world while the former simply does not reveal his sexual desires as part of his social identity. MSM and gay men both would engage in same-sex activity. However those who assign themselves as subject to SSA suggest that they resist same-sex relationships. Therefore individuals are working towards denying aspects of their instinctive sexual desires. It's not surprising that the SSA men in *My Husband Is Not Gay* reject SSA, as they identify themselves as Mormon and follow a religious order where homosexuality may be considered as deviant.

Despite this, in *My Husband Is Not Gay* forbidden sexual desire and the notion of gay identity, rather than MSM, are foregrounded. Notably, in a sequence where the main male characters encounter gay-identified males in a clothing shop, a tension is foregrounded which challenges the dominant reading of the text, as denying gay identity. Although this sequence could be read as a shopping trip for the main cast of SSA men, the composition and context of the sequence offer a glimpse of gay identity in relation to sexual desire. Specifically, when the characters encounter a couple of attractive gay men, initially observing them then actually conversing with them, a certain tension erupts within the group.

At the start of the sequence, which is set up as a shopping trip for Tom, who has an upcoming date with a girl, despite his SSA, the friendship group of Pret, Curtis and Jeff initially are connoted as queer. This is evident where they are initially depicted as in close vicinity to colourful handbags, and then Pret tries to persuade Tom to try on a pink shirt, coding them as effeminate. However Tom, Pret, Curtis and Jeff suspend shopping after they observe two attractive men on the other side of the shop, indicating a particular attraction for one of them.

> Jeff: Hey you see that guy over there. What do you think?
>
> Pret: He's a good-looking guy for sure!
>
> Tom: I kind of like guys that are more athletic, fit, like myself . . . Is he your type?
>
> Jeff: I think that he is a great-looking guy, but I like the swimmer's build . . .
>
> Curtis: Neither of those two fit my imperative.
>
> Pret: So what kind of guy are you into?
>
> Curtis: Usually taller, like Ryan Reynolds.
>
> Jeff: I am with you there.
>
> Pret: Who isn't!

This conversation foregrounds sexual desire, by relating notions of desirable physical form, evident in the preference of a 'type', and the notion of being 'into' a particular type. Also there is a consensus in sharing preferred models or types, in considering the notion of a swimmer's build, and the assessment of a well-known actor (Ryan Reynolds). These connotations prioritise the notion of natural desire, even though the characters suggest that they do not act on these desires.

However, when Jeff and Pret suggest that they know the guy whom they have been observing, and the group engage in conversation with the couple, it becomes apparent, that Jeff may have had sexual relations with one of the two observed guys, Jay. This is apparent when in conversation Jay acknowledges that he knows Jeff, and Jay offers a bemused expression, when Jeff calls Jay a 'man of mystery', and Tom questions whether Jeff might have not known if Jay was gay. Notably, Jay and his friend Shaun as the only gay-identified men in the documentary offer a commentary on the SSA men. Jay reveals that he had attempted to reject his gay identity as part of trial connected to the Mormon religion and the notion of SSA, but had come to terms with his gay identity, considering this as enabling, rather than problematic. Notably, Shaun, who is not connected to a history of identifying as subject to SSA, offers a criticism of the group, suggesting that they should act on their sexual desires, and, on hearing of Tom's impending date with a woman, sarcastically advises him, 'Good luck with *that*'.

Hence, although *My Husband Is Not Gay* seems to reject gay identity, at the same time it foregrounds irresistible queer desire, offering a sense of ambivalence. Although Jeff is the only character who acknowledges that he has had sex with men, the subliminal and liminal framing of desire for the male body constructs the male participants in the programme as queer men. These men, however, are resolutely supported by straight girls, who acknowledge their husband's queer desires (if not queer identities), and are bonded through deep emotional connectivity.

In *My Husband Is Not Gay*, this is profoundly evident where Pret and his wife Megan discuss the birth of their second child, Stella, a few months before the recording of the documentary. Pret and Megan discuss how they found out before the birth of the child that there would be problems with Stella, knowing that she would not survive for long. They discuss how they held Stella for twenty minutes after she was born, with her dying in their arms. Such a tragic and emotional narrative clearly reveals a bond between Pret and Megan that transcends notions of sexual desire, and engages with aspects of mortality, and the desire for eternity, evident in deep and respectful shared humanity. This sense of eternal bonding through shared experience and the acceptance of difference is also apparent in the representation of Cynthia and gay-identified Matt in *Fag Hags: Women Who Love Gay Men*.

Cynthia and Matt are represented as close friends who had known each other for many years since their time together in university. In many ways they had formed a close family unit, including often sleeping together as friends, and caring for a dog called Hazel, who is represented as a child figure to them. Cynthia tells us:

> I was quite devoted to [Matt]. At the end of the day he was the one I was comfortable with. He was the one I went to with all my problems and stories, and joys and tribulations . . . We would sleep in the same bed, and sit and chat when one of us was in the bath, and there was just a feeling that we were at ease with each other physically.

Accompanying this discourse, old photographs are presented showing Matt, Cynthia and their dog Hazel as living together, seeming like an intimate family unit. This sense of familial intimacy is foregrounded, relating their connection to Hazel, with Cynthia commenting on one of the old pictures,

'That's you sleeping on an air mattress in my bedroom, with Hazel sleeping in a basket. But she would tilt the basket over so she could get her head on your shoulder.' In this sense Hazel represents the child that they could have created between them, which was an option that they had discussed. Also Hazel offers a representation of intimacy similar to the feeling felt by Cynthia for Matt. A sense of familial, physical, social and intellectual comfort is represented, implying certain devotion that would not end. This is also evident where Matt and Cynthia discuss their possible funeral arrangements, indicating that each would ensure that the other's wishes were honoured with the appropriate choice of music. They recall this knowledge, with Matt saying that he was supposed to sing *Softly and Tenderly Jesus Is Calling* at her funeral, and Cynthia was supposed to play the *Mary Tyler Moore Show* theme tune for Matt's funeral.

Despite this deep connection reflecting the acceptance of diverse tastes and life worlds, a few years back Cynthia had expressed unhappiness, asking for some validation that they had a deep relationship which was like a marriage, writing a letter to Matt when he was working away on a cruise liner. This had resulted in Matt feeling defensive, needing to support his own gay male relationship, and then writing back to Cynthia, suggesting that they would not continue to see each other. However, despite this, later when Cynthia had developed cancer, the couple had reconnected, and the documentary represents them as eternally bonded despite difficult times in their relationship. This frames Matt in the present as helping Cynthia with her cancer treatment, and being there for her.

The notion of the lasting bond, similar to the relationship between Carrington and Lytton within the biographical documentary drama, forms a central strand, in considering the constitution of the straight girl and queer guy relationship. At the same time the eternal bond between the straight girl and the queer guy can be more directly familial. For example, in *My Husband Is Gay* the representation of Ajay, a middle-aged Asian gay man who has only recently came out, reveals the construction of the straight girl as not the wife who is absent but the daughter who encourages her father to find a suitable gay male partner, accompanying him to Gay Pride events. Hence the straight girl not only potentially presents a close emotional, physical or familial bond with the queer guy but also may be an enabler, or performative agent, in supporting the queer guy. This is particularly noticeable in *Would Like to Meet*, where the straight girl offers insight and support to the queer guy, not only in terms of improving social skills but also in defining a liminal framework.

WOULD LIKE TO MEET

The notion of advice or support to queer men by straight girls forms a central context in an episode of the reality television series *Would Like to Meet* (BBC 2001–4, UK), a series which focused on helping a different individual each week gain confidence in personal dating skills. I am examining an episode featuring a gay male, Richard Smith, where a cast of experts offer advice and support. I have selected this specific episode not only because it represents a 'queer male' but also because it foregrounds the relationship between the straight girl and the queer guy, seeming to invert the 'normative' dynamic. While later I discuss *Queer Eye for the Straight Guy* – which in many ways uses a similar format, but in this case the queer guy helps the straight girl and straight guy – the popularity of the dating and personal grooming show offers a key context in addressing mainstream audiences. Hence the address of these 'personal help' television formats not only engages with domesticity and female identity (see Chapter 4) but also directly integrates performative aspects of gender and sexuality. In addressing mainstream audiences, seeming to reflect the dominant representational world, these programmes tend to be heterocentric. If *Would Like to Meet* were to focus on the desires of a gay man, this be an exception within the dominant focus of the series: not surprisingly, female heterosexual identity offers a key context in mediating the discourse.

The series includes two female presenters, Tracey Cox as a relationship expert and Jay Hunt as a stylist. These may be considered as the straight girls, offering support to the queer guy, Richard Smith. The programme seems to invert the normal relationship between the straight girl and the queer guy, as the straight girl offers support and advice to the queer guy, while the normative tradition, as discussed in this book, is the reverse of this. While this suggests that there may be some progressive insight, presenting the straight girls as a commodity to the queer guy, at the outset of the episode we are aware that the queer guy is coded as failing to meet the stereotypical signification of a gay man. Richard Smith is represented as a schoolteacher from a rural location who is not self-confident and has poor fashion sense, rather than following the 'stereotypical norm' of a gay man, as an individual connected to an urban environment who is self-assured and has good fashion sense. While the later case study on *Queer Eye for the Straight Guy* productively engages in this signification for the queer man as useful to the straight girl, in *Would Like to Meet* the queer guy is represented as needing reformation to meet these expectations.

Notably, early in the episode, Jay, the style expert, advises Richard about the connection that gay men have to fashion, relating this to discerning who is gay or straight in attempting to find a partner in public space. She advises him that gay men are able to read 'subtle signals' in decoding aspects of sexuality, through reading the associations that apparel may provide.

> Jay: Gay men do notice these signals. They are very clothes-conscious. You don't have to give off a massive signal [in selecting what to wear. Fortunately] you are in a peer group who are going to 'clock it'.

In this way Jay makes an allusion to the performance of the archetypal gay man, as possessing 'fashion sense'. Also she suggests that certain clothes may be read as gay, offering the ability to code yourself in this way, to make your sexual identity obvious. As part of this she transforms his clothes selection, presenting closer fitting, and more casual clothes, which are coded as gay, encouraging him to stop wearing his looser-fitting and more formal clothes, which are coded as straight. This transformation is presented as useful, since Richard has had problems dating and wants to find men in his local rural environment, where it is imagined that there are few gay men. Hence the skill of reading clothes is presented not only as a liminal frame but as also offering the ritual potential of affirming an identity, providing the means to find a suitable partner.

While this seems to emulate the liminal potential of heterosexual males and females to follow discernible types of gender performance, which may also be coded in the selection of personal apparel in order to find a suitable partner, there is an emphasis on female discourse. At the same time, the straight girl seems to be a substitute for a gay man, offering advice in an area that is disconnected not only from her gender but also from her sexuality. Through the coding of the female experts as gay men, there is an unusual tension regarding gender performativity.

This is particularly noticeable in a sequence where Tracey accompanies Richard in public space. While earlier Jay had been offering fashion tips to Richard in order to code himself as gay, this was set in the domestic household space, framing the domestic medium of television, at the same time referencing the female audience as part of this. When Tracey and Richard arrive in Old Compton Street in Soho in London, an area considered to be frequented by gay men, the notion of the public is foregrounded, framing issues of sexual promiscuity. As part of this Tracey represents herself as an expert in stimulating sexual attraction.

> Tracey: What we are going to do today is learning to cruise. It's a very, very, specific gay body language thing. What it will enable you to do is to tell who is gay, and who is straight, in predominantly straight environments.

As part of this Tracey then instructs him, while walking in public space towards a desirable male, to engage in eye contact for at least three seconds, then to drop his gaze, walk a little further, then look back to see if there is a reciprocal glance. If this happens she assures him that the man he had encountered would be gay. Although it's possible that Tracey had learned these skills either by observing gay men 'cruising' or by reading about this, or potentially she does this herself, it is the signification that this forms a specific code of sexual practice in terms of ritual which is central. While what a gay man cruising for sex does may be relevant (see Berlant and Warner 1998), she conflates a promiscuous gay sexual ritual with the notion of finding a romantic partner. As part of this she presents herself as a masquerade for a stereotypical promiscuous gay man, who is an expert in cruising for sex. While such skills might be useful to Richard in his quest to find a partner, it is the hyper-representation of a female acting as a gay man which offers hybrid instability in challenging the authenticity of the queer guy himself.

Such a challenge to authenticity, I argue, is apparent in *Would Like to Meet*, attempting to fix the identity of the queer guy, as different to the straight male, and at the same time as a commodity to the straight girl. If Richard remains in the countryside, finds his romantic partner there and continues to wear unfashionable clothing, for a mainstream audience he is neither comprehensible nor a commodity. While *Would Like to Meet* does foreground the queer guy as needing support, the straight girl expects the adherence of certain normative expectations. This similarly takes place in *Queer Eye for the Straight Guy*: however, the straight male acts as a resource for modernisation, situated between, but connecting the straight girl and the queer guy.

QUEER EYE FOR THE STRAIGHT GUY

Queer Eye for the Straight Guy is a reality television format that has been sold worldwide (TV Barn 2004). It is indicative of television broadcaster Bravo's interest in exploring gay social worlds, which includes other shows such as *Fire Island* (1998), a series which focused on wealthy gay men and women holidaying away from Manhattan on the island, *Gay Weddings* (2003), a series that followed a range of gay and lesbian same-sex marriage ceremonies and *Boy Meets Boy* (2003) (which is discussed below), a dating show which foregrounded a gay man in search of an ideal partner.

Queer Eye for the Straight Guy is a makeover reality television programme, focusing on services provided by a cast of five gay males who support a straight man, offering lifestyle and cultural advice, in an attempt either to impress his female partner or to succeed in heterosexual social affairs. Whilst this suggests that the queer guy is foregrounded in the narrative, there is no evidence of social reciprocity. Queer men are service providers to straight men, and not generally vice versa.⁴ At the same time the notion of service to the straight girl is foregrounded in the narrative, where the main aim is to improve the aesthetic and cultural potential of her straight guy partner.

Although the series seems to focus on the notion of service to the straight guy, an address to females is apparent in the narrative, particularly evident in the title sequences, which includes a popular song, sung by a female, with the lyrics 'Things keep getting better for me when you are around', implying that the queer guy is in support of the straight girl. Aspects of femininity and camp performance are also evident in the aesthetics of the title sequences. The queer males termed the 'fab five' are individually identified with synthesised visual images of the cast, and graphics, highlighting their roles. These images seem like hyper-real stylised personal performances, evident where the fashion expert Carson Kressley is depicted as leaving a department store through a revolving door, laden with shopping bags; he spins around on his heels and strikes a dramatic pose. At the same time the grooming expert Kyan Douglas throws a hairdryer in the air, then grabs it, making it seem like a revolver, instantly putting his sunglasses on, seeming like James Bond.

These aesthetic constructions seem hyper-real in terms of gender performance, offering a camp 'feminised' or 'masculinised' representation, suggesting that the bodily stance of the gay performer is extraordinary. Whilst this method of representation is commonplace in the iconography associated with pop stars and celebrities, the stylised representation of the participants not only signifies their dissimilarity to the heterosexual clients, it provides a divide which highlights aspects of 'difference' and 'incongruity' between queer and straight identities. This is particularly evident in the closing stages of the title sequence where no pretence is made that homosexual and heterosexual lives are on the same pathway. This is vividly evident with the depiction of street signs, which indicate 'Straight Street' and 'Gay Street' as leading in different directions. Whilst these visual representations may be considered as a metaphor for the series, suggesting different pathways for homosexual and heterosexual lives, they are bonded in the service provider identity of the queer guy, for the straight girl.

For example, if we consider an episode of *Queer Eye for the Straight Guy* from the first series, which foregrounds the straight guy John Zimmerman IV and his girlfriend Sylvia, who are both professional ice skaters, we see that a central focus is made at the outset on the usefulness of the makeover team for the straight girl. Kyan Douglas grooming expert, Ted Allen food and wine expert, Jai Rodriquez culture expert, Tom Filicia interior design expert and Carson Kressley fashion expert converse together in a car on their way to meet the couple. During this 'establishing' conversation, oppositions are made between the straight girl and the straight guy, indicating that the straight guy is in need of improvement, and the straight girl is already 'fully formed'. For example, the team foreground John as from Birmingham, Alabama, and Sylvia as from Italy, coding John as a 'country boy' and unsophisticated, in comparison with Sylvia as cultured, coming from Italy. Kyan sums this up, saying, 'On the one hand we have Rome, glamour, gorgeous, and on the other we have Alabama, country toad'.

They also state that Sylvia is in need of support, advising that John 'needs to step up to the plate and start taking care of his lady girl'. As the programme progresses, whilst to some degree the queer male cast comment on the 'straight social world' as lacking sophistication, evident in their reviewing the state of the home environment, and evident cultural signifiers there, the straight guy is coded as lacking cultural and social refinement, not the straight girl. Hence the straight girl inhabits the same cultural world as the queer guys, and, despite separate social worlds, only the queer guy is able to transform the straight guy into some ideal partner.

Hence, the final sequence of the show foregrounds a romantic social event, which has been designed by the queer guys, purely in service of meeting the social and cultural needs of the straight girl. For John and Sylvia, at the romantic dinner that John has prepared for Sylvia with the support of Ted the food and wine expert, this showcases not only the culinary skills of the queer guy but also the appreciation of the straight girl for this. This is evident when all the team are watching a transmission of the dinner event, offering the chance for them to comment on the success of the evening. Sylvia tastes the food prepared by John, saying, 'The tomatoes taste so good', and Ted comments to the *Queer Eye* team, observing the meal, 'It's the expressway to her heart, that pasta'. Therefore, whilst there is no explicit union between the straight girl and the queer guy, they are intimately connected, in the service element provided by the queer guy for the straight girl, manifest in the improved social, cultural and aesthetic development of the straight guy.

While this focuses on the notion of service, and the context of the straight guy as a third party in this transaction, there is little reciprocal support for the queer guy given by the straight girl. This might be apparent, as the straight girl has a romantic sexual partner; at the same time the notion of the straight girl who is coupled to a heterosexual partner does not exclude the notion of support for the queer male. Hence in comparison, in *Boy Meets Boy*, not only is the service focus on the queer guy rather than the straight guy, but also the series foregrounds the dynamics of the straight girl who, while she is already coupled, resolutely supports the queer guy.

BOY MEETS BOY

In the opening sequences of *Boy Meets Boy*, the audience are not only introduced to the central performer, James Getzlaff but also they are provided with information concerning a format twist:

> Dani Behr (host): One exceptional man.
>
> James: I want to make a huge attempt at finding a connection [with a male partner].
>
> Dani Behr: Fifteen extraordinary suitors all vying for his affection ... But appearances aren't always what they seem. What neither the gay suitors nor the leading man know is that some of the suitors are straight men – pretending to be gay, competing to win a cash prize. In a world where gay is the norm and straight men must stay in the closet ... Can stereotypes be shattered? Will romance prevail?

Whilst this foregrounds the notion of a psychological, sociological and cultural experiment, at the same time a tension is raised that James is an isolated figure, unaware at the outset of the format twist. Despite this, the series couples him with his straight female best friend, Andra, who is coded as a political and social supporter to James. Such a union is exhibited in their discourse. Notably, James confides to Andra:

> If I can get one person to understand there is no difference between [gay and straight people] except for who we love, we should be able to marry, ... we should be able to do what everybody else does.

James, like many other gay and lesbian social actors, involved himself as a performer in reality television for the purpose (amongst other reasons) of reforming dominant ideas concerning sexual identity (see Pullen 2007a). When James finds out about the format twist, this strengthens his relationship with Andra, to resolve his search for romance, and to promote his political address to mainstream audiences. As part of this, Andra tells James that she wants him to have the romantic potential that she has with her husband. Hence, unlike *Queer Eye for the Straight Guy*, where the already coupled straight girl is the beneficiary of support from a gay man to improve her social and sexual life, the reverse takes place in *Boy Meets Boy*, where the straight girl is an accomplice with the queer guy, attempting to gain equality for him.

Such drive to equality is presented by the openly gay series producer Douglas Ross, who tells us, 'It's impossible to tell who's gay and who's straight' (quoted in Sigesmund 2003: 52), and that the programme might challenge the appropriateness of stereotypes that may be applied to both gay and straight men. As part of this, *Boy Meets Boy* appears to have influenced the development of the reality series *Playing It Straight* (Fox 2005, US), which similarly offered the premise of breaking down stereotypes by suggesting that you cannot tell who is gay or straight. In *Playing It Straight*, however, a heterosexual female must select an ultimate date from a group of male suitors where a number of them are gay but acting straight. Despite this, there was no representation of queer and straight coupling in *Playing It Straight*. Whilst the series inevitably reached larger audiences than *Boy Meets Boy* as a product broadcast on Network TV (despite its early cancellation),[5] the representation of the straight girl as a key protagonist in supporting a queer guy is central in *Boy Meets Boy*, relative to the constrictions and the opportunity of the format twist as political, something not developed in *Playing It Straight*.[6]

At the outset of *Boy Meets Boy*, James and Andra are not aware of anyone's sexual identity, they believe that all the participants are gay until episode four, when James is told that one of the remaining three is straight (see Figure 5.2). While the original main line-up of fifteen competitors consisted of a balance between gay and straight men, only the straight participants pretending to be gay were aware that there was a format twist. In earlier episodes, only the audience are able to discern who is actually gay or straight, as this is revealed after their elimination. Although James and Andra give the impression that

Figure 5.2   *Andra Stasko expresses emotional support to James Getzlaff in the reality television series* Boy Meets Boy, *on discovering the format twist, that one of the remaining suitors for James is heterosexual, and that James may be fooled into selecting him as his ultimate date.*

James is able to select a possible gay male partner, through gradually eliminating potential suitors, the discourse of the series changes after episode four. The focus shifts from the notion of finding romance and fulfilment to the need to resist humiliation, should he choose a final date who is a straight man, and be rejected. Consequently on discovering the plot twist, James and Andra go on the offensive, in order to discern who is gay or straight, rather than who would make an ideal partner. The three contestants left are Franklin, Brian H and Wes, one of which is straight while the other two are gay.

Andra plays a major role in working with James, to try and detect who is straight or gay. James had suggested earlier to Andra that Franklin might be the straight guy. In order to test this he arranges a date with Franklin, which may be seen to test Franklin's imagined heterosexual discomfort, as they go to a sauna, and are seen in close physical proximity. Although James does not conclude (before the finale) if this revealed Franklin to be the outsider, Andra further confronts Franklin, although she is not able to reveal the twist to any of the participants. In a scene where Andra suggests that she would be unhappy if anyone were lying to her best friend (James), the finalists discuss stereotypes which surround gay identity. Franklin recalls his history of identification as a sexual rather than a social object, and tells us, 'There is nothing more I wanted to hear [from gay men] than about a person's day, not about how pretty I am!' Andra responds, 'You're pretty?' Andra's aggressive riposte manifests her close, protective alliance to James and her possible identification of Franklin as the outsider.[7]

Later, after James with the support of Andra, decides whom to eliminate, he identifies Franklin as the outsider. This reveals a sense of closure, and at the same time irony and displeasure.

> James: From the bombshell of the twist, I assumed you were the straight guy. Because of that I didn't choose you.
>
> Franklin: I am sorry, you are correct. I am relieved; I have been scared all day.
>
> James: [tilts his head and looks unimpressed]
>
> Franklin: I got involved in this to discontinue stereotypes, but this became personal . . .
>
> James: There is so much that we as gay men have to fight against already, to just have a glimmer of acceptance. The fear that we could be infiltrated for *another* goal in something that we thought it was just about love, uh, hurts!

James identifies his potential to be humiliated, at the same time framing Franklin's motives for financial reward, rather than necessary support to challenge gay stereotyping.[8] A sense of performative inversion takes place, where the straight outsider is revealed, and, whilst James goes on to select Wes, who is gay, as his final date, there is an uneasy tension in the final outcome. Andra's persistent support for James – not only making connections to the equality that he deserves but also emotively challenging with the producers, whom she was discontented with because of the 'humiliating twist' – reveals the final couple not as James and Wes (evident in the culmination of the series in coupling with a gay guy) but as James and Andra, evident in her determined support for him and his respect for her.

Hence while the liminal frame of romance is defined, supporting the notion of same-sex attraction, the potential for ritual advancement is denied or deferred. The format twist distorts the liminal frame, which, while it seemed to accommodate same-sex romantic opportunities, in fact created resistant motives and actions. However, through the notion of sacrifice, some liminoid potential is created, reforming or challenging dominant notions of emotional engagement, relating the straight girl and queer guy relationship. Hence the deep bond between James and Andra is tested and worked through. While in some ways this seems like an unsatisfactory outcome, it iterates senses of alliance, which may endure, rather than offering ephemeral moments of romance, disconnected from investment.

The relationship between James and Andra is not so dissimilar to the relationship between Carrington and Lytton in *Carrington*, through foregrounding the straight female partner as a central ally, enabler and supporter of the queer guy. Whilst *Would Like to Meet* and *Queer Eye for the Straight Guy* in some senses parody this relationship, at the same time the format expectations of reality television stimulates contextual references, placing the queer guy alongside the straight girl, appearing as a formidable union, in reinventing the dating show.

Conclusion

The documentary representation of the straight girl and the queer guy offers certain significance, in framing connections to social reality, and verisimilitude. In exploring the case studies in this chapter, I have deliberately juxtaposed representations in regular documentary form, documentary drama and reality television. At the same time I have foregrounded the theoretical significance of documentary, and that of performance studies. While the notions of documentary and performance seem antithetical, as the former suggests some access to actuality and the latter seems to recognise a determined subjectivity, I argue that they are inherently entwined. The liminal potential of male and female representations offers scope for the straight girl and the queer guy, in challenging the meaning of normative relationships. While in many ways the liminal frame remains, I consider that liminoid potential is equally apparent, particularly evident in considering the profound commitment of the straight girl and the queer guy.

Dora Carrington and Lytton Strachey may be represented in biographical documentary drama, which suggests that a certain dramatic licence is apparent in *Carrington* in conveying historical accounts. The married couples in *My Husband Is Not Gay* seem to be ironically framed within contemporary documentary form, implying a disingenuous prospect that hides a social or sexual reality. The alliance between James and Andra in *Boy Meets Boy* is vivified in responding to stereotypical norms, production format surprises and the notion of the game rather than the reality. Despite this, I argue that adherence to historical realism, establishing a reading that has no irony, and finding out what is behind the format, are not necessarily appropriate issues to consider. Social realism is not found in determining some kind of truth; it is decoding the signifiers and sensing the actions or feelings of the social agents (or their representations).

This largely relates to reviewing the life stories of the performers, participants and representations, juxtaposing the potential for textual analysis in reading between the lines. The ultimate prospect is that only the media text remains, and any reading must be contextual. Biographical documentary drama, reality television and regular documentary form seem to imply a world full of feints, complications, trials, tribulations and compromises, in conveying some social reality. Notably, the format premise of *Queer Eye for the Straight Guy* deliberately ignores the life chances of queer men, yet at the same time such absence reveals a need for presence.

Such need and urge for immediacy in framing this absence is intense in *Carrington* when Dora Carrington decides to end her life, as she cannot go on living without Lytton Strachey, and in *My Husband Is Not Gay* is apparent when Pret and Megan, a married couple, discuss the tragic loss of their baby. These are visceral and complex tragic moments that foreground eternal dedication, not mortality, a specific end or a real meaning. We can't judge what should happen, or the reasons why these events took place, we can only consider our affective relationship with each other, which may be complex, unknowable or alien.

The diverse representation of the straight girl and the queer guy within documentary form may seem like a freak show, where we seem to determine what's the problem, or what's really happening. Despite this we can only be thankful that a diverse range of individuals have inscribed their mark, even if it's hard to read, or seems incomprehensible. The notion of fixing a meaning to social realism is complex, and, as we discover in the last chapter of this book, relationships to fiction and fact are blurred, and not necessarily direct, in working through political potentials within media form. Youth identity and the stylistic conventions of social realism potentially offer new ways of looking, at the same time framing the need for representation and the context of lived experience and social networks of support.

Notes

1. The initial discussion in this chapter on documentary and performance develops a theoretical framework that was originally presented in my book *Documenting Gay Men: Identity and Performance in Reality Television and Documentary Film* (2007).
2. It's important to note that within the Bloomsbury Set there was also another devoted coupling of a straight girl and a queer guy, evident in the long-term relationship between fine arts painters Duncan Grant and Vanessa Bell (see Spalding 1998). Bell was the sister of Virginia Woolf, who lived with Grant for forty years. Their child Angelica was conceived in a brief time when they shared sexual relations. While Grant and Bell play minor roles in the film *Carrington*, in 2015 the BBC produced a three-part high-quality drama largely focused on the couple entitled *Life in Squares*.
3. It's important to note that Sky Television produced a different documentary also titled *My Husband Is Gay*, as part of its *Forbidden Love* series, broadcast in 2014 in the United Kingdom.
4. Despite this, there have been two episodes that did focus on gay men, as the makeover subject: one in season two, episode five, titled 'Queer Eye for a Not-So-Straight Guy: Wayne H' (broadcast in June 2004), and the other in season four, episode four, titled 'Bringing Out the Inner Fab: Jeff B' (broadcast in June 2006). In addition there has been an episode focusing on a male transgendered person in season four, episode nine, titled 'Trans-form this Trans-man: Miles G' (broadcast in August 2006).
5. *Playing It Straight* was cancelled after three episodes in the United States (see Reality TV Planet 2004). Despite this, the UK adaptation of the series produced by Channel 4 was reasonably successful, running for two complete series in 2005 (set in Mexico) and 2012 (set in Spain).
6. These texts potentially influenced the production of the reality television series *Girls Who Like Boys Who Like Boys* (Sundance TV 2010–12, US), which ran for two series framing the domestic and social environment of the straight girl and the queer guy, set respectively in New York and Nashville.
7. Also this sequence foreshadows Franklin's admission (at the end of the finale) of why he engaged in the show: he had been wrongly identified as gay before (because of his cultural interests). Franklin later goes on to tell James (after being outed) that this misidentification was the reason he did the show (saying he wanted to break down stereotypes).
8. A prize award would have gone to Franklin had James selected him as the final date.

CHAPTER 6

Youth, Realism and Form

John Hill (1986), in discussing the influence of teen identity within British social realist cinema of the late 1950s and early 1960s, tells us:

> Central to the imagery of the 'affluent teenager' was the idea of dissolution of old class barriers and the construction of a new collective identity based on teenage values . . . Teenagers, indeed, represented a new 'class' whose very badge of identity was their rejection of traditional class boundaries. (11)

Hence the representation of young people or teenagers within film (and television) might be traced to their identity as breaking down class boundaries, at the same time challenging sexual identity norms. For example the representation of the queer youth Geoffrey who forms a bond with Jo in *A Taste of Honey*, wanting them to raise a child together (discussed in Chapter 1), offers insight into this transgressive potential for the representation of the queer guy and the straight girl who challenge identity norms. As part of a cultural movement from the early 1960s, which foregrounds new opportunity for social realism, I argue that the representation of queer youth in the company of the straight girl extends from these potentials, offering new scope in diverse contemporary forms.

Hence, this chapter explores case studies that are potentially influenced by the transgressive potential of social realism, founded through earlier ideological frames and formats of the early 1960s. As part of this I examine two groundbreaking films; Jonathan Harvey's *Beautiful Thing* (Hettie MacDonald 1996, UK) and Daniel Ribeiro's *The Way He Looks* [*Hoje eu quero voltar sozinho*] (2014, Brazil), which, though separated by nineteen years in terms of production, offer similar insight into the representation of the queer guy and the straight girl, framing the affective youthful queer body as a site of feeling and agency. At the same time, I examine the revolutionary television series *Glee* (Fox 2009 to present, US) for its focus on the straight girl and queer guy relationship, within school (and university) drama, where contextual narratives foreground the abject position of the queer guy and the straight girl. Finally I look at *Gayby* (Jonathan Lisecki 2012, US) and *G.B.F.* (Darren Stein 2013, US), where the notion of the gay best friend for the straight female engages with discourses of youth in the former, and dating in the latter, relating the notion of having a child, and involves issues of commodity and masquerade. However, it is first important to consider the historical framing of youth and queer identity relative to realism evident in the 1960s.

Social Realism, Queer Identity and Youth in 1960s Film

Notions of social realism have always been problematic, with regards to the representation of queer men. The concept of the hetero media gaze has consequently framed the queer male as outside and abject, rather than as included and central. Although this book frames the increasing appearance of the queer male in the company of the straight girl, suggesting inclusivity, generally the queer male is subordinate to heterosexual order. As part of this Vito Russo (1987) reports in his groundbreaking book *The Celluloid Closet* that the representation of gay men and lesbians within Hollywood film had historically relied on stereotypical forms. For the queer man this often involved associations with effeminacy, deviancy or threat, constructing the queer male as abject and peripheral. Russo reports that gay men in Hollywood film were often represented as entertaining 'others' (Hall 1997), as 'sissies' (Bergling 2001) or as disposable murder victims, or as murderers themselves. While Russo's work considers films up to the late 1980s, even more recent films, which purport to offer a better sense of realism, such as *Brokeback Mountain* (Ang Lee 2005, US) and *A Single Man* (Tom Ford 2009, US), still foreground notions of otherness, difference and tragedy. Hence, although *Brokeback Mountain* presents a love story between two queer men, they are represented as outsiders, alone, and one must die; also, while *A Single Man* foregrounds a queer man as an accomplished, socially integrated central character, ultimately he loses his life. Although *A Single Man* is a positive representation of queer male life, in the original book by Christopher Isherwood a deep sense of tragedy is present. This is apparent where, when the lead character George meets his soulmate Jim, Isherwood notes that George's arteries began to harden, which we presume results in his demise in the film, where he dies of a heat attack (see Pullen 2014c). Hence these films still rely on reductive stereotypical notions of isolation, and punishment. This is problematic, as Richard Dyer ([1993] 2000) tells us that stereotypes 'do not only, in concert with social types, map out the boundaries of acceptable and legitimate behaviour, they also insist on boundaries exactly at those points where in reality there are none' (16). As Michael Pickering succinctly observes in his work *Stereotyping: The Politics of Representation* (2001):

> The stereotypical act of descriptive compression and assessment as it is serially reiterated serves to externalize, distance and exclude those so designated.

> It does so through constructing their 'difference' in terms which diverge from what is taken to be central, safe, normal and conventional. (48)

The reduction of personal character to simple traits of identity or recognition in this sense allows dominant groups to identify subordinate groups as bearing signs of 'difference', coding outsiders as disconnected to the mainstream.

While it may be difficult to imagine a film that does not rely on stereotypes, as they are often used as short cuts in relating social identities, there is a need to consider the representational needs of diverse minority groups, relative to issues of respect, social justice, equality and inclusivity. As Dyer ([1993] 2000) attests:

> How we are seen determines in part how we are treated; how we treat others is based on how we see them; such seeing comes from representation. [Therefore,] negative designations of a group have negative consequences for the lives of members of that grouping. (1–3)

For queer men (and lesbians), the reliance on stereotypes in film and television has limited the opportunities for positive and/or diverse identifications, restricting the construction of role models, which might offer some better sense of plurality and social realism to queer and mainstream audiences.

Despite this, attempts by media producers to integrate queer characters within political social settings, which may connect to new narratives of social realism, are evident not only in films of the New Queer Cinema (see Chapter 2); they also may be related to origins in transgressive independent cinema within the UK, relative to the focus on youth. While I have already discussed *A Taste of Honey* for its sympathetic representation of queer youth in this regard (see above, and Chapter 1), it is the subcultural iconographic potential of young adults, as framed within the transgressive films of 1960s UK, which offers such scope (see Hill 1986; Murphy 1992). For example, while a film like *The Leather Boys* (Sidney J. Furie 1964, UK) might foreground a queer youth for his desire to link with another male, it is more the focus on notions of youth rebellion and personal agency in finding the self which are central in defining a political discourse. At the same time a film like *To Sir, with Love* (James Clavell 1967, UK) may not explicitly represent queer identity, but through foregrounding young learners at school, willing to find their own pathways, inspired by an inspirational black teacher, notions of rebellion and individuality are central, framing youth as the new order. I argue that the British social realist films of the 1960s offered a new political and representational movement that defined young people as new storytellers.

As part of this the teenager is represented as a citizen, defined by financial commodity, relating to emergent new independence. As John Hill (1986) reports, the idea of the teenager 'was coined in the 1940s by American market researchers who wished to describe young people with money to spend on consumer goods' (10). The representations in the 1960s social realist films frame this potential for independence, set within a mise en scène of rebellion and a need to escape. Hence the youth characters in *A Taste of Honey*, *The Leather Boys* and *To Sir, with Love* are all represented as being in lower-class social and impoverished environments, as needing to escape and improve themselves. Following the notion of the 'kitchen sink drama', which in the 1960s foregrounded lower-class domestic environments as the setting where conversation would take place but there was a need to escape, these films offered hope for self-improvement. While such architectural iconography, focusing on the kitchen, related a need to modernise older buildings that had become run down or damaged since the Second World War in the United Kingdom, and there was need for new buildings, this domestic environment offered a sense of intimacy, and immediacy in forming new social realist narratives.

Central within this is the notion of subcultures, relative to the formation of social realist contexts:

> [S]ubcultures exist in relationship to the society from which they emerge, ... their existence may provide an insight into the experiences of young people, especially in areas of education work and leisure ... [C]ontemporary subcultures are involved in the act of self definition: groups of young people may collectively develop ways of differentiating themselves from others and, in the process of doing so, constitute and define themselves as a subcultural group. (Kehily 2007: 25)

Often subcultural groups are related to mass social communities, such as in the 1960s 'Skinheads', 'Mods' and 'Rockers', and more recently 'Punk', 'Emo' and 'Goth', which follow certain stylistic, cultural and social group membership conventions, often exhibited in public space (see Hebdige 1979). Despite this, there may be more introspective potential exhibited by queer youths who may not feel comfortable in joining mainstream subcultural groups. As part of this, queer young people might form their own subcultural worlds online (see Pullen 2014c; Pullen and Cooper 2010), framing a need for anonymity and self-protection. At the same time, queer young people may openly express their identities at home, in school and in the wider social world, despite not having the mainstream networks of support that may be afforded to heterosexual children or young people.[1] This is particularly evident in the representation of queer young people in *Glee* (discussed further below), where explicit subcultural potential is presented at school, framing issues of restriction and denial. As contextual to this I argue that *Beautiful Thing* and *The Way He Looks* engage with this potential, framing the youthful queer body, not only as needing exploration and respect but also in doing this foregrounding the straight girl as an enabler or an accomplice.

BEAUTIFUL THING AND THE WAY HE LOOKS

Jonathan Harvey's 1993 celebrated play *Beautiful Thing* was adapted, and released as a film in 1995. Produced by Channel 4 television and with the participation of Tony Garnett, a producer renowned for realist discourse (see Lacey 2012), *Beautiful Thing* offers an intimate connection between television and film realism. This is apparent in Channel 4's public service remit as a broadcaster and film producer to be innovative and to reflect public diversity (Annan Committee 1977), evident in Channel 4's early development through groundbreaking programming (Harvey 2000; Hobson 2008) representing queer identity. This included the prior production of the film *My Beautiful Laundrette* (Stephen Frears 1985, UK) (Geraghty, 2005), which focused on Hanif Kureishi's exploration of homosexuality, race and contemporary politics in the 1980s. Also it included Terence Davies's autobiographical film *The Long Day Closes* (1992, UK), which focuses on a queer youth growing up, identifying with cinema as an escape from isolation.

Daniel Ribeiro wrote the screenplay and directed the film *The Way He Looks*, releasing this in 2014, with the original title in Portuguese *Hoje eu quero voltar sozinho*. Produced and set in Brazil, *The Way He Looks* is a development of an earlier short film produced in 2010 by Ribeiro, with the original title in Portuguese *Eu não quero voltar sozinho*. It may be considered as contextual to his first short film *Café com leite* (2007) which foregrounds homosociality in relation to child care. As a product of a Brazilian independent film company, Lanuna Films, whilst *The Way He Looks* has received heightened attention on the international festival circuit, it has not been distributed in mainstream cinemas. Ribeiro's work may be considered as self-reflexive, as it includes narratives of his own life, particularly evident in *The Way He Looks* where he references a story concerning a male school friend who deliberately left his 'hoodie' with him, which led to their kissing, which appears in the film (Rogers 2015).

Although *Beautiful Thing* and *The Way He Looks* seem like entirely different texts, produced in different time frames, and coming from different countries with different original languages, I am discussing them together, for their relationship to the youthful queer body and the context of the straight girl. Both texts employ a straight girl as an ally or enabler within the text. However unlike the mainstream films *My Best Friend's Wedding* and *The Object of My Affection* (see Chapter 4), a central focus is placed upon the queer male rather than the straight girl. Hence, through the medium of social realism and

Figure 6.1 *Fabio Audi (left) as Gabriel, Tess Amorim (middle) as Giovana and Ghilherme Lobo (right) as Leonardo, a key friendship group in Daniel Ribeiro's* The Way He Looks. *Image courtesy of Daniel Ribeiro.*

independent cinema, the desires of the queer male are foregrounded, over those of the straight girl.

In *Beautiful Thing*, the central queer couple of Jamie and 'Ste' (Steve) are related to Leah, a young girl who is a neighbour to them, whose interest in the music of the 1960s group The Mamas & the Papas offers context to their relationship. In the *Way He Looks*, the best friend of the central character of Leonardo is a young girl called Giovana, who not only supports him with his disability as a blind person but also offers empathy, and finally resolve, after Leonardo couples with Gabriel (see Figure 6.1). Central within this is the context of domestic architecture and social space, which may be related to iconographic histories within the films of British social realism.

In *Beautiful Thing*, the narrative of Jamie and Ste, who develop a same-sex romantic and sexual attachment, frames them as neighbours within the setting of a low-income council housing 'tower block' estate (filmed in Thamesmead, south-east London). The straight girl Leah offers escape from this environment, through publicly broadcasting the music of The Mamas & the Papas, by playing her record player at high volume. In *The Way He Looks*, Leonardo, who is blind, is restricted in his domestic and social environment, needing the support of Giovana to take him from school, helping him navigate the journey to return home safely. As part of this, issues of tactility and empathy are central in both texts.

In *Beautiful Thing*, although Leah is not represented as physically, or necessarily socially, close to Jamie and Ste, references are made, through the couple identifying with her as wanting to escape the environment, overhearing her play *Make Your Own Kind of Music* by Momma Cass, as transgression, and self-identification. In contrast in *The Way He Looks*, Leonardo has direct physical contact with Giovana, who holds his hand to guide him safely back home. At the same time it is this learned trust with Giovana that enables Leonardo to then trust Gabriel, evident when he then takes over Giovana's role in guiding him home.

This juxtaposition of the body related to trust and feeling, contained within the domestic environment, is particularly evident in *Beautiful Thing*. Jamie harbours an internalised romantic affection for his schoolmate Ste, but is unable to demonstrate this within the public social space. However, Jamie and Ste are drawn together when Jamie's mother (a single parent) offers to protect Ste by allowing him to lodge in her household, when his family threatens him. Jamie and Ste have to share a bed (because of a lack of space in the household), and this stimulates a physical closeness, where through undressing Jamie discovers the signs of physical abuse on Ste's body, in bruises inflicted by his brother and father. Jamie applies 'peppermint' ointment to soothe Ste's bruised body, and the two become physically and emotionally close, resulting in an intimate relationship. Central within this is the notion of escape, in the manner that young people are represented as wanting to 'play their own kind of music', as emblematic of the music preferred by Leah.

This sense of rebellion and need to escape is also apparent in *The Way He Looks*, where Leonardo confides to Giovana that he wants to leave his local town, wishing to move to Los Angeles, through an exchange programme in the school. Also we understand that this is unlikely to be easily achieved, such a desire to leave his hometown is related to his feelings as an outsider, as both blind and queer. Giovana is represented as a central force in helping Leonardo achieve his goals, telling her career adviser that she wishes to do this with Leonardo, even though she is represented as preferring to stay at home. At the same time, the confidence that Leonardo has gained through his tactile relationship with Giovana, in her guiding him home, is developed when he gets closer to Gabriel. Notably, when Leonardo shows Gabriel how to read Braille, this enables them to get closer. Although at this point there is no explicit sexual desire between them, a sense of romance is developed through increased tactility. Gabriel jokes with Leonardo that he cannot understand Braille, and Leonardo may be making it up. Leonardo takes Gabriel's hand to show him how to read using his fingers, and while this happens Leonardo's mother enters the room to offer refreshments as they are studying, and they withdraw their hands as if implying embarrassment through realising their increased physical closeness.

Such a denial of physical closeness, however, is only temporary in *Beautiful Thing* and *The Way He Looks*, as both films close with a demonstration of same-sex intimacy in public space. Hence, while within interior domestic space, tactility, or the drive to tactility, is represented, both films offer a political representation of social realism, determining the need for a public demonstration of physical closeness.

In the closing sequences of *Beautiful Thing*, Jamie and Ste dance intimately together in the central social space of their tower block community, to the music of *Dream a Little Dream of Me* by The Mamas & the Papas. Offering an allusion to the final dance at a school disco, where the 'slow dance' is usually the closing musical number, Jamie and Ste invert the heterosexual norm, of hooking up with any leftover suitable sexual partner, and instead reference the romantic movies that Jamie and his mother enjoy watching on television together, connoting endurance and unending love. Making a link to the notion of youth rebellion, but framing this with regard to same-sex romantic encounters, the couple at the same time are joined in their dance, with Leah and Jamie's mother also dancing together. Hence two straight girls, a female friend and a mother, join in their transgressive public performance.

Similarly in *The Way He Looks*, public social space is queered, with the support of the straight girl. Leonardo, Gabriel and Giovana are represented as leaving the school building, passing the other school students, who include those who have taunted and oppressed Leonardo for being blind, and Giovana for being a reserved girl. While Giovana and Leonardo had fallen out earlier, as Giovana had expressed feelings for Gabriel, unaware at the time that he had feelings only for Leonardo, they are represented as reunited. As they pass the bullies, one of them shouts out, 'Look at that, Leonardo! The relationship is going strong, huh?' Gabriel is guiding Leonardo as they walk together, allowing the upper part of his arm to be held in order to aid this. Giovana accompanies the couple, walking alongside. On hearing this taunt, all three briefly stop walking, and are viewed from the rear, as if pausing in freeze frame. The camera closes in on Leonardo's hand, as it gently unclasps Gabriel's upper arm, as it gently slides down to hold his hand with a light caress of his thumb, in the manner that a romantic couple hold hands together in public. All three walk off confidently together, as the bullies laugh at each other in embarrassment. At this point the song *There Is Too Much Love* by Belle and Sebastian gradually fades in, referencing the first time that the couple danced together and became physically close. Within entirely different time frames and cultural settings, *Beautiful Thing* and *The Way He Looks* foreground the straight girl as in support of the queer guy. As part of this, I argue that both texts employ the conventions of social realism, as evident in the iconography and settings within 1960s British film. The focus on domestic social space, and the prioritisation of youth narratives, as an enabling force for change and rebellion, I argue, offers transgressive potential. At the same time the context of popular culture, and notably the significance of popular music, plays a central role, which I argue is also apparent in the following case study on *Glee*.

GLEE

Although unlike the other texts within this chapter *Glee* is a television series rather than a film, I am exploring its potential, relative to the notion of youth culture, and the drive to social realism. Also, while *Glee* represents a product of American culture – and may be considered as quite removed from *Beautiful Thing* as a contemporary British social realist film, and from *The Way He Looks* as an independent film produced in Brazil, reflecting social issues – I argue that linkages can be made regarding young people, queer identity and a focus on realism, as a stylistic convention that extends from ideologies within televisual form in the 1960s.

As part of this, John Caughie (2000) considers the emergence of 'serious drama' in the 1960s and 1970s, which reflected a shift in British television drama as reliant on formats of naturalism defined by the historical influence of theatre, and the emergence of realism, produced as a stylistic convention. Tracing the influence of Troy Kennedy Martin, who argued that 'television drama . . . is ultimately not created by writers who write scripts for actors to speak, but by directors who integrate sound, lighting, editing and design into images and movement' (2000: 97), Caughie records the changing form of television drama which would more explicitly connect with issues of performance and framing in attempting to create a political social realism. Such processes involving the improving technology of the television camera, able to be more mobile and less fixed to the static studio environment, allied drama more close to documentary. This influenced opportunities for mise en scène, where there was less of a reliance on confined studio-based sets, where traditional plays were often staged to seem like the normative domestic environment, and more mobility was offered, broadening the representational scope. As George Brandt (1981) reports, 'the new flexibility made it possible, in the manner of Italian neorealism, to bring in non professionals, to tap greater spontaneity in the actors, and give a greater feeling of verisimilitude to a production all around' (19). Hence, evoking the cinematic potential of Italian neorealism, where a film like *Bicycle Thieves* (Vittorio de Sica 1948, Italy) foregrounded non-professional actors, and the camera moved freely within diverse social settings, a new sense of stylistic realism was created. In *Bicycle Thieves*, telling the story of a family where through unemployment the father has to take a lower-paid job cleaning windows, issues of abjection, morality and pride are central in mediating a visceral story of human struggle and responsibility.

The British television drama *Cathy Come Home* (BBC 1966, UK), which involved Jeremy Sandford as the screenwriter, Tony Garnett as the producer and Ken Loach as the director, evoked this potential, telling the story of a young couple who become homeless due to problems in the welfare state at a time of unemployment (see Leigh 2002). Including an aesthetic realism evident in a diverse range of outdoor shooting locations, using mobile cameras, and including documentary footage intercut with scripted and improvised content, the drama would offer significant political impact to mainstream audiences. As a result of foregrounding this personal story, framing the abject oppression of everyday people, changes in the law were made, offering better support to families where the father had become unemployed. While it is not my intent to provide links between representations in film or television drama and possible responses from audiences that might lead to social change, the development of television drama in relation to aesthetic and stylistic realism, particularly evident in the 1960s, I argue, offers a cultural foundation which is enduring. This has included a diverse range of socially aware television dramas that have represented queer youth, such as *Oranges Are Not the Only Fruit* (BBC 1990, UK) and *The Buddha of Suburbia* (BBC 1993, UK), the soap opera *Brookside* (Channel 4 1982–2003, UK), the school educational drama *The Two of Us* (BBC 1987, UK), and the teen dramas *As If* (Channel 4 2001, UK), *Sugar Rush* (Channel 4 2005–6, UK) and *Dawson's Creek* (Warner Bros 1998–2003, US) (see Pullen 2007b; 2014c).

Notably, the focus on the straight girl and the queer guy within contemporary televisual dramatic form connects to new notions of politicised social realism, extending from this foundation, where the opportunities for youth are presented as some new kind of veracity. In the manner that stylistic conventions were challenged by the opportunity of new modes of social realist drama, I argue that *Glee* connects to this potential, through framing outsiders as challenges to order, integrating popular cultural references through the medium of the popular song.

As a popular television drama series which in 2015 is currently in production, *Glee* frames notions of diversity in referencing mainstream culture. Originally broadcast in 2009 on the Fox network in the United States, at the outset the series focuses on the life chances of a diverse range of teenage school students, and their engagement with a glee club, a social club organised in school where students may sing and dance, in recreation and competition. After the fourth series the setting changes from the school environment set in Lima, Ohio, to include New York, where a number of the students have moved to develop their singing and dancing careers. The regular cast of characters includes an inspirational teacher as a leader (Will Schuester) and a diverse range of school students. Central within this is the focus on social diversity, with particular attention to sexual diversity, including the characters of Kurt Hummell and Blaine Anderson as a gay male couple, Santana Lopez as a lesbian and Brittany S. Pierce as a female bisexual. The lead heterosexual female character is Rachel Berry.

While in terms of genre *Glee* seems like a light entertainment teen drama, for its focus on organised and coached singing performances (see Sarkissian 2014), I argue that it offers senses of social realism in its attempt to represent social and sexual diversity. Hence, in the manner that the British social realist dramas of the 1960s advanced the constituent conventions of the form, through blending drama and documentary forms, *Glee*, in its focus on diverse youth, uses the notion of performance to signify veracity, in relation to subaltern identity. As part of this, the coupling between the central straight girl Rachel Berry (played by Lea Michele) and the central queer guy Kurt Hummell (played by Chris Colfer) offers a dynamic of engagement, challenging the notion of the hetero media gaze.

Rachel is coded as a supporter of queer identity at the outset of the first series, as we are aware that she has two male parents who are gay. While we rarely see her queer fathers, she is constructed as a straight girl who has familial connection to queer identity politics, inherent in family ties. Despite this intimate connection to queerness, in the first series Rachel is cast as in competition to her peer Kurt, the central queer guy in *Glee*. This is primarily evident, as both characters want to be the lead singer of the musical group that they perform in within the glee club, The New Directions. While later, as the series develops, Rachel and Kurt become best friends, living together in New York, as they pursue their dreams in higher education and the entertainments industry, their relationship may be coded as the archetypal straight girl and queer guy alliance. However, following the social realist conventions of the series, their relationship is mediated through performance sequences, as much as through quotidian dialogue.

However the central relationship between Rachel and Kurt forms a mirror reflecting and contextualising its gaze, referencing social realist narratives, not explicitly connected to the main characters. For example the narrative of queer youth suicide is referenced to Kurt, reflecting the vulnerability of queer youth, evident in the story of a fellow student, David Karofsky, who in season three attempts suicide in response to being identified as gay. Kurt is represented as bullied by David, who suppresses his homosexual desires, but ultimately it is Kurt who supports David after his suicide attempt. In many ways, this is directly related to the life experience of the actor Chris Colfer, who works with the Trevor Project (2011), an organisation that supports suicidal queer youth. In this sense, although Kurt is not represented as a vulnerable suicidal youth himself, this contextual narrative vivifies the discursive possibilities of the subject area, through mirroring by placing this on another character as contextual. At the same time, Rachel is also subject to this process, of reflective identification contextualising social realism, specifically apparent in the episode titled 'Choke'.

This eighteenth episode of season three is significant with regard to the relationship between Rachel and Kurt. In this episode both characters have auditions for NYDA (the New York Academy of Drama and Arts), a fictional higher education performing arts body. This represents the culmination of all their engagement with the glee club, as graduating to NYDA would allow them to embark on a higher level of study, potentially leading to professional careers as singers and performers. The notion of mirroring is evident at the outset, where the title sequence of the episode closes with Rachel gazing at herself in a dressing room mirror, saying to herself. 'You are a star Rachel Berry, and in just two days from now, you are going to shine so bright on that stage, that the sun is going to cry with envy. You know when your time is, and it's now.' This sense of egoistic representation seems unusual, but it forms part of the structural conventions of the series, which involves fast editing pace, moving from one sequence to another with punctuation and haste, evident where this sequence closes with the sound of a drum roll, as if providing an ironic exclamation mark.

Hence, the episode frames the lead character of Rachel, as confident in her pursuits, opening the episode with her discourse. At the same time, her desires are inherently linked to Kurt, who also has an audition. However, Kurt is represented as unsure of his ability, evident when he decides to change his choice of audition song, but Rachel offers him advice on this.

> Rachel: I just talked to Blaine and he told me about [you singing] *Not the Boy Next Door*. You cannot sing that for your NYDA audition.
>
> Kurt: I need to be excited about this, and this is the first time that I have been inspired in this process.
>
> Rachel: It's too controversial. You can't repeat Peter Allen's gold lamé pants!
>
> Kurt: It was too controversial in 1962. Look, the play, and that song, won Hugh Jackman a Tony, and NYDA is a Broadway school.
>
> Rachel: But you haven't rehearsed it enough. I am not singing *Don't Rain on My Parade* as it's my go-to song, and because it's impossible for me not to cry when I sing it, but because I have been belting out that song since I was two years old. This is the biggest moments of your lives. We cannot be taking risks.
>
> Kurt: Isn't that the exact moment to take a risk?

This exchange between Rachel and Kurt foregrounds Rachel's reliance on comfort and the everyday, rejecting the idea of taking risks and going against the grain. However, Kurt wants to parody his identification as a queer male through singing a controversial song, involving an over-stylised performance, wearing lamé shorts and thrusting his body in a provocative and sexualised way. By the point of his audition he had heeded the advice of Rachel, and was going to sing a song he was familiar with, *Phantom of the Opera*. However, after sensing the uninterested response of the teacher holding the audition, implying that this might not be so interesting, he reverts to his original plan, and does perform *Not the Boy Next Door*, in the manner described above.

While the teacher responds well to Kurt's audition, Rachel follows her own advice in singing *Don't Rain on My Parade*, but in doing this falters, ruining her audition. While we find out later in the series that Kurt's performance was not sufficient to get him into NYDA, and conversely Rachel gets another chance at an audition, and does go to NYDA, it is the focus on Rachel which is central here. Although Rachel's desires to advance her career seem central in this episode, I argue that a contextual narrative of violence against females in fact counterpoints and contextualises Rachel's emotion and feelings, suggesting a different narrative bias.

This narrative is evident where the school sports coach, Beiste, a female character who presents a masculinised appearance, arrives in school with bruising to her face. While some students make jokes about this, Sue Sylvester, the leader of the cheerleading squad, advises students not to make fun of the notion of domestic abuse. Initially Coach Beiste tells the students that her bruises were not domestic abuse but were the result of an accident. However, when the students are 'taken to task' to understand the problems of domestic abuse, and they perform a seemingly inappropriate musical number where a female punishes an abusive male, Coach Beiste tells Sue Sylvester that in fact she has been abused by her male partner. While later it appears that Coach Beiste has moved out of her abusive domestic environment, and is praised by her friends at school for her bravery, we find out that in fact she has returned to her abusive partner.

Hence, the reflective mirror where Rachel gazes upon herself, although seeming like a reference to her ego, in fact is a reference to her insecurity as a female. The representation of Coach Beiste as subject to domestic violence is not a counterpoint in a different place, it is a reflection of female vulnerability, evident in Rachel's own failing to perform well in her audition. These contextual points of emotional stress and abuse frame a social realist narrative, that of feminine vulnerability. Although Rachel herself is not represented as subject to domestic violence, her humiliation within the audition process is a saturated site of feeling which connects the two narratives. In a similar manner that Kurt is connected to David Karofsky as a suicidal queer teen, Rachel is inherently bonded to Coach Beiste, as subject to feelings of isolation and vulnerability.

Hence, through counterpointing narratives of stylistic performative excess, in union with and alongside social realist narratives, such as exploring queer youth suicide and domestic abuse against females (evident in the case studies above), the series offers a complex site of performance and feeling. While the straight girl and the queer guy in *Glee* seem like observers and outsiders to the visceral problems of isolation, confrontation and periphery that might be shared by females and queer men alike, it is the performative juxtaposition of youth, as evident in these case stdies, that frames as much as providing answers. Such a focus on problems is also evident in the final case studies in this chapter, focusing on *Gayby* (2012) and *G.B.F.* (2013); however, there are more explicit references to masquerade and commodity, evident in the independent film form.

GAYBY AND G.B.F.

Produced within two years of each other, *Gayby* (2012) and *G.B.F.* (2013) reflect a changing filmic representational landscape for the straight girl and the queer guy. This includes not only the films discussed in Chapter 4 and *Beautiful Thing* (1995) (see above) but also *A Single Man* (Tom Ford 2009, US), which foregrounded the female best friend as a narrative device in considering the life world of an older academic who is contemplating suicide (see above), and *Clueless* (Amy Heckerling 1995, US), a school-based drama where a central female character presents herself as an expert in matchmaking but discovers that her love interest is actually gay. Hence, an appetite for the gay best friend had evolved, stimulated by a shifting representational landscape within both film and television. Central within this might be the emergence of the television series *Glee* (see above) for its youth-oriented cast and a wide range of friendship networks supporting gay and lesbian sexuality.

Certainly the influence of *Glee* and the precedence of *Clueless* may be apparent in considering the textual content of *G.B.F.*, which focuses on the notion of the gay best friend within high school. At the same time, whilst *Gayby* focuses on characters who are aged between mid and late twenties, the film evokes the context of the teenager and youthfulness, evident in a naivety expressed towards dating and the notion of raising a child. Despite this, although *G.B.F.* and *Gayby* may seem disparate in context, provenance and representation, I argue that, in signalling diverse social worlds, school and early adult life, they are inherently connected, not only as regards the time frame but also in foregrounding confidence in representing the life chances of queer males. Hence, rather than assigning the queer male as a sidekick, or as a lesser valued social construct, as may be apparent in films like *My Best Friend's Wedding*, *The Object of My Affection* and *The Next Best Thing* (see Chapter 4), the representation of the queer male in these two films is more developed, with him seeming to take an equal or shared role as storyteller. Notably, *G.B.F.* foregrounds the personal narrative of the central gay male character, evident in the use of voiceover, as if reading the dialogue from a diary. While in *Gayby* it seems that the straight girl is the central character; both characters are represented as working together with equality.

Both films offer a critique of contemporary life, framing the life chances of the queer guy and the straight girl, who might engage with the queer guy. While in *Gayby* the critique mostly concerns the desires of the straight girl, who wants to produce a child with her gay best friend, in *G.B.F.* the notion of possessing a gay best friend is critiqued. Despite this, both films involve diverse generic influences in creating these critiques.

G.B.F. may be considered as a whimsical, popular-culture-oriented school teen drama. Foregrounding two gay male youth characters who have been concealing their sexuality, the central narrative revolves around the seemingly comical desires of a range of diverse straight girls, who want to have a gay best friend as a social trophy. Such a desire is apparent, as supposedly within the school there are no openly gay males. The lead queer youth male character, Tanner (who provides the narrative voiceover), is encouraged by his gay friend Brent to create a profile on Guydar (an allusion to Gaydar, a gay dating site) in order to find a boyfriend. However, the school's Gay Straight Alliance, in wanting to trace gay kids for the group, detects the GPS location of his phone and as a consequence makes Tanner come out at school. However, rather than his joining the alliance, a range of popular girls vie for his attention, wanting him to be part of their social group as their gay best friend. While Tanner initially socialises with these girls, and they encourage him to adopt the stereotypical persona, fashion sense and deportment of the imagined gay best friend (see Figure 6.2), this distances him from his best friend Brent, who prefers to be anonymous. Later at the school prom, when Tanner and Fawcett (one of the popular girls) win the prom king and prom queen awards, he realises his failure to support Brent, and the film closes with a suggestion that Tanner and Brent will become romantically involved.

In contrast, *Gayby* may be considered as a quirky, eccentric social realist drama, focusing on gay male Matt and his female best friend Jenn, whom he once had sex with when they were at college. Significantly the roles of Jenn and Matt are played by actors Jenn Harris and Matt Wilkas, adding senses of realism, through the characters adopting, the real-life names of the actors. At the same time the openly gay director Jonathan Lisecki also appears in the

Figure 6.2 *The queer male youth character Tanner (Michael J. Willett, centre) is coached on what images he should include on his phone by his new friendship group of straight girls: Fawcett (Sasha Pieterse, back left), Caprice (Xosha Roquemore, back centre) and 'Shley (Andrea Bowen, back right) in* G.B.F.

film as a supporting character, Nelson, offering a self-reflexive context with regard to production and acting. The narrative focuses on Jenna, who wants to have a baby with Matt, and they embark on a utilitarian routine of having sex together so this will happen. Matt and Jenn have a number of close gay male friends, who offer support to them both in their desire to have a baby. At the same time whilst they are attempting this process, both Matt and Jenn attempt to date, and/or have sex with, imagined ideal partners. As part of this Jenn has sex with a man who is decorating her apartment, and, when a condom accidentally breaks, it makes it possible that he could be the father of her child, when she finds out that she is pregnant. When Matt finds out about this, he rejects Jenn, as there was an agreement that she would not have unprotected sex while they were trying for a baby. Later both Matt and Jenn make up, and the film closes with a scene one year later, when both Jenn and Matt are happy with their baby and their respective new partners, and there is no concern whether Matt is the father or not.

Both films critique the notion of the gay best friend as a commodity. While in *Gayby* this concerns a focus on the ability to provide sperm, and to provide help in raising a baby, in *G.B.F.* this concerns the actual cultural capital that girls may gain through 'possessing' a gay best friend. Notably in *G.B.F.*, a key sequence early in the film foregrounds this potential, framing the idea of possession. Tanner has just come out as gay at school (after the incident discussed above), and a straight guy is manhandling him, holding him up in front of the school lockers. Fawcett (one of the popular girls) rescues Tanner, by threatening to punish the oppressor, by spreading details of his small penis to the school if he does not let go. In the manner that an effeminate or lesser abled prisoner might be rescued or 'bought' within prison, Tanner is owed to Fawcett. In the following sequence, he socialises, drinking coffee with Fawcett and other popular girls who are competing for his friendship:

> Fawcett: So you're a gay now.
>
> Tanner: Not now, I mean I have always been. Just now everybody knows.
>
> Caprice: Are you going to audition for the spring musical? Cos we are going to do the *Wiz*, and we are going to need as many minorities as we can get.
>
> Tanner: I am not much for the whole singing, or dancing or being on stage thing.
>
> Caprice: Are you sure you're a mo? I mean what gay stuff you like, like?
>
> Tanner: I am into comics.
>
> Fawcett: Like Kathy Griffin? She's hilar.
>
> Tanner: No, like comic books.
>
> Fawcett: That's not gay. That's just lame! You don't even sound like the [gays] on Bravo. Say the word 'Fierce'.
>
> Tanner: I don't really say that word.

This scene foregrounds stereotypical ideas connected to the gay best friend. This includes the stereotypes of 'being' a gay, as if assuming a performed identity and being interested in performing; having a connection to gay men (or supporters of gay men like Kathy Griffin) who appear in popular entertainment, such as appearing on the television channel Bravo; and not being interested in regular cultural things such as comic books, and consequently not appearing as gay.

This parodist and ironic sequence clearly critiques the idea that gay men appear as, or necessarily naturally assume, a homogeneous identity in the everyday world. At the same time in terms of the gaze, whilst the popular girls gaze upon the queer guy as a cultural and social asset, they imagine him as a stereotypical form, in a sense displaced from the reality of the person they are gazing upon. Hence, there is a duality in the gaze related to wish-fulfilment and determination, questioning the ability to contain or possess. Even when they transform Tanner to appear as the ideal gay best friend, taking him to fashionable clothing shops and changing his attire, Tanner actually rejects this signification, desiring instead to make amends with the friends he had neglected. Hence the notion of transformation is in fact a stereotypical imagination, which is revealed to be insubstantial. Whilst such a failure of the oppressive heterocentric gaze does not necessarily transform the 'normative' world, the film raises questions about the role of stereotypes evident in the formation of the gaze.

Similarly to the earlier films that focus on the straight girl and queer guy (see Chapters 1 and 3), the stereotypical composition of the gaze as inherently focused on the adherence of normative gender roles is central here. Not only in *G,B,F,* does Tanner reveal himself to be rather more masculine than had initially been determined by the straight girls who are interested in him, but also in *Gayby* the gaze and the deportment of the straight girl offers interesting intersections between feminine and masculine stereotypical forms that challenge notions of social reality.

This is particularly noticeable in a sequence where Jenn comes over to Matt's apartment, while Matt is meeting a new date, Adrian, whom Matt is unsure of, due to Adrian's excessive interest in sex. Jenn arrives, sitting on the sofa between the two possible queer male lovers, in some senses saving Matt from an inappropriate sexual encounter which is unlikely to be romantic.

> Matt: Jenn, this is . . .
>
> Adrian: . . . is Adrian! . . .
>
> Jenn: Matt always forgets names when he meets people. His mom smoked when she was pregnant.
>
> Matt: Jenn!
>
> Jenn: What, it's true! Oh [and I brought my suitcases here as] I am having my apartment painted, and it's not good for me to be around the fumes when we are having a baby . . .
>
> Adrian: Oh the city needs more children.
>
> Jenn: [to Matt] So can I stay for a few days? . . . Oh and I think today is day one, I thought that is was going to be tomorrow, but the thermometer says it's today. [Jenn looks at Adrian with relish]
>
> Adrian: This is so my cue to leave. [Adrian gets up to leave]
>
> Jenn: Thanks for getting him ready.
>
> Adrian: Sure, have fun breeding.

Hence Jenn's gaze directs the social environment, intervening in the romance and sex life of Matt, suggesting that Adrian might be useful in stimulating Matt's sexual arousal, so he can efficiently perform when she and Matt have sex for the purpose of procreation. At the same time she breaks the imagined rules of Jenn and Matt's arrangement, which was supposed to preserve their individuality. While in many ways her overdetermination is part of the stylistic convention of the film, which employs eccentric and quirky dialogue, a focus is made upon Jenn as the major narrative force, while Matt remains a subsidiary. Such a relationship frames Jenn as the more masculine and the beholder of the dominant gaze, particularly evident when Matt describes her as 'the only man for me', after defending his reason for rejecting Adrian.

Similarly to the straight girls in *My Best Friend's Wedding* and *The Object of My Affection* (see Chapter 3), Jenn appears to masquerade as the heterosexual male within the relationship. As part of this she represents a queering of male and female subjectivity, in some senses coding the queer male as more vulnerable than her. As Mark Finch discusses with regards to representations of the male body:

> It seems to me that the pleasure for female spectators is in seeing men treated like women, rather than the pleasure of seeing nudity itself: a textual equality to match representations of strong women. (Finch 1986: 28)

While Jenn and Matt often appear in bed, seeming subject to each other's gaze, and both characters appear coy and inexperienced, Jenn is suggested as possessing the dominant gaze. Notably, early in the film when Jenn and Matt first get into bed, and Matt masturbates on his side of the bed in order that he can achieve sexual arousal through thinking of male sexual partners before inseminating her, Jenn asks to look at his penis, commenting on its large size. Hence from the outset, while both seem vulnerable and there is a sense of equality, Jenn is constructed as possessing the dominant gaze, presented as a masquerade of male identity.

However, as Mary Anne Doane (1982) suggests with regards to female masquerade as offering a philosophical context (see Chapter 1), Jenn foregrounds traits of masculine identity and authority, blending her excessive female identity as a potential mother and object of procreation, making connections as much as revealing distances. Hence through Jenn masquerading as male, evident in possessing the dominant gaze, rather than necessarily subjecting the queer male as feminine and abject, she reflects problems inherent in the dominant masculine gaze itself.

Ultimately this is apparent in the film, where the audience are denied knowledge as to the paternity of the baby, connoting a social realist ethic that care of a child is more important than knowledge of its essential parenthood. While it is suggested that Matt may not be the father of the child, as Jenn had sex with the decorator of her apartment and the condom broke, no attempts are made to ascertain who is the 'real' father. Also Matt, as a retailer and an author of graphic novels, produces a new comic that foregrounds the baby as a science fiction superhero, in a magazine titled 'Gayby', framing a disconnection from social reality.[2] Hence the child produced by the sexual and social engagement between the straight girl and the queer guy remains outside the forensic symbolic, cultural and social order. This narrative culmination establishes the desiring sexual gaze as uncertain and unfulfilled. While in *The Object of My Affection* and *The Next Best Thing* (see Chapter 3), issues of biological paternity are central in determining how the queer guy relates to the notion of fatherhood, in *Gayby* a sense of suspension remains. I argue that this sense of suspension denies the fulfilment of the gaze. Whether Jenn masquerades as a man or a heterosexual man or alternatively a queer man is the father of the child, seems irrelevant, it is not the gender performative possibilities that are central but the realisation that working together makes more sense than knowing exactly who we are.

Hence, *G.B.F.* and *Gayby* negotiate complex issues of social identity that frame young people, or young adults, as central protagonists in challenging the 'normative' dominant order. Through connecting the queer guy with the straight girl, not only is a sense of alliance and union presented but also mutual respect is learned or worked through, in establishing some kind of order. Whether living your life out within school, or considering the need to raise a child, the queer guy in concert with the straight girl expresses the insightfulness and immediacy of teen and youth identity, in sharing their lived worlds and working towards goals.

Conclusion

Youth and teen identity may be seen as a central force in addressing mainstream audiences, with regards to the contemporary narratives of growing up and working towards adulthood. The notion of the teenager as a cultural commodity, able to break down barriers of class and identity, offers scope for the democratic representation of sexual diversity. *Beautiful Thing* and *The Way He Looks*, although diverse in form, context and cultural provenance, foreground the potential for queer male same-sex romance, in a social realist manner. Focusing on the queer body as an affective site of feeling and emotion, making connections to rightful citizenship, the straight girl plays a central role in framing this narrative potential, establishing herself as a central supporter, rather than as a dominant protagonist.

Although this places the emphasis on the life chances of the queer male rather than the straight girl, duality is present, through positioning the female as abject, alongside the queer male. This sense of veracity, which I argue connects to the formal and stylistic foundations of 1960s British social realism in film and television, is equally present in the television series *Glee*. Although a teen-focused school drama, which utilises popular cultural references and particularly uses the popular song, *Glee*, like the transgressive television dramas of the 1960s, which blended documentary and fictional forms, offers political commentary on meaningful social issues. Hence, although *Glee* seems to focus on the life chances of youthful, but indulgent, light entertainment performers, through performative juxtaposition and context the series counterpoints meaningful social narratives such as queer youth suicide and the domestic abuse of females (see above). Through exploring these important issues, as contextual to the main characters, the social realist potential is emboldened through association, offering an indirect emotional context, rather than explicit direction.

This sense of emotional context, rather than direct address, I argue, is an important factor in addressing mainstream audiences. The central characters represent the mainstream audience, and it is for them to try and understand, to place the narrative world within a wider context that they can understand or feel. For teen audiences this is particularly pertinent, as they are working through their life chances, trying to understand the way ahead. As Jenn and Matt in *Gayby* try to have a baby, at the same time incorporating their preferred dating regime with others, and the characters of *GBF* try to comprehend that the gay best friend is not an asset, or resource but a person 'just like you', some sense of context, and distance, in looking upon or watching over, is needed to put these ideas in place.

Like the 1960s social realist films and television dramas, there is an acknowledgement that 'reality' is never achievable, and only an understanding of representational context and politics, in reference to the larger cultural and social world, makes sense. Teen identity, relative to notions of ritual, consumption and determination, offers a wide scope of possibility, and engagement, in working through these ideas. The fact that the lead character, Leonardo, in *The Way He Looks* is not only a queer male youth but is also blind suggests that he may be doubly abject and peripheral: it is his ability to touch as much as see that enables him to place in context not only the frame that he may sense but also the distance from the frame that informs his sense of understanding, and feeling.

The teen and youth representation of the straight girl and the queer guy within film and television contextualises the way ahead, building upon the formal potential of social realism. This does not necessarily reveal the way it is, or the way it should be, seen, but does imply the importance of context, distance and questioning, in working through the lived potentials that may be possible.

NOTES

1. Clearly queer young people are vulnerable, particularly with regard to the instance of suicide (Dorias and Lajeunesse 2004; Cover 2012). As part of this, the Trevor Project (2011) offers a support network to queer young people contemplating suicide. Also the It Gets Better Project (2011) offers a resource designed for varying individuals to upload personal videos of support.
2. It's interesting to note that prior to *G.B.F.* within *Queer as Folk* (discussed in Chapter 5) lead characters Justin and Michael similarly produce a queer superhero graphic magazine, entitled *Rage*.

Conclusion

The representation of the straight girl and the queer guy within film and television is a complex source of identification. This book has offered a glimpse into this subject area, foregrounding the notion of the hetero media gaze, which may be considered as the dominant viewing processes of western media production worlds that address, and try to represent, heterosexual audiences. This may be coded as both post-feminist and neoliberal (see Introduction), for its focus on dominant identity forms relating use and exchange, as much as a potential for transgression. As part of this, and subject to, the hetero media gaze, the 'unlikely coupling' of the straight girl and the queer guy is contiguous of everyday male and female coupling, seeming like a coding of 'normality'.

However, there is a bias of representation that foregrounds not only heterosexuality as the dominant coupling form but also male identity as the ultimate force. For the representation of the straight girl and the queer guy, a sense of instability is apparent, in that both the straight girl and the queer guy are independently and separately coded as the 'superior' identity form. The female being heterosexual may be connected to the everyday, and especially within the medium of television may be considered as the focus of attention, and also the subject that domestic media address (see Chapter 4). While the queer guy does not have the privilege of heterosexuality, nevertheless, as male he bears the cultural and social capital of masculine order, and consequently can exert a sense of power.

Hence, there is a bifurcated potential within the union of the straight girl and the queer guy, which reveals both characters as vying for attention, even if they are seemingly in collaboration. However, generally the straight girl is represented as the dominant identity, and hence, in many representations within this book, the focus is upon her life chances, potentially limited (but in some cases enriched) through her coupling with the queer guy. This is not so surprising, as mainstream media do address dominant audiences, and there is an expectation of mirroring, or at least respect for them. Hence, considering Hollywood film, from the early subliminal queer films of Doris Day (see Chapter 1) through to more recent explicit representations in films starring

Julia Roberts, Jennifer Aniston and Madonna (see Chapter 3), a female focus saturates the celluloid frame, offering little scope for meaningful queer representation, or challenge to order. This is not so dissimilar in television, where from early texts such as *Love Sidney* through to later texts such as *Will and Grace*, and more complicated contemporary 'bisexual' texts such as *Bob and Rose* and *Girls*, heterosexual female sexual desire is not only dominant and overarching but also insidious and invasive, suggesting that it cannot be resisted.

Despite this, not only do the films of the New Queer Cinema such as those by Derek Jarman and Gregg Araki foreground queer male desire in the context of heterosexual female identity (see Chapter 2) but a substrate exists that needs little excavation to find stronger queer male roles, and there is a better sense of union with the straight girl. For example, not only does the contemporary television series *Looking* (see Chapter 4) offer a developed relationship between the straight girl and the queer guy but also films of independent cinema such as *Beautiful Thing* and *The Way He Looks* (see Chapter 6) offer an affective presence where the queer body is represented as feeling, and fully functioning.

However, mainstream media prefer to contain the relationship between the straight girl and the queer guy as somewhere in stasis, rather than as offering a prospect to arrive, for either party. This sense of in-betweenness or impossibility is vividly represented in the documentary and reality television texts (see Chapter 5). The real-life 'straight girl' Dora Carrington's eternal bond to the 'queer guy' Lytton Strachey is represented as impossible, despite such deep devotion between the two. Carrington's final act of suicide punctuates this sense of destiny, through foregrounding the notion of loyalty. At the heart of this is the concept of alliance relating shared experience. Even in the controversial documentary *My Husband Is Not Gay*, which supplants the positive prospect of gay identity for the problem of same-sex attraction, the straight girl and the queer guy are bonded through feeling and shared humanity, rather than shared desires for the male body, and ephemeral camaraderie. Pret and Megan's shared grief for the loss of their child foregrounds a union based on deep mutual respect, relative to shared experience, something that transcends the problem, or opportunity, of sexual desire.

Hence while the hetero media gaze frames the straight girl and the queer guy as objects of the dominant desiring gaze, a sense of transgression and rebellion comes not from relating their co-dependent situation as outside, implying that they are near, or possibly could just fit within, the frame, but rather it is evident in relating their context as bodies that *are* absent.

While it is possible to argue that the straight girl and the queer guy are present, clearly evident in the many instances discussed in this book, in the manner that liminal performance actually reiterates the frame (see Chapter 5) there is little use in possessing an identity that is subordinate to another identity. The representation for the straight girl and the queer guy may seem like a substitute for a real representation between a heterosexual man and woman, but I would argue that it is only through recognising their absence from the frame that we can progress.

Each bearing the signification of power, but also otherness; the straight girl as heterosexual, but also female, and the queer guy as male, but also queer, share a vivid sense of presence as absence, within the hetero media gaze. In the manner that Geoffrey within the social realist drama *A Taste of Honey* (see Chapter 1) appears like a ghost after he is expelled from the possible domestic home where he might have raised a child with a straight girl, as simulacrum he can never be the real thing but always a representation. The promise of Geoffrey's life was taken away, but he remains for ever fixed in the audience's imagination as a ghostly form, wandering around a bonfire in the presence of children playing and socialising as the night draws in around him.

Even though the ghostly form may be vivified, seeming to become real, like the dilemma of presenting the real, the relationship between what really exists and what we can really represent reveals the importance of absence more than presence. The straight girl and the queer guy as an absent coupling in the mainstream does not rely on how we might read it, or even what it might mean in post-feminist and neoliberal contexts, but it reveals that the gaze does not result in an identity. As part of this the gaze upon the straight girl and the queer guy is process-based, implying that this coupling is not fully formed nor homogeneous.

Despite this, the representation of the straight girl and the queer guy, as an incomplete continuum, may continue to 'resonate' in varying media forms, through recognising absence, rather than presence. In the manner that the character of Leonardo in *The Way He Looks*, as blind, cannot rely on sight, but sees things clearly, social and cultural space is formed through understanding, rather than creation. This sense of stylistic and process-based 'social realism', foregrounded in relation to young people, offers not only new ways of seeing but also ways of seeing-through, redefining absence as presence.

Select Filmography

Beautiful Thing (1996), film drama, 85 minutes. Director: Hettie MacDonald. Screenwriter: Jonathan Harvey. Producers: Tony Garnett and Bill Shapter. Film Four, UK.

Bob and Rose (2001), television drama series, 6 × 47 minutes. Directors: Joe Wright and Julian Farino. Screenwriter: Russell T. Davies. Producer: Ann Harrison-Baxter. Co-producer: Russell T. Davies. Red Production Company, UK.

Boy Meets Boy (2003), reality television series, 6 × 50 minutes. Creators: Douglas Ross, Dean Minerd and Tom Campbell. Executive Producers: Douglas Ross, Greg Stewart, Kathleen French and Dean Minerd. Co-executive Producers: Tom Campbell and Kirk Marcolina. Evolution Film and Tape for NBC/Bravo, US.

Cabaret (1972), film drama, 124 minutes. Director: Bob Fosse. Screenwriter: Jay Presson Allen. Original source writing credits: Christopher Isherwood, Joe Masteroff and John Van Druten. Producer: Cy Feueur. Associate Producer: Harold Nebenzal. Allied Artists Pictures, US.

Caravaggio (1986), biographical film drama, 93 minutes. Director: Derek Jarman. Screenwriter: Nicholas Ward Jackson. Writing credit: Derek Jarman. Producer: Sarah Radclyffe. Executive Producers: Colin MacCabe and Nicholas Ward Jackson. Development Producer: James McKay. British Film Institute, UK.

Carrington (1995), biographical film drama, 121 minutes. Director: Christopher Hampton. Screenwriter: Christopher Hampton. Original writer of biography: Michael Holroyd. Producers: John McGrath and Ronald Shedlo. Associate Producer: Chris Thompson. Executive Producers: Frances Boespflug, Phillippe Carcassonne and Fabienne Vonnier. Polygram Filmed Entertainment, UK.

Carry On Camping (1969), film drama, 88 minutes. Director: Gerald Thomas. Screenwriter: Talbot Rothwell. Produced: Peter Rogers. Rank Organisation, UK.

Carry On Cleo (1964), film drama, 92 minutes. Director: Gerald Thomas. Screenwriter: Talbot Rothwell. Original writer: William Shakespeare. Produced: Peter Rogers. Associate Producer: Frank Bevis. Anglo Amalgamated, UK.

Carry On Constable (1960), film drama, 86 minutes. Director: Gerald Thomas. Screenpwriter: Norman Huddis. Original idea: Brock Williams. Produced: Peter Rogers. Anglo Amalgamated, UK.

Carry On Doctor (1967), film drama, 92 minutes. Director: Gerald Thomas. Screenwriter: Talbot Rothwell. Produced: Peter Rogers. Rank Organisation, UK.

Darling (1965), film drama, 128 minutes. Director: John Schlesinger. Screenwriter: Frederic Raphael. Original narrative concept: John Schlesinger, Frederic Raphael and Joseph Janni. Producer: Joseph Janni. Associate Producer: Victor Lyndon. Joseph Janni Productions, UK.

Edward II (1991), biographical film drama, 87 minutes. Director: Derek Jarman. Screenwriters: Derek Jarman, Stephen McBride and Ken Butler. Producers: Steve Clark-Hall and Antony

Root. Executive Producers: Takashi Asai, Simon Curtis and Sarah Radclyffe. BBC Films, UK.

Fag Hags: Why Women Love Gay Men (2005), documentary film, 52 minutes. Director: Justine Pimlott. Writer and Producer: Maya Gallus. Red Queen Productions, Canada.

Gayby (2012), film drama, 89 minutes. Director and Screenwriter: Jonathan Lisecki. Produced: Amy Hobby and Anne Hubbell. Associate Producers: Townes Coates, Maureen Stanton and Pierre Stefanos. Executive Producers: Zeke Farrow and Laura Heberton. HubbHobb, US.

G.B.F. (2013), film drama, 92 minutes. Director: Darren Stein. Screenwriter: George Northy. Produced: Richard Bever, Stephen Israel, George Northy and Darren Stein. School Pictures, US.

Gimme Gimme Gimme (1999–2001), television situation comedy series, 19 × 30 minutes. Creator: Jonathan Harvey. Tiger Aspect Productions, UK.

Girls (2012 to present), television drama series, 42 × 30 minutes (series 1–4). Creator Lean Dunham. Apatow Productions, US.

Glee (2009 to present), television drama series, 109 × 44 minutes (series 1–5). Creators: Ryan Murphy, Ian Brennan and Brad Falchuk. Ryan Murphy Productions, US.

The Heidi Chronicles (1995), television film drama, 100 minutes. Director: Paul Bogart. Screenwriter: Wendy Wasserstein. Producer: Leanne Moore. Co-producer: Steven J. Brandman. Executive Producer: Michael Brandman. Turner Network Television, US.

The Living End (1992), film drama, 84 minutes. Director and Screenwriter: Gregg Araki. Producers: John Gerrans and Marcus Hu. Cineplex Odeon Films, US.

Looking (2014–15), television drama series, 18 × 30 minutes. Creator: Michael Lannan. Directors: Andrew Haigh, Jamie Babbit, Ryan Flack, Joe Swanberg and Craig Johnson. HBO, US.

Love Sidney (1981–83), television situation comedy series, 44 × 30 minutes. Executive Producers: George Eckstein, Rod Parker and Hal Cooper. Warner Bros Television, US.

Lover Come Back (1961), film drama, 107 minutes. Director: Delbert Mann. Screenwriters: Stanley Shapiro and Paul Henning. Producers: Martin Melcher and Stanley Shapiro. Executive Producer: Robert Arthur. Universal International Pictures, US.

My Best Friend's Wedding (1997), film drama, 105 minutes. Director: P. J. Hogan. Screenwriter: Ronald Bass. Producers: Ronald Bass and Jerry Zucker. Associate Producers: Patricia Cullen and Bill Johnston. Executive Producers: Gill Netter and Patricia Witcher. Tristar Pictures, US.

My Husband Is Gay (2005), television documentary, 50 minutes. Director and Producer: Benetta Adamson. Assistant Producer: Faye Maclean. Executive Producers: Dean Palmer and Bridget Boseley. Caledonia TV, UK.

My Husband Is Not Gay (2015), television documentary, 50 minutes. TLC, US.

Mysterious Skin (2004), film drama, 105 minutes. Director, Screenwriter: Gregg Araki. Original writer of novel: Scott Heim. Produced by Gregg Araki, Mary Jane Skalski and Jeffrey Levy-Hinte. Antidote Films, US.

The Next Best Thing (2000), film drama, 108 minutes. Director: John Schlesinger. Screenwriter: Thomas Ropelewski. Producers: Leslie Dixon, Linne Radmin, Tom Rosenberg. Lakeshore Entertainment, US.

The North Star (1943), film drama, 108 minutes. Director: Lewis Milestone. Screenwriter: Lillian Hellman. Producer: Samuel Goldwyn. Associate Producer: William Cameron. Samuel Goldwyn Company, US.

The Object of My Affection (1998), film drama, 111 minutes. Director: Nicholas Hytner.

Screenwriter: Wendy Wasserstein. Original writer of novel: Stephen McCauley. Producer: Laurence Mark. Co-producer: Diana Pokorny. Associate Producer: Petra Alexandria. Twentieth Century Fox, US.

Pillow Talk (1959), film drama, 102 minutes. Director: Michael Gordon. Screenwriter: Stanley Shapiro and Maurice Richlin. Idea: Russell Rouse and Clarence Greene. Universal International Pictures, US.

Queer as Folk (2000–5), television drama series, 5 seasons (83 × 48 minutes). Creators: Ron Cowen and Daniel Lipman. Original narrative concept: Russell T. Davies. Showtime, US.

Queer Eye for the Straight Guy (2003–7), reality television series, 100 × 50 minutes. Creators: David Collins and David Meltzer. Scout Productions for NBC/Bravo, US.

Rope (1948), film drama, 80 minutes. Director: Alfred Hitchcock. Screenwriter: Arthur Laurentis. Adaptation: Hume Cronyn. Writer of original play: Patrick Hamilton. Producers: Sidney Bernstein and Alfred Hitchcock. Transatlantic Pictures, US.

Send Me No Flowers (1964), film drama, 100 minutes. Director: Norman Jewison. Screenwriter: Julius J. Epstein. Writers of original play: Norman Barasch and Carrroll Moore. Producer: Harry Keller. Executive Producer: Martin Melcher. Universal Pictures, US.

Sex in the City (1998–2004), television drama series, 94 × 30 minutes. Creator: Darren Star. Executive Producer: Michael Patrick King. HBO, US.

Sidney Shorr: A Girl's Best Friend (1981), television film drama, 120 minutes. Director: Russ Mayberry. Screenwriter: Oliver Hailey. Story concept: Marilyn Cantor Baker. Producer: George Ekstein. Associate Producer: Maria Padilla. Warner Bros. Television, US.

Suddenly Last Summer (1959), film drama, 114 minutes. Director: Joseph L. Mankiewicz. Screenwriters: Gore Vidal and Tennessee Williams. Writer of original play: Tennessee Williams. Producer: Sam Spiegel. Columbia Pictures Corporation, US.

Sunday Bloody Sunday (1971), film drama, 110 minutes. Director: John Schlesinger. Screenwriter: Penelope Gilliatt. Producer: Joseph Janni. Associate Producer: Edward Joseph. United Artists Corporation, US.

Swoon (1992), biographical film drama, 80 minutes. Director Tom Kalin. Screenwriters: Tom Kalin and Hilton Als. Producer: Christine Vachon. Co-producer: Tom Kalin. Associate Producer: Thomas Wentworth. Executive Producers: James Schamus and Lauren Zalanick. American Playhouse, US.

Tales of the City (1993), television drama, 302 minutes. Director: Alistair Reid. Screenwriter: Richard Kramer. Original narrative concept: Armistead Maupin. Producer Alan Poul. Executive Producers: Richard Kramer, Armistead Maupin, Sigurjon Sighvatsson and Tim Bevan. Channel 4, UK/US.

A Taste of Honey (1961), film drama, 100 minutes. Director and Producer: Tony Richardson. Screenwriters: Shelagh Delaney and Tony Richardson, based on the play by Shelagh Delaney. British Lion Films, UK.

Torchwood (2006–11), television drama series, 41 × 50 minutes. Creator: Russell T. Davies. Executive Producers: Russell T. Davies and Julie Gardner. BBC Wales, UK.

The Way He Looks [original title: *Hoje eu quero voltar sozinho*] (2014), film drama, 96 minutes. Director and Screenwriter: Daniel Ribeiro. Producers: Daniel Ribeiro and Diana Almeida. Lacuna Films, Brazil.

Will and Grace (1998–2006), television situation comedy series, 188 × 22 minutes. Creators: David Kohan and Max Mutchnick. Director: James Burrows. KoMut Entertainment, US.

Would Like to Meet (2001–2003), reality television series, 3 series, 27 × 60 minutes. Presented by Tracey Cox, Jay Hunt and Jeremy Milnes. Series Producer: Alannah Richardson. Series Editor: Daisy Goodwin. Director: Will Parry. Talkback Production for BBC, UK.

Zee and Co. (1972), film drama, 110 minutes. Director: Brian G. Hutton. Screenwriter: Edna O'Brien. Producers: Alan Ladd Jr and Jay Kanter. Executive Producer: Elliott Kanter. Columbia Pictures Corporation, UK.

References

Aaron, M. (ed.) (2004), *New Queer Cinema: A Critical Reader*, New Brunswick, NJ: Rutgers University Press.
Aitkenhead, D. (2001), 'Village People', *Guardian*, G2, 24 October, p. 7.
Akass, K. and McCabe, J. (eds) (2003), *Reading Sex and the City*, London: I. B. Tauris.
Aldridge, M. and Murray, A. (2008), *T Is For Television: The Small Screen Adventures of Russell T. Davies*, London: Reynolds & Hearn Ltd.
Andrews, M. (2012), *Domesticating the Airwaves: Broadcasting, Domesticity and Femininity*, London: Continuum.
Annan Committee (1977), *Home Office Report of the Committee on the Future of Broadcasting*, London: HMSO.
Arthurs, J. (2004), *Television and Sexuality*, London: Open University Press.
Auslander, P. (2006), *Performing Glam Rock: Gender and Theatricality in Popular Music*, Ann Arbor: University of Michigan Press.
Avert (2015), Men who have sex with men (MSM) and HIV/AIDS, http://www.avert.org/men-who-have-sex-men-msm-hiv-aids.htm [Accessed 30 April 2015].
Baker, P. (2002), *Polari: The Lost Language of Gay Men*, London: Routledge.
Barbie, P. (1998), *The World of the Castrati: The History of an Extraordinary Operatic Phenomenon*, London: Souvenir Press.
Baudrillard, J. (1981) *For a Critique of the Political Economy of the Sign*, trans. Charles Levin, St Louis: Telos Press.
Baudrillard, J. (1994), *Simulacra and Simulation*, trans, Sheila Faria Glaser, Ann Arbor: University of Michigan Press.
Beck, U, Giddens, A. and Lash, S. (1995), *Reflexive Modernization: Politics, Tradition and Aesthetics in the Modern Social Order*, Cambridge: Polity Press.
Beemyn, B. and Steinman, E. (2002), *Bisexual Men in Culture and Society*, New York: Haworth Press.
Benshoff, H. and Griffin, S. (eds) (2004), *Queer Cinema: The Film Reader*, New York: Routledge.
Berger, R. (2010), 'Out and about: slash fic, re-imagined texts and queer commentaries', in C. Pullen and M. Cooper (eds), *LGBT Identity and Online New Media*, London: Routledge, pp. 173–84.
Bergling, T. (2001), *Sissyphobia: Gay Men and Effeminate Behavior*, New York: Harrington Park Press.
Bergman, D. (ed.) (1993), *Camp Grounds: Style and Homosexuality*, Amherst: University of Massachusetts Press.
Berlant, L. and Warner, M. (1998), 'Sex in public', *Critical Inquiry*, 24 (2), pp. 547–66.
Bosworth, P. (1978), *Montgomery Clift: A Biography*, New York: Harcourt, Brace Jovanovich.
Bourdieu, P. (1984), *Distinction: A Social Critique of the Judgement of Taste*, London: Routledge.

Bourne, S. (1996), *Brief Encounters: Lesbians and Gays in British Cinema 1930–1971*, London: Cassell.
Brandt, G. (1981), *British Television Drama*, Cambridge: Cambridge University Press.
Brewster, B. (1975), 'Editorial', *Screen*, 16 (3), pp. 4–5.
Bruzzi, S. (2000), *New Documentary: A Critical Introduction*, London: Routledge.
Buckley, C. (2015), 'The liminal rhetorical space of the fag hag: bridging rhetoric and queer theory within Sex and the City', http://eds.b.ebscohost.com/eds/pdfviewer/pdfviewer?sid=280005c7-4589-4286-ab77-cd4250d0b3f1%40sessionmgr110&vid=4&hid=117 [Accessed 30 April 2015].
Bucknell, K. (2000), 'Who is Christopher Isherwood?' in J. J. Berg and C. Freeman (eds), *The Isherwood Century: Essays on the Life and Works of Christopher Isherwood*, Madison: University of Wisconsin Press, pp. 13–29.
Butler, J. (1999), *Gender Trouble*, rep., London: Routledge.
Campbell, M. (2002), *Carry On Films*, Harpenden: Pocket Essentials.
Capsuto, S. (2000), *Alternate Channels: The Uncensored Story of Gay and Lesbian Images on Radio and Television*, New York: Ballantine Books.
Carlson, M. (1996), *Performance: A Critical Introduction*, London: Routledge.
Carroll, N. (1996), *Theorizing the Moving Image*, Cambridge: Cambridge University Press.
Caughie, J. (2000), *Television Drama: Realism, Modernisation and British Culture*, Oxford: Oxford University Press.
Cho, M. (2002), *I'm The One that I Want*, New York: Ballantine.
Cleto, F. (ed.) (2002), *Camp: Queer Aesthetics and the Performing Subject: A Reader*, Ann Arbor: University of Michigan Press.
Clum, J. M. (2000), *Still Acting Gay*, rev. ed., New York: St Martin's Griffin.
Colebrook, C. (2004), *Irony*, London: Routledge.
Coppock, V., Haydon, D. and Ritchter, I. (1995), *The Illusions of Post-Feminism: New Women, Old Myths*, London: Routledge.
Cover, R. (2012), *Queer Youth Suicide, Culture and Identity: Unbearable Lives?* Farnham: Ashgate Publishing.
Creed, B. (2000), 'Film and psychoanalysis', in J. Hill and P. Church Gibson (eds), *Film Studies: Critical Approaches*, Oxford University Press, pp. 75–88.
Davis, G. (2008), *Queer as Folk*, London: BFI
DeAngelis, M. (ed.) (2014), *Reading the Bromance: Homosocial Relationships in Film and Television*, Detroit: Wayne State University Press.
De La Cruz, M. and Dolby, T. (eds) (2007), *Girls Who Like Boys Who Like Boys: True Tales of Love, Lust, and Friendship Between Straight Women and Gay Men*, New York: Dutton.
Deleuze, G. (1986), *Cinema 1: The Movement Image*, Minneapolis: University of Minnesota Press.
Doane, M. A. (1982) 'Film and the masquerade: theorizing the female spectator', *Screen*, 23 (3–4), pp. 74–87.
Doane, M. A., Mellencamp, P. and Williams, L. (1984), 'Feminist film criticism: an introduction', in M. A. Doane, P. Mellencamp and L. Williams (eds), *ReVision: Essays in Feminist Film Criticism*, Frederick: University Publications of America, pp. 1–17.
Dorias, M. and Lajeunesse, S. L. (2004), *Dead Boys Can't Dance: Sexual Orientation, Masculinity, and Suicide*, Montreal: McGill-Queen's University Press.
Doty, A. (1993), *Making Things Perfectly Queer: Interpreting Mass Culture*, Minneapolis: University of Minnesota Press.
Dyer, R. (ed.) (1984), *Gays and Film*, rev. ed., New York: Zoetrope. Dyer, R. (1986), *Heavenly Bodies: Film Stars and Society*, London: BFI.

Dyer, R. (2000), *The Matter of Images*, second rep., London: Routledge.
Dyer, R. (2001a), *Stars*, rep., London: BFI.
Dyer, R. (2001b), *Culture of Queers*, London: Routledge.
Ellis, J. (1982), *Visible Fictions*, London: Routledge.
Ellis, J. (2009), *Derek Jarman's Angelic Conversations*, Minneapolis: University of Minnesota Press.
Fackler, M. F. and Salvato, N. (2012), 'Fag hag: a theory of effeminate enthusiasms', *Discourse*, 34 (1), pp. 59–92.
Farmer, B. (2000), *Spectacular Passions: Cinema, Fantasy, Gay Male Spectatorships*, Durham, NC: Duke University Press.
Finch, M. (1986), 'Sex and address in *Dynasty*', *Screen* 27 (6), pp. 24–42.
Finnegan, R. (1997), 'Storying the self: personal narratives and identity', in H. Mackay (ed.), *Consumption and Everyday Life*, London: Sage, pp. 65–112.
Fiske, J. (1989), *Understanding Popular Culture*, London: Routledge.
Fiske, J. (1994), *Television Culture*, rep., London: Routledge.
Foucault, M. (1995), *Discipline & Punish: The Birth of the Prison*, New York: Vintage.
Frackler, M. F. and Salvato, N. (2012), 'Fag hag: a theory of effeminate enthusiasms', *Discourse*, 31 (1), pp. 59–92.
Fuss, D. (1995), *Identification Papers*, London: Routledge.
Gale, P. (1999), *Armistead Maupin*, Bath: Absolute Press.
Gambaudo, S. (2012), 'From scopophilic pleasure to the jouissance of the madonna: the mother's maternal gaze in three photographic examples', *Women's Studies*, 41 (7), pp. 781–804.
Gamman, L. (1998), 'Watching the detective: the enigma of the female gaze', in L. Gamman, L. and Marshment, M. (eds), *The Female Gaze*, London: Women's Press, pp. 8–26.
Gauntlett, D. (2002), *Media, Gender and Identity: An Introduction*, London: Routledge.
Gaze, D. (ed.) (2001), *Concise Dictionary of Women Artists*, London: Routledge.
Genz, S. and Brabon, B. A. (2012), *Postfeminism: Cultural Texts and Theories*, Edinburgh: Edinburgh University Press.
Geraghty, C. (1991), *Women and Soap Opera: A Study of Prime Time Soaps*, Cambridge: Polity Press.
Geraghty, C. (2005), *My Beautiful Launderette*, London: I. B. Tauris.
Giddens, A. (1992), *Modernity and Self Identity: Self and Society in the Late Modern Age*, rep., Cambridge: Polity Press.
Giddens, A. (1995), *The Transformation of Intimacy: Sexuality, Love and Eroticism in Modern Societies*, rep., Cambridge: Polity Press.
Giles, J. (2004), *The Parlour and the Suburb: Domestic Identities, Class, Femininity and Modernity*, London: Berg.
Giroux, H. A. (2011), 'The crisis of public values in the age of the new media', *Critical Studies in Media Communication*, 28 (1), pp. 8–29.
Granger, F. and Calhoun, R. (2007), *Include Me Out: My Life from Goldwyn to Broadway*, New York: St Martin's Press.
Grant, B. K. (2008), *Auteurs and Authorship*, Oxford: Blackwell.
Gross, L. (2001), *Up From Visibility: Lesbians, Gay Men, and the Media in America*, New York: Columbia University Press.
Hall, S. (1997), 'The spectacle of the "other"', in S. Hall (ed.), *Representation: Cultural Representations and Signifying Practices*, London: Sage, pp. 223–79.
Handbag (2015), Handbag: the documentary, http://www.handbagthemovie.com/ [Accessed 6 May 2015].
Hart, K. P. (2000), *The AIDS Movie: Representing a Pandemic in Film and Television*, New York: The Haworth Press.

Hart, K. P. (2010), *Images for a Generation Doomed: The Films and Career of Gregg Araki*, Lanham: Lexington Books.

Hart, K. P. (2014), 'Looking at complicated desires: gay male youth and cinematic representations of age-different relationships', in C. Pullen (ed.), *Queer Youth and Media Cultures*, Basingstoke: Palgrave Macmillan, pp. 197–208.

Harvey, S. (2000), 'Channel Four Television: from Annan to Grade', in E. Buscombe (ed.), *British Television: A Reader*, Oxford: Oxford University Press, pp. 92–117.

Hayman, R. (1993), *Tennessee Williams: Everybody Else in an Audience*, New Haven: Yale University Press.

Heath, S. (1978), 'Difference', *Screen*, 19 (3), pp. 51–111.

Hebdige, D. (1979), *Subculture: The Meaning of Style*, London: Routledge.

Heim, S. (1995), *Mysterious Skin*, New York: HarperCollins.

Higdon, H. (1999), *Leopold and Loeb: The Crime of the Century*, Urbana: University of Illinois Press.

Hight, C. (2010), *Television Mockumentary: Reflexivity, Satire and a Call to Play*, Manchester: Manchester University Press.

Hill, J. (1986), *Sex, Class and Realism: British Cinema 1956–1963*, London: British Film Institute.

Hill J. (1994), *The Art of Dora Carrington*, London: The Herbert Press.

Hobson, D. (2008), *Channel 4: The Early Years and the Jeremy Isaacs Legacy*, London: I. B. Tauris.

Holroyd, M. (2004), *Lytton Strachey*, London: Chatto and Windus.

Howe, D. J. and Walker, S. J. (2003), *The Television Companion: The Unofficial and Unauthorised Guide to 'Doctor Who'*, London: Telos.

Hudson, R. and Davidson, S. (2007), *Rock Hudson: His Story*, New York: Carroll & Graf Publishers Inc.

Human Rights Campaign (2015), The lies and dangers of efforts to change sexual orientation or gender identity, http://www.hrc.org/resources/entry/the-lies-and-dangers-of-reparative-therapy [Accessed 30 April 2015].

Independent (1995), Obituary: Larry Grayson, 9 January, http://www.independent.co.uk/news/people/obituary-larry-grayson-1567199.html [Accessed 5 May 2015].

Isherwood, C. (1947), *Lions and Shadows: An Education in the Twenties*, Norfolk, CT: New Directions.

Isherwood, C. (1977), *Christopher and His Kind*, London: Methuen.

Isherwood, C. (1978), *Goodbye to Berlin*, St Albans: Triad/Panther.

It Gets Better Project (2011), http://www.itgetsbetter.org/ [Accessed 28 May 2011].

Ivakhiv, A. J. (2013), *Ecologies of the Moving Image: Cinema, Affect, Nature*, Waterloo: Wilfrid Laurier University Press.

James, D. (2015), *Picturing the Closet: Male Secrecy and Homosexual Visibility in Britain*, New York: Oxford University Press.

Jameson, F. (1991), *Postmodernism or The Cultural Logic of Late Capitalism*, London: Verso.

Jarman, D. (1987), *The Last of England*, London: Constable.

Jarman, D. (1991), *Derek Jarman: Today and Tomorrow*, London: Salmon.

Jarman, D. (1992), *Modern Nature: Journals of Derek Jarman*. London: Vintage.

Jarman, D. (1993), *At Your Own Risk: A Saint's Testament*, London: Vintage.

Jarman, D. (2001), *Smiling in Slow Motion: Diaries, 1991–94*, London: Vintage.

Jermyn, D. (2009), *Sex and the City*, New York: Wayne State University Press.

Jones, C. (1994), *Living Proof: Courage in the Face of AIDS*. Foreword by Ian McKellen, New York: Abbeville Press Publishers.

Joseph, S. (2005), *Social Work Practice and Men Who Have Sex With Men,* New Delhi: Sage.
Kassabian, A. (2001), *Hearing Film: Tracking Identifications in Contemporary Hollywood Film Music,* London: Routledge.
Kehily, M. J. (2007), 'A cultural perspective', in M. J. Kehily (ed.), *Understanding Youth: Perspectives, Identities and Practices,* London: Sage, pp. 11–43.
Kennedy, L. (2000), *Race and Urban Space in Contemporary American Culture,* Edinburgh: Edinburgh University Press.
King, C. S. (2014), '*A Single Man* and a tragic woman: gender politics and the fag hag', *Feminist Media Studies,* 14 (2), pp. 190–205.
Kolb, E. (2004), *The Weimar Republic,* London: Routledge.
Kristeva, J. (1977), *About Chinese Women,* London: Marion Boyars.
LaValley, L. (1985), 'The great escape: gays and film', *American Film,* 10 (6), pp. 28–71.
Lacan, J. (1968), *Symbol and Language: The Language of the Self,* Baltimore: The Johns Hopkins University Press.
Lacey, S. (2012), *Tony Garnett,* Manchester: Manchester University Press.
Lechte, J. (2000), *Fifty Key Contemporary Thinkers: From Structuralism to Postmodernity,* London: Routledge.
Leigh, J. (2002), *The Cinema of Ken Loach: Art in the Service of the People,* New York: Columbia University Press.
Lyotard, J., F. (1979), *The Postmodern Condition: A Report on Knowledge,* Manchester: Manchester University Press.
Maddison, S. (2000), *Fags, Hags and Queer Sisters: Gender Dissent and Heterosocial Bonding in Gay Culture,* Basingstoke: Palgrave Macmillan.
Maitland, S. (2007), 'Fag hags: a field guide', *Critical Quarterly,* 33 (2), pp. 19–24.
Manlove, C. T. (2007), 'Visual "drive" and cinematic narrative: reading gaze theory in Lacan, Hitchcock, and Mulvey', *Cinema Journal,* 46 (3), pp. 83–108.
Mann, W. J. 2004. *Edge of Midnight: The Life of John Schlesinger,* London: Hutchinson.
Marinucci, M. (2010), *Feminism Is Queer: The Intimate Connection Between Queer and Feminist Theory,* London: Zed Books.
Marks, L. U. (2000), *The Skin of the Film: Intercultural Cinema, Embodiment, and the Senses,* Durham, NC: Duke University Press.
McHarry, M. (2010), 'Identity unmoored: Yaoi in the west', in C. Pullen and M. Cooper (eds), *LGBT Identity and Online New Media,* London: Routledge, pp. 185–98.
Meyer, M. (1994), 'Introduction: reclaiming the discourse of camp', in M. Meyer (ed.), *The Politics and Poetics of Camp,* New York: Routledge, pp. 1–22.
Modleski, T. (2005), *The Women Who Knew Too Much: Hitchcock and Feminist Theory,* New York: Routledge.
Moon, D. (1995), 'Insult and inclusion: the term fag hag and "gay male community"', *Social Forces,* 74 (2), pp. 487–511.
Moore, S. (1998), 'Here is looking at you kid', in L. Gamman and M. Marshment (eds), *The Female Gaze,* London: Women's Press Ltd, pp. 44–59.
Morris, C. E. (ed.) (2011), *Remembering the AIDs Quilt,* East Lansing: Michigan State University Press.
Mulvey, L. (1975), 'Visual pleasure and narrative cinema', *Screen,* 16 (3), pp. 6–18.
Mulvey, L. (1981), 'Afterthoughts on "Visual pleasure and narrative cinema" inspired by *Duel in the Sun*', *Framework,* 15–17, pp. 12–15.
Munford, R. and Waters, A. (2013), *Feminism and Popular Culture: Investigating the Postfeminist Mystique: Explorations in Post-feminism,* London: I. B. Tauris.

Murphy, R. (1992), *Sixties British Cinema*, London: BFI.
Murray, R. (1998), *Images in the Dark: An Encyclopedia of Gay and Lesbian Film and Video*, London, Titan Books.
Neale, S. (1983), 'Masculinity as spectacle', *Screen*, 24 (6), pp. 2–17.
Nichols, B. (1991), *Representing Reality*, Bloomington: Indiana University Press.
Nichols, B. (1994), *Blurred Boundaries: Questions of Meaning in Contemporary Culture*, Bloomington: Indiana University Press.
Nichols, B. (2001), *Introduction to Documentary*, Bloomington: Indiana University Press.
Nietzsche, F. (1974), *Thus Spoke Zarathustra*, London: Penguin.
Nietzsche, F. (2008), *The Birth of Tragedy*, rep. translated by Douglas Smith, Oxford: Oxford University Press.
Nixon, S. (1997), 'Circulating culture', in P. Du Gay (ed.), *Production of Culture/Cultures of Production*, London: Sage, pp. 221–34.
Pickering, M. (2001), *Stereotyping: The Politics of Representation*, Basingstoke: Palgrave.
Plummer, K. (1997), *Telling Sexual Stories: Power, Change and Social Worlds*, rep., London: Routledge.
Princess Diana Remembered (2015), http://www.princess-diana-remembered.com/diana-news-blog/memories-of-diana-dianas-smile-gives-hope-to-aids-victims [Accessed 7 May 2015].
Pullen, C. (2007a), *Documenting Gay Men: Identity and Performance in Reality Television and Documentary Film*, Jefferson: McFarland.
Pullen, C. (2007b). 'Non-heterosexual characters in post war television drama: from covert identity and stereotyping, towards reflexivity and social change', in D. Godiwala (ed.), *Alternatives within the Mainstream II: Queer Theatres in Post War Britain*, Newcastle: Cambridge Scholars, pp. 272–99.
Pullen, C. (2010), '"Love the coat": bisexuality, the female gaze and the romance of sexual politics', in A. Ireland (ed.), *Illuminating Torchwood: Essays on Narrative, Character and Sexuality in the BBC Series*, Jefferson: McFarland, pp. 135–52.
Pullen, C. (2011), Heroic gay characters in popular film: tragic determination, and the everyday', *Continuum: Journal of Media & Cultural Studies*, 25 (3), pp. 397–413.
Pullen, C. (2012), *Gay Identity, New Storytelling and the Media*, rev. ed., Basingstoke: Palgrave Macmillan.
Pullen, C. (2014a), 'Sensing the place of British queer social realism: tower blocks, architectural space and the affective body', paper presentation at the MECCSA conference Bournemouth, 10 January.
Pullen, C. (2014b), 'Self-reflexive screenwriting and LGBT identity: framing and indirectly reading the self', in C. Batty (ed), *Screenwriters and Screenwriting*, Basingstoke: Palgrave Macmillan, pp. 271–87.
Pullen, C. (ed.) (2014c), *Gay Identity, Queer Youth and Media Cultures*, Basingstoke: Palgrave Macmillan.
Pullen, C. and Cooper, M. (eds) (2010), *LGBT Identity and Online New Media*, New York: Routledge.
Rabinowitz, P. (1994), *They Must be Represented: The Politics of Documentary*, New York: Verso.
Reality TV Planet (2004), Playing it straight news: cancelled due to poor ratings, http://www.realitytvplanet.com/shows03/playing_it_straight_news.php [Accessed 3 June 2004].
Ritch, B. R. (2013), *New Queer Cinema: The Director's Cut*, Durham, NC: Duke University Press.
Rogers, N. (2015), Interview: Daniel Ribeiro on his international hit film 'The Way He Looks',

http://www.towleroad.com/2014/11/interview-daniel-ribeiro.html [Accessed 30 April 2015].

Russo, V. (1987), *The Celluloid Closet*, rev. ed., New York: Harper & Row.

Saad-Filho, A. and Johnson, D. (eds) (2005), *Neoliberalism: A Critical Reader,* London: Pluto Press.

Samuels, R. (1998), *Hitchcock's Bi-textuality: Lacan, Feminisms and Queer Theory*, New York: State University of New York Press.

Sarkissian, R. (2014), 'Queering TV conventions: LGBT teen narratives on Glee', in C. Pullen (ed.), *Queer Youth and Media Cultures*, Basingstoke: Palgrave Macmillan, pp. 145–57.

Schechner, R. (2002), *Performance Studies: An Introduction*, London: Routledge.

Seigworth, G. J. and Gregg, M. (2010), 'An inventory of shimmers', in G. J. Seigworth and M. Gregg (eds), *The Affect Theory Reader*, Durham, NC: Duke University Press, pp. 1–26.

Shilts, R. (1987), *And the Band Played On: Politics, People, and the AIDS Epidemic*, New York: St Martin's Press.

Sigesmund, B. J. (2003), 'Boys R Us', *Newsweek*, 21 July 2003, pp. 52–3.

Sinfield, A. (1994), *The Wilde Century: Effeminacy, Oscar Wilde and the Queer Movement*, New York: Columbia University Press.

Spalding, F. (1998), *Duncan Grant: A Biography*, London: Pimlico.

Spigel, L. (1992), *Make Room for TV: Television and the Family Ideal in Postwar America*, Chicago: University of Chicago Press.

Stacey, J. (1987), 'Desperately seeking difference', *Screen*, 28 (1), pp. 48–61

Stacey, J. (1993), *Star Gazing: Hollywood Cinema and Female Spectatorship*, London: Routledge.

Stallybrass, P. and White, A. (1995), *The Politics and Poetics of Transgression*, rep., New York: Cornell University Press.

Stevens, C. (2010), *Born Brilliant: The Life of Kenneth Williams*, London: John Murray.

Strachey, L. (1918), *Eminent Victorians*, London: Chatto and Windus.

Stugart, H. (2003), 'Reinventing privilege: the new (gay) man in contemporary popular media', *Critical Studies in Media Communication*, 20 (1), pp, 67–91.

SWISH (2015), http://swishallyfund.org/ [Accessed 5 May 2015].

Taddeo, J. A. (2011), *Lytton Strachey and the Search for Modern Sexual Identity: The Last Eminent Victorian*, New York: Haworth Press.

Tarr, C. (1985), '*Sapphire*, *Darling* and the boundaries of permitted pleasure', *Screen*, 26 (1), pp. 50–65.

Thompson, D. (2004), 'Calling all fag hags: from identity politics to identification politics', *Social Semiotics*, 14 (1), pp. 37–48.

Thompson, L. (2015), 'Diana, Princess of Wales was one of the most remarkable icons of the twentieth century', http://www.express.co.uk/news/uk/272/Diana-The-legacy [Accessed 7 May 2015].Tracy, K. (1999), *The Real Story of Ellen*, Toronto: Birch Lane Press.

Trevor Project (2011), http://www.thetrevorproject.org/ [Accessed 18 July 2011].

Turner, V. (1982), *From Ritual to Theatre: The Seriousness of Human Play*, New York: Performing Arts Journal Publications.

TV Barn (2004), NBC PR: 'Queer Eye' sold in 20 countries, http://www.tvbarn.com/ticker/archives/017809.html [Accessed 14 May 2004].

Van Zoonen, L. (1994), *Feminist Media Studies*, London: Sage.

Vorlicky, R. (ed.) (1998), *Tony Kushner in Conversation*, Ann Arbor: University of Michigan Press.

Wartenberg, T. E. (1999), *Unlikely Couples: Movie Romance as Social Criticism*, Boulder: Westview Press.

Weedon, C. (1999), *Feminism, Theory and the Politics of Difference*, Oxford: Blackwell Publishers.

Weeks, J. (1990), *Coming Out: Homosexual Politics in Britain from the Nineteenth Century to Present*, rev. ed., London: Quartet Books.
Weston, K. (1991), *Families We Choose: Lesbians, Gays, Kinship*, New York: Columbia University Press.
Westwood, R. and Rhodes, C. (eds) (2007), *Humour, Work and Organization*, London: Routledge.
White, J. D. (2002), 'Bisexuals who kill: Hollywood's bisexual crimewave, 1985–1998', in B. Beemyn and E. Steinman (eds), *Bisexual Men in Culture and Society*, New York: Haworth Press, pp. 39–54.
Williams, R. (1992), *Television, Technology and Cultural Form*, London: Routledge.
Wilson, B. (2012), *Daily Telegraph*, London, 6 October 2012, p. 8.
Woolen, R. (1996), *Derek Jarman: A Portrait*, London: Thames and Hudson.
Yar, M. (2003), 'Panoptic power and the pathologisation of vision: critical reflections on the Foucauldian thesis', *Surveillance & Society*, 1 (3) (September), pp, 254–71.
YouTube (2015), Princess Diana funeral – Elton John – Candle In The Wind (Goodbye Englands Rose), https://www.youtube.com/watch?v=A8gO0Z818j4 [Accessed 7 May 2015].

Index

Aaron, Michele, 52
abject, 5, 7, 13, 40, 49, 67, 82, 85, 87, 93, 104, 106, 109, 123–5, 147, 148, 155–6, 165–7
abortion, 81, 92–4, 127–8
absence of identity, 8, 11, 13, 39–40, 44, 46–8, 50, 52, 54, 56, 62–4, 145, 171
Adair, Peter, 4
AIDS/HIV, 3, 56–9, 61, 111
alcohol, 32, 80, 101
Alien, 21
Allen, Ted, 139–40
ambivalence, 15, 23, 93, 104, 112, 117, 131, 134
androcentric, 19, 33, 39, 117
androgynous, 111, 126
An Ideal Husband, 82
Andrews, Maggie, 89
Aniston, Jennifer, 82–4, 87, 170
Another Country, 82
archetype/archetypal, 2, 10–11, 52, 80, 85, 93, 137, 157
As If, 156
autobiography, 44, 76

baby (child raising), 34, 38, 78, 81, 84–5, 92, 94, 145, 162, 164–5, 167
Basic Instinct, 111
Baudrillard, Jean, 23–4
Baxter, Anne, 8–9, 13
'Beard', 4
Beautiful Thing, 11, 99, 147, 150–5, 160–6, 170
Beemyn, Brett, 110
Behr, Dani, 141
Bell, Vanessa, 146
Bergman, David, 67
Beverley Hills 90210, 103
Bicycle Thieves, 155

bisexuality, 8, 12, 34, 44–5, 47, 57, 75–7, 79, 90, 96, 106–8, 110–12, 114, 116–19, 157, 170
biography, 75, 125–6
Bloomsbury Set, 126, 146
Blue, 57
Bob and Rose, 12, 90, 110–12, 114–18, 170
body
  male, 12, 15–16, 19, 29, 133, 165, 170
  female, 16, 18, 22, 36, 69, 113
Bogarde, Dirk, 35
Bolan, Marc, 111
Bowen, Andrea, 162
Bowie, David, 111
Boy Meets Boy, 12, 120, 130, 138, 140–2, 145
Brandt, George, 155
Brewster, Ben, 16
Brief Encounter, 116
Brokeback Mountain, 148
'bromance', 3
Bryan, Dora, 34
The Buddha of Suburbia, 156
Burrows, James, 102
Butler, Judith, 67

Cabaret, 10–11, 65, 74–7, 79, 81, 87–8
Caine, Michael, 35
camaraderie, 16, 74, 77, 83, 85, 110, 129, 170
camp, 14, 65–72, 74, 87, 139
Campbell, Mark, 69
Candle in the Wind, 3
Capsuto, Steven, 92
Carravaggio, 42, 57–61, 63–4
Carrington, 10, 12, 120, 124–30, 135, 144–5, 170
Carrington, Dora, ii, 10, 34, 120, 124–6, 128, 145, 170

Carry On Films, 11, 65, 68, 70, 74, 87
Carry On at Your Convenience, 70
Carry On Camping, 70, 72
Carry On Cleo, 73
Carry On Constable, 70
Carry On Dick, 70
Carry on Doctor, 70, 72–3, 87
Carry On Loving, 70
Carry On up the Khyber, 70
Cathy Come Home, 156
Caughie, John, 155
The Celluloid Closet, 146, 148
Channel 4, 96, 107, 146, 151
Cheers, 102
Cho, Margaret, 3, 129–30
Christie, Julie, 35
Christopher and His Kind, 75, 88
Cleto, Fabio, 68
Clooney, George, 101
Clueless, 160
Colebook, Claire, 130
Colfer, Chris, 157
consumption, 11, 15–19, 23, 36, 40, 42, 64, 89, 117, 167
Cox, Tracey, 136–8
Curram, Roland, 35

Danquah, Paul, 34
Darling, 11, 16, 32–40, 74
Davidson, Monica, 4
Davies Russell T., 90, 103, 111–12, 117–18
Davies, Terrence, 151
Davis, Gina, 21
Dawson's Creek, 156
Day, Doris, 8, 11, 16, 25–30, 32, 40, 65, 82, 169
Degeneres, Ellen, 98
Delaney, Shelagh, 34
Desperately Seeking Susan, 21
The Devils, 56
devotion, 80, 120, 125–6, 129, 135, 170
Dionysian and Apollonian tragedy, 49
Doane, Mary Ann, 20–2, 165
Doctor Who, 111, 113, 119
documentary, 1, 4, 11–12, 24, 46, 49, 53, 58, 102, 104–6, 129–35, 144–6, 156–7, 167, 170
domesticity, 11–12, 29, 32, 55, 88, 117, 136
Douglas, Kyan, 139–40

Dunham, Lena, 102–3, 106
Dyer, Richard, 15, 65, 148

Edward II, 42, 57–61, 63–4
effeminate, 16, 35, 67–70, 95, 99, 101, 106, 111, 123–4, 133, 148, 163
Ellen, 89, 98, 117
Ellis, John, 41, 90
Eminent Victorians, 126
ER, 101
Everett, Rupert, 82–3, 86–7
exclusion, 20, 36, 97

Fackler, Maria F., 96
Fag Hag, 2–3, 82–3, 87, 96–7, 111, 121, 115, 117, 129
Farmer, Brett, 66–7
feminism, 5, 7, 13, 20
Feminism Is Queer: The Intimate Connection Between Queer and Feminist Theory, 5
Filicia, Tom, 139
Finch, Peter, 78
Fire Island, 138
Fiske, John, 8, 19, 90
Frankenstein, 52
Franks, Robert, 44, 54
Freud, Sigmund, 15, 17
Fuss, Diana, 8

Gambaudo, Sylvie, 93
Gamman, Loraine, 20
Garland, Judy, 65, 82
Gauntlett, David, 19
gay best friend, 4, 81–5, 105, 147, 160–3, 167
Gay Weddings, 138
The Generation Game, 3
G.B.F., 12, 81, 147, 160–2, 166
Geraghty, Christine, 24
Gertler, Mark, 126
Getzlaff, James, 141–4, 146
Giddens, Anthony, 75–6, 91
Giles, Judy, 91
Gimme Gimme Gimme, 12, 89, 95, 98–9, 117
Girls, 89, 102–10, 117–18
Girls Who Like Boys Who Like Boys, 146
Giroux, Henry, 8
Glee, 12, 147, 150, 155–8, 160, 166–7
Gok Wan, 3
Gok's Fashion Fix, 3

Goodbye to Berlin, 10, 75–6, 79, 88
Granger, Farley, 8–9, 13, 44
Grant, Duncan, 146
graphic magazine, queer, 168
Grayson, Larry, 3, 14
Gregg, Melissa, 58
gynocentric, 117–18

Haigh, Andrew, 103–4
Hamilton, Patrick, 44
Handbag, 4
Harris, Jenn, 161
Harry Potter, 14
Hart, Kylo Patrick R., 24
Hart, Phoebe, 4
Harvey, Jonathan, 99, 147, 151
Harvey, Laurence, 35
Hawtrey, Charles, 69–71, 73–4
Hayes, Sean, 100
Head, Murray, 77
Heath, Stephen, 17
The Heidi Chronicles, 5–7, 13
heterocentric, 8, 16–17, 20, 66, 116, 136, 164
Hill, John, 147, 149
Hitchcock, Alfred, 12, 15, 19, 44, 47–8, 128
Hollywood cinema, 10–11, 16, 18–19, 22, 25, 26, 30, 43–4, 46, 63, 65–6, 75, 81, 111, 119, 148, 169
holograms, 25, 36, 40
Holroyd, Michael, 125
How to Look Good Naked, 3
How to Survive a Plague, 4
Hudson, Rock, 8, 11, 16, 25–32, 40, 65
Hulce, Tom, 6
Hunt, Jay, 136–7
Hutton, Brain G., 33

I Am a Camera, 88
identity politics, 5, 8, 13, 157
irony, 52, 65, 68, 73, 130, 132, 143, 145
Isherwood, Christopher, 10, 66, 74–6, 87–8, 148
It Gets Better Project, 168
Ivakhiv, Adrian J., 61

Jackson, Glenda, 77
Jacques, Hattie, 65, 70, 72–4, 87
Jarman, Derek, 12, 24, 53, 56–9, 63–4, 170
Jewish identity, 55, 76, 79–81, 92

John, Elton, 3, 111
Judaism, 81

Kamen, Nick, 15–16, 36
Kassabian, Annahid, 131
Kelly's Heroes, 33
Kennedy Martin, Troy, 155
The Kids are All Right, 13
kinship, 86, 92, 109
Kissing Jessica Stein, 13
Kressley, Carson, 139
Kristeva, Julia, 20

The L Word, 13
Lacan, Jacques, 15, 17, 43, 47
Lannan, Michael, 103
LaValley, Al, 66
The Leather Boys, 149–50
Lee Curtis, Jamie, 6
Leopold, Nathan, 42, 44, 46, 53–4, 56
Life in Squares, 146
liminal, 11, 58, 88, 118, 121, 123–7, 129–30, 134, 137, 144, 171
liminoid, 124, 144
Lions and Shadows, 75, 88
Lip Service, 13
Lisecki, Jonathan, 161
The Living End, 42, 57–9, 64
Loeb, Leopold, 42, 44, 46, 53–4
The Long Day Closes, 151
The Long Kiss Goodnight, 21
long shot (camera), 44, 47, 54
Looking, 10, 12, 90, 102–3, 107–9, 117–18, 170
Love Sidney, 12, 89, 92–3, 95, 117, 170
Love Sidney, Sidney Shorr: A Girl's Best Friend, 93

Madonna, 82–3, 86–7, 170
Make You Own Kind of Music, 153
Manlove, Clifford T., 15–17, 43
Marinucci, Mimi, 5
Marks, Laura U., 58
Marlowe, Christopher, 57
marriage, 34–5, 70, 83–4, 101, 120, 129–30, 135, 138
Maupin, Armistead, 96
McGill, Donald, 69
Melrose Place, 102
Melvin, Murray, 34
men who have sex with men (MSM), 132

Michele, Lea, 157
Minelli, Liza, 79
mockumentary, 132
Modeleski, Tania, 19–20, 119
Momma Cass, 153
Moore, Suzanne, 19, 21
morals/morality, 38, 46, 92, 95, 101, 124, 155
Mormon religion, 129, 132, 134
Mullally, Megan, 100
Mulvey, Laura, 11, 15–16, 18–19, 22
My Best Friend's Wedding, 11, 66, 81–3, 85–6, 151, 161, 165
My Husband Is Gay, 12, 129–31, 135, 146
My Husband Is Not Gay, 12, 120, 129–30, 132, 134, 145, 170
masquerade, 21–2, 28, 30, 32, 84, 86, 87, 93–4, 106, 114, 138, 148, 160, 165–6
maternal, 21, 29, 93, 97
Mysterious Skin, 42, 57–9, 61–4

The Names Project (The AIDS Quilt), 4
Narcissism, 42–3, 51, 53, 63–4
Nazi Germany, 79–80
Neoliberalism, 5, 7, 8, 13, 169, 171
New Queer Cinema, 41–2, 52–3, 56–8, 63–4, 149, 170
New York City Pride, 4
The Next Best Thing, 11, 82, 86
Nietzsche, Frederick, 45, 49, 54
Nixon, Sean, 23
The North Star, 8–9, 13
Nyman, Michael, 128

The Object of My Affection, 11, 66, 81–7, 115, 151, 161, 165–6
Oedipus complex, 20, 93
oppositional, 23, 28, 93, 95
Oranges Are Not the Only Fruit, 156
ostracism, 111
other/otherness, 5, 7, 12, 17, 19–20, 36, 49, 51, 89, 93, 104, 107, 108–9, 117–18, 148–9, 171

The Pacific Sun, 96
Panopticon, 22–3, 30, 49, 51
Paris is Burning, 52
parody, 12, 65, 68, 71–2, 74, 130, 132, 144, 159
Partridge, Ralph, 126, 128
paternal, 7, 97

Penrose, Beacus, 126–8
phallus, 17, 31, 43, 48, 74, 101
Pieterse, Sasha, 162
Platonic, 3, 6, 12, 26, 87, 114, 126, 129
Playgirl, 61
Playing It Straight, 142, 146
Polari, 10, 68–9
political economy, 22–3
post-feminism, 5, 7, 33, 102
postmodernity, 5, 18, 23, 25, 90
poverty, 34
pregnant, 16, 30, 34, 81, 83, 89, 105, 114, 127, 162, 164
Price, Jonathan, 125
Princess Diana, 3–4
procreation, 7, 92, 95, 97, 123, 164–5
prototypical representation, 12, 16, 41

Queer as Folk, 12, 90, 102–3, 107–9, 112, 117–18
queer gaze, 11–12, 40, 41, 40–4
queer male as substitute, 93, 171, 81

Rabinowitz, Paula, 120
Randall, Tony, 11, 16, 25–7, 29, 31, 32, 40, 92
Rannells, Andrew, 106
Rear Window, 19–20, 43, 128
Reynolds, Ryan, 133
Robert, Julia, 82–3, 87, 170
Rodriquez, Jai, 139
romantic comedy, 32, 84
Rope, 10, 12, 41–8, 52–6, 63–4
Roquemore, Xosha, 162
Ross, Douglas, 141
Round the Horne, 68
Rowlands, Patsy, 70
Rudd, Paul, 83–4

Salvato, Nick, 96
same sex attraction (SSA), 129–30, 132–3, 144, 170
Samuels, Robert, 43–3, 47
The San Francisco Chronicle, 96
Schlesinger, John, 33–4, 66, 74–7, 85–7
Sebastiene, 56
seduce/seduction, 25–6, 30, 35–7, 72–3, 80, 84–5, 87, 105, 107, 113
Seigworth, Gregory J., 58
self-reflexivity, 7, 87, 103
Sex and the City, 12, 102–5, 107–8, 110, 117

Showgirls, 111
Showtime, 13, 96, 102, 107
Sims, Joan, 65, 70, 73–4, 87
simulacra, 23–5, 30–1, 132
Sinfield, Alan, 95, 101
A Single Man, 83, 148, 160
Sisco King, Claire, 82
situation comedy, 82, 92, 98, 99, 102, 127
slash fiction, 14
Smith, Richard, 136–8
social realism, 11–13, 32–3, 35, 52, 145–6, 149, 151–2, 154–6, 157–8, 166–7, 171
  British social realism, 32–3, 147, 149, 152, 155, 157, 166
soulmate, 1, 59, 81, 87, 99, 107, 115–16, 148
Spectacular Passions: Cinema, Fantasy, Gay Male Spectatorships, 66
spectatorship, 11, 16–19, 21, 41, 65–6, 69, 87, 90, 165
Spigel, Lynn, 91
St Clair, Isla, 3
Stacey, Jackie, 20–1, 40
Stallybrass, Peter, 124
Standing, John, 35
Star, Darren, 102–3
Star Trek, 14
stars/celebrities, 3, 11, 16, 35, 40, 64–5, 67, 69, 74, 82, 87, 92, 95, 101, 139
Stasko, Andra, 141–4
Steiner, John, 76
Steinman, Erich, 110
stereotyping, 143, 148
Stereotyping: The Politics of Representation, 148
Stewart, James, 47, 128
Strachey, Lytton, 10, 120, 124–9, 135, 144–5, 170
straight girl and queer guy
  as alliance or union, 3–5, 7, 8, 10, 13, 26, 49, 62, 65, 67, 70, 80, 83, 85–9, 92, 96, 98, 104, 107, 118, 120–2, 124, 126–7, 130, 140–1, 143–5, 157, 166, 169, 170
  as shared political vision, 5, 109
  as unlikely couple, 2, 169
straight girl as substitute, 137, 171, 81
Straight Women in Support of Homos (SWISH), 4

struggle (political/human), 17, 89, 104, 108, 155
Stugart, Helene, 83
subculture, 120, 150
sublimation, 93
Suddenly Last Summer, viii, 41, 43–9, 51–2, 64
Sugar Rush, 156
Sunday Bloody Sunday, 34, 65, 74–8, 81, 87
Swoon, 12, 42, 52–4, 56–7, 59, 64

Tales of the City, 95–6, 98, 117, 118
Tarr, Connie, 39
A Taste of Honey, 11, 16, 32–4, 36, 38–40, 147, 149–50, 171
Taylor, Elizabeth, 35, 52
televisual glance, 11–12, 90–3, 95, 99–100, 103–4, 110, 117–18
Thompson, Deborah, 82
Thompson, Emma, 125
To Sir With Love, 149–50
Tongues Untied, 52
Torchwood, 12, 90, 110–14, 116–19
transient, 92, 67, 78
The Trevor Project, 157, 168
Turner, Victor, 124
Tushingham, Rita, 34
The Two of Us, 156

unattainability, 9, 77, 85, 87
use and exchange value, 18, 20, 23, 25, 36, 37

Van Zoonen, Liesbet, 18

Ward Jackson, Adrian, 4
Ward Jackson, Nicholas, 57
Wasserstein, Wendy, 5–6
The Way He Looks [*Hoje eu quero voltar sozinho*], 1–2, 12–13, 147, 155–5, 166–7, 170–1
Weaver, Sigourney, 21
Weedon, Chris, 5
Weekend, 103
Weimar republic, 79
Where Eagles Dare, 33
White, Allon, 124
Wilde, Oscar, 82, 95
Wilkas, Matt, 161
Will and Grace, 12, 81, 89, 95, 98–102, 114, 117, 131, 170

Willett, Michael J., 162
Williams, Kenneth, 11, 14, 65, 68–75, 87
Williams, Raymond, 90
Williams, Tennessee, 44, 45–6
Windsor, Barbara, 65, 70
The Wizard of Oz, 66
Word is Out: Stories of Our Lives, 49

Would Like to Meet, 12, 120, 130, 135–6, 138, 144

Yaoi culture, 14
Yar, Majid, 22–3
York, Michael, 79
York, Susannah, 35

Zee and Co., 11, 32–40

EU representative:
Easy Access System Europe
Mustamäe tee 50, 10621 Tallinn, Estonia
Gpsr.requests@easproject.com

www.ingramcontent.com/pod-product-compliance
Lightning Source LLC
Chambersburg PA
CBHW051100230426
43667CB00013B/2380